Books by John R. Wilch

Concordia Commentary: A Theological Exposition of Sacred Scripture

    Ruth, 2006

As Consultant

    The Lutheran Study Bible

Hebrew Grammars from Concordia

    Fundamental Biblical Hebrew and Aramaic
    Fundamental Biblical Hebrew and Aramaic Workbook
    Intermediate Biblical Hebrew

Concordia Commentaries: Hebrew Scriptures

    Leviticus
    Joshua
    Ruth
    Ezra and Nehemiah
    Proverbs
    Song of Songs
    Ezekiel
    Amos
    Jonah

Concordia Hebrew Reader: Ruth

CONCORDIA HEBREW READER

RUTH
רוּת

JOHN R. WILCH

Peer Reviewed

CONCORDIA PUBLISHING HOUSE • SAINT LOUIS

ABOUT THE COVER: The ancient Hebrew text on the cover is based on a stock image of 1QIsa^a showing most of Isaiah 1:26b–2:14a.

Peer Reviewed

Published 2010 Concordia Publishing House
3558 S. Jefferson Ave., St. Louis, MO 63118-3968
1-800-325-3040 · www.cph.org

Text © 2006 Concordia Publishing House.

The text of this reader is based on the translation and textual notes from the Ruth Concordia Commentary © 2006 Concordia Publishing House.

All rights reserved. No part of this publication may be reproduced, stored in a retrieval system, or transmitted, in any form or by any means, electronic, mechanical, photocopying, recording, or otherwise, without the prior written permission of Concordia Publishing House.

Unless otherwise indicated, Scripture quotations are the author's translation.

Biblia Hebraica Stuttgartensia, edited by Karl Elliger and Wilhelm Rudolph, Fifth Revised Edition, edited by Adrian Schenker, © 1977 and 1997 Deutsche Bibelgesellschaft, Stuttgart. Used by permission.

Scripture quotations marked RSV are from the Revised Standard Version of the Bible, copyright 1952, © 1971, by the Division of Christian Education of the National Council of the Churches of Christ in the United States of America. Used by permission. All rights reserved.

Scripture quotations marked ESV are from The Holy Bible, English Standard Version, copyright © 2001 by Crossway Bibles, a division of Good News Publishers. Used by permission. All rights reserved.

Scripture quotations marked NIV are taken from the HOLY BIBLE, NEW INTERNATIONAL VERSION®. NIV®. Copyright © 1973, 1978, 1984 by International Bible Society. Used by permission of Zondervan Publishing House. All rights reserved.

Scripture quotations marked NASB are taken from the NEW AMERICAN STANDARD BIBLE®. Copyright © 1960, 1962, 1963, 1968, 1971, 1972, 1973, 1975, 1977, 1995 by The Lockman Foundation. Used by permission.

The SymbolGreek II, NewJerusalem, and TranslitLS fonts used to print this work are available from Linguist's Software, Inc., PO Box 580, Edmonds, WA 98020-0580, USA; telephone (425) 775-1130; www.linguistsoftware.com.

Manufactured in the United States of America

1 2 3 4 5 6 7 8 9 10   19 18 17 16 15 14 13 12 11 10

Contents

Foreword	ix
How to Use this Reader	xiii
Abbreviations and Reference Works Cited	xv
Books of the Bible	xv
Books of the Apocrypha	xv
Reference Works and Scripture Versions	xvi
Bibliography	xix
Text, Translation, and Notes	
Chapter 1	
Ruth 1:1–5	2
Ruth 1:6–22	14
Excursus: Faithfulness	46
Chapter 2	
Ruth 2:1–17	50
Ruth 2:18–23	84
Chapter 3	
Ruth 3:1–6	100
Ruth 3:7–18	114
Chapter 4	
Ruth 4:1–12	136
Ruth 4:13–22	164

FOREWORD

The study of Biblical Hebrew continues to flourish in seminaries and universities worldwide. The cultural and religious significance of the Hebrew Bible, no less than its literary quality, have made it a focus of meticulous study and careful translation for over two millennia. Each new generation brings with it students who eagerly embark on learning its language so that they might read it for themselves. The most recent generation of elementary Hebrew grammars has made significant advances, both linguistically and pedagogically, over standard grammars of the past. New ways of presenting old material have piqued interest in acquiring an understanding of this ancient language. Attentiveness to different learning styles has produced new and effective strategies for instruction and has motivated the development of new models for teaching Biblical Hebrew. Computer-assisted analysis of Biblical Hebrew texts has provided new access and new insights into Hebrew forms and structures and their functions. Our understanding of Hebrew syntax and semantics has grown exponentially over the last few decades.

The development of new resources for the study and reading of Biblical Hebrew texts has made it possible for all who desire to cultivate and maintain their understanding of Biblical Hebrew to do so. Such is the contribution of the Concordia Hebrew Reader series, an impressive new resource for the study of Biblical Hebrew. This first volume, on the Hebrew text of Ruth, has been prepared by Professor John Wilch, and it is an exceptional teaching resource.

The format and organization of the volume is ambitious and engaging. Students will appreciate the conciseness and clarity of the explanations. Teachers will welcome its carefully conceived layout, which reinforces the solid linguistic foundation and pedagogical orientation of the book. The inclusion of the entire Hebrew Masoretic Text in large segments not only encourages the reading of the full biblical text throughout—an essential, albeit often neglected, aspect of learning Biblical Hebrew!—but also encourages and facilitates analysis of the biblical text in its immediate and broader contexts. The accompanying literal English translation for each segment enables the user quickly to grasp the basic sense of the Hebrew text. Detailed textual notes offer succinct contextual explanations of forms and their function. The volume's commitment to analyzing words and phrases at the clause level and in collocation with other constituents affords the user a more accurate, linguistically informed understanding of the Hebrew text than is available in previous works of this type.

The distinctiveness of this volume is the way in which it unifies and integrates a full complement of interrelated grammatical, historical, and theological insights. Grammatically, no stone is left unturned. This particular feature will be met with gratitude and enthusiasm by all users, whether one is currently learning Biblical Hebrew or attempting to revitalize Hebrew once learned! Full identification and explanation of forms and their contextual meaning is provided for each verse. Clarification of syntactic structures throughout makes the presentation a very positive, constructive resource for a broad spectrum of users. Literary observations derived from the Hebrew text provide additional depth and texture to the analysis and demonstrate the kind of rich insight afforded by the Hebrew text to those who are able to navigate it. Attentiveness to the Hebrew text is evidenced further by the decision to identify and explore interpretive issues and to elucidate even text-critical matters, including important Kethib/Qere readings, making this volume all the more useful as a learning resource. Clear and concise explanations of matters often regarded as too complex even to consider provide parameters for understanding the issues and point the way to resolution.

A laudable feature of the textual notes is that they are generously referenced, providing the user with trajectories for further study. Professor Wilch has read widely, researched carefully, and scoured the important secondary literature on Ruth. Occurrences of a key form or lexeme or collocation found elsewhere in the Hebrew Bible are regularly noted. References to the standard Hebrew lexicons and major intermediate and advanced Hebrew grammars are numerous and illuminating. Interaction with other commentators on Ruth is extensive and insightful, and engagement with other substantive secondary literature is correlated in an impressive way.

In addition to its thorough grammatical treatment of Ruth, the Concordia Hebrew Reader also provides, where necessary, helpful historical information. Brief descriptions and explanations within the textual notes give clarity to specific social customs of the time, geographic locations that figure prominently in the story, tools and techniques that pertain to ancient agricultural life, and everyday norms and practices that would easily elude a modern reader. Theologically, the volume does not shy away from encouraging reflection on the meaning and significance of the story here told, particularly as it relates to the theme of faithfulness. Observations and conclusions reached in the annotation serve as a foundation for contemplation and a consideration of theological implications inherent in the story.

Learning the essentials of Biblical Hebrew is its own challenge. But a challenge far greater than mastering the rudiments of the language—verb forms, noun endings, vocabulary—is developing and nurturing an understanding of how Hebrew works. The Concordia Hebrew Reader on Ruth explains how the Hebrew of the book of Ruth works. All that one has learned in a beginning Hebrew class or an elementary Hebrew course sequence is here reinforced and enriched by the careful, insightful, and methodical analysis offered by Professor Wilch.

The benefit to be gained from this exceptional learning resource is there for all. Whether one has finally reached the threshold of exploring a Biblical Hebrew text, or is attempting to resuscitate Hebrew once learned, or simply desires to explore more extensively the Hebrew text of the book of Ruth, the guidance provided by the Concordia Hebrew Reader will not disappoint.

> Dennis R. Magary, Ph.D.
> Chairman, Department of Old Testament
>   and Semitic Languages
> Trinity Evangelical Divinity School
> Deerfield, Illinois

HOW TO USE THIS READER

This reader is designed to increase proficiency in Biblical Hebrew for one who has studied, or is now learning, an introductory grammar. The entire Hebrew Masoretic Text of Ruth from *Biblia Hebraica Stuttgartensia* appears in large sections. Each section is accompanied by a literal English translation drawn from the acclaimed scholarly Concordia Commentary series. Detailed textual notes on the Hebrew follow. The features of this book enable the user to gain fluency through several different pedagogical methods.

First, the layout enables one to rapidly read the Hebrew sections even without consulting the textual notes. Each unit of Hebrew text is placed with its corresponding English translation on the facing page. This enables one to easily glance at the facing page for a translation of any unfamiliar Hebrew word or phrase. To help this process, the Hebrew and English are aligned more precisely by starting each new verse (of both the Hebrew and the English) on a new line. Moreover, a vertical rule | in the English translation indicates each point where a Hebrew line ends. As a further suggestion, one can read the Hebrew text aloud (and even memorize units for oral recital) to enhance one's grasp of the language.

Second, one who desires to study the Hebrew text in detail (perhaps at a slower pace) will find the textual notes to be a treasure trove of insights. Each textual note begins by citing the relevant portion of Hebrew text. To teach the contextual meaning of Hebrew properly, the notes normally treat whole clauses or phrases rather than isolated words. The notes furnish phonetic, lexical, morphological, semantic, and syntactical information, and engage text-critical issues, including important Qere/Kethib variants (as in the fourth note on 4:5). Abundant references to standard Hebrew lexica and advanced Hebrew grammars, plus occasional citations of commentaries and related works, point the way for further research. The textual notes are not simply cobbled together from other sources. Instead, they are the fruit of many years of proprietary scholarship not available elsewhere except in the unabridged Concordia Commentary series.

Third, the user has room to add comments and references by hand. A space of approximately one inch separates the textual notes for each verse and the margins are ample.

Fourth, the textual notes are not devoid of theological implications, but invite one to ponder matters of faith. Additionally, a short excursus on faithfulness probes one of the key themes of Ruth and helps deepen the understanding of its vocabulary, characters, and context.

The publishers hope and pray that this reader may foster the study of sacred Scripture in the original language, both for the sake of academic excellence and an increase in faithful comprehension. קָרוֹב אֵלֶיךָ הַדָּבָר (Deut 30:14).

                Christopher W. Mitchell, Ph.D.
                Editor, Concordia Commentary Series

Abbreviations and Reference Works Cited

Books of the Bible

Gen	2 Ki	Is	Nah	Rom	Titus
Ex	1 Chr	Jer	Hab	1 Cor	Philemon
Lev	2 Chr	Lam	Zeph	2 Cor	Heb
Num	Ezra	Ezek	Hag	Gal	James
Deut	Neh	Dan	Zech	Eph	1 Pet
Josh	Esth	Hos	Mal	Phil	2 Pet
Judg	Job	Joel	Mt	Col	1 Jn
Ruth	Ps (pl. Pss)	Amos	Mk	1 Thess	2 Jn
1 Sam	Prov	Obad	Lk	2 Thess	3 Jn
2 Sam	Eccl	Jonah	Jn	1 Tim	Jude
1 Ki	Song	Micah	Acts	2 Tim	Rev

Books of the Apocrypha and Other Noncanonical Books of the Septuagint

1–2 Esdras	1–2 Esdras	Ep Jer	Epistle of Jeremiah
Tobit	Tobit	Azariah	Prayer of Azariah
Judith	Judith	Song of the Three	Song of the Three Young Men
Add Esth	Additions to Esther	Susanna	Susanna
Wis Sol	Wisdom of Solomon	Bel	Bel and the Dragon
Sirach	Sirach / Ecclesiasticus	Manasseh	Prayer of Manasseh
Baruch	Baruch	1–2 Macc	1–2 Maccabees

3–4 Macc	3–4 Maccabees	Odes	Odes
Ps 151	Psalm 151	Ps(s) Sol	Psalm(s) of Solomon

REFERENCE WORKS AND SCRIPTURE VERSIONS

ABD — *The Anchor Bible Dictionary.* Edited by D. N. Freedman. 6 vols. New York: Doubleday, 1992

ANEP — *The Ancient Near East in Pictures Relating to the Old Testament.* Edited by J. B. Pritchard. 2d ed. Princeton: Princeton University Press, 1969

ANET — *Ancient Near Eastern Texts Relating to the Old Testament.* Edited by J. B. Pritchard. 3d ed. Princeton: Princeton University Press, 1969

BDB — Brown, F., S. R. Driver, and C. A. Briggs. *A Hebrew and English Lexicon of the Old Testament.* Oxford: Clarendon, 1979

Brockelmann — Brockelmann, C. *Hebräische Syntax.* Neukirchen: Kreis Moers, Verlag der Buchhandlung des Erziehungsvereins, 1956

DCH — *The Dictionary of Classical Hebrew.* Edited by D. J. A. Clines. Sheffield: Sheffield Academic Press, 1993–

ESV — English Standard Version of the Bible

ET — English translation

GKC — *Gesenius' Hebrew Grammar.* Edited by E. Kautzsch. Translated by A. E. Cowley. 2d ed. Oxford: Clarendon, 1910

HALOT — Koehler, L., W. Baumgartner, and J. J. Stamm. *The Hebrew and Aramaic Lexicon of the Old Testament.* Translated and edited under the supervision of M. E. J. Richardson. 5 vols. Leiden: Brill, 1994–2000

IDB — *The Interpreter's Dictionary of the Bible.* Edited by G. A. Buttrick. 5 vols. Nashville: Abingdon, 1962, 1976

Jastrow	Jastrow, M., comp. *A Dictionary of the Targumim, the Talmud Babli and Yerushalmi, and the Midrashic Literature.* 2 vols. Brooklyn: P. Shalom, 1967
Joüon	Joüon, P. *A Grammar of Biblical Hebrew.* Translated and revised by T. Muraoka. 2 vols. Subsidia biblica 14/1–2. Rome: Editrice Pontificio Istituto Biblico, 1991
KJV	King James Version of the Bible
LEH	Lust, J., E. Eynikel, and K. Hauspie. *A Greek-English Lexicon of the Septuagint.* Rev. ed. 2 vols. Stuttgart: Deutsche Bibelgesellschaft, 2003
NASB	New American Standard Bible
NIV	New International Version of the Bible
NT	New Testament
OT	Old Testament
RSV	Revised Standard Version of the Bible
TDNT	*Theological Dictionary of the New Testament.* Edited by G. Kittel and G. Friedrich. Translated by G. W. Bromiley. 10 vols. Grand Rapids: Eerdmans, 1964–1976
TDOT	*Theological Dictionary of the Old Testament.* Edited by G. J. Botterweck, H. Ringgren, and H.-J. Fabry. Translated by J. T. Willis et al. 14 vols. at present. Grand Rapids: Eerdmans, 1974–
TLOT	*Theological Lexicon of the Old Testament.* Edited by E. Jenni and C. Westermann. Translated by M. E. Biddle. 3 vols. Peabody, Mass.: Hendrickson, 1997
TWOT	*Theological Wordbook of the Old Testament.* Edited by R. L. Harris, G. L. Archer Jr. and B. K. Waltke. Chicago: Moody, 1980

WA DB	Weimar Ausgabe Deutsche Bibel ("German Bible"). *Luthers Werke: Kritische Gesamtausgabe. Deutsche Bibel.* 12 vols. Weimar: Hermann Böhlau, 1906–1961
Waltke-O'Connor	Waltke, B. K., and M. O'Connor. *An Introduction to Biblical Hebrew Syntax.* Winona Lake, Ind.: Eisenbrauns, 1990
Williams	Williams, R. J. *Hebrew Syntax: An Outline.* 2d ed. Toronto: University of Toronto Press, 1976

BIBLIOGRAPHY

Aistleitner, Joseph. *Wörterbuch der ugaritischen Sprache*. Edited by Otto Eissfeldt. 4th ed. Berlin: Akademie, 1974.

Andersen, Francis I. *The Sentence in Biblical Hebrew*. Janua Linguarum, Series Practica, 231. The Hague: Mouton, 1974.

Barber, Cyril J. *Ruth: An Expositional Commentary*. Chicago: Moody, 1983.

Beattie, Derek R. G. "The Book of Ruth as Evidence for Israelite Legal Practice." *Vetus Testamentum* 24 (1974): 251–67.

———. "Ruth III." *Journal for the Study of the Old Testament* 5 (1978): 39–48.

Berlin, Adele. *Poetics and Interpretation of Biblical Narrative*. Sheffield: Almond, 1983.

Bledstein, Adrien J. "Female Companionships: If the Book of Ruth Were Written by a Woman ..." Pages 116–33 in *A Feminist Companion to Ruth*. Edited by Athalya Brenner. Feminist Companion to the Bible 3. Sheffield: Sheffield Academic Press, 1993.

Block, Daniel I. *Judges, Ruth*. The New American Commentary 6. Nashville: Broadman & Holman, 1999.

Boecker, Hans Jochen. *Law and the Administration of Justice in the Old Testament and Ancient East*. Translated by Jeremy Moiser. Minneapolis: Augsburg, 1980.

Bons, Eberhard. "Die Septuaginta-Version des Buches Rut." *Biblische Zeitschrift* 42 (1998): 202–24.

Brichto, Herbert Chanan. "Kin, Cult, Land and Afterlife—A Biblical Complex." *Hebrew Union College Annual* 44 (1973): 1–54.

Bruppacher, Hans. "Die Bedeutung des Namens Ruth." *Theologische Zeitschrift* 22 (1966): 12–18.

Bush, Frederic W. *Ruth, Esther*. Word Biblical Commentary 9. Dallas: Word, 1996.

———. "Ruth 4:17: A Semantic Wordplay." Pages 3–14 in *Go to the Land I Will Show You: Studies in honor of Dwight W. Young.* Edited by Joseph E. Coleson and Victor H. Matthews. Winona Lake: Eisenbrauns, 1996.

Campbell, Edward F., Jr. "Naomi, Boaz and Ruth: *Hesed* and Change." *Austin Seminary Bulletin* 105 (1990): 64–74.

———. *Ruth.* Anchor Bible 7. Garden City, N.Y.: Doubleday, 1975.

Carasik, Michael. "Ruth 2,7: Why the Overseer Was Embarrassed." *Zeitschrift für die alttestamentliche Wissenschaft* 107 (1995): 493–94.

Cassel, Paulus Stephanus. *Ruth.* Translated by P. H. Steenstra. A Commentary on the Holy Scriptures. Vol. 4, no. 3 of the Old Testament. Edited by J. P. Lange. Repr., Grand Rapids: Zondervan, 1960.

Collins, C. John. "Ambiguity and Theology in Ruth: Ruth 1:21 and 2:20." *Presbyterion* 19 (1993): 97–102.

Dalman, Gustaf. *Arbeit und Sitte in Palästina.* Vols. 1–4 (vol. 1 in 2 parts). Gütersloh: C. Bertelsmann, 1928–1935.

Driver, S. R. *An Introduction to the Literature of the Old Testament.* 9th ed. Gloucester: P. Smith, 1913.

Enns, Paul P. *Ruth.* Bible Study Commentary. Grand Rapids: Zondervan, 1982.

Fontinoy, Charles. *Le duël dans les langues sémitiques.* Paris: Société d'édition "Les Belles Lettres," 1969.

Galli, Barabara E. "Time, Form, and Content: Franz Rosenzweig and the Secret of Biblical Narration." *Judaism* 44 (1995): 467–76.

Gerleman, Gillis. *Ruth, Das Hohelied.* Edited by Siegfried Herrmann and Hans Walter Wolff. 2d ed. Biblischer Kommentar: Altes Testament 18. Neukirchen-Vluyn: Neukirchner, 1981.

Gibson, John C. L. *Textbook of Syrian Semitic Inscriptions.* Vol. 1: *Hebrew and Moabite Inscriptions.* Oxford: Clarendon, 1971.

Gordis, Robert. "Love, Marriage and Business in the Book of Ruth." Pages 241–64 in *A Light unto My Path: Old Testament*

Studies in Honor of Jacob M. Myers. Philadelphia: Temple University Press, 1974.

———. "Personal Names in Ruth: A Note on Biblical Etymologies." *Judaism* 35 (1986): 298–99.

Gordon, Cyrus H. *The World of the Old Testament*. 2d rev. ed. London: Phoenix, 1960.

Gow, Murray D. *The Book of Ruth: Its Structure, Theme and Purpose*. Leicester: Apollos, 1992.

Gray, John. *Joshua, Judges, Ruth*. New Century Bible. Grand Rapids: Eerdmans, 1986.

Gressmann, Hugo. "Ruth." In *Die Anfänge Israels*. Vol. 1, part 2, of *Die Schriften des Alten Testaments*. Göttingen: Vandenhoeck & Ruprecht, 1914.

Hamilton, Victor P. *The Book of Genesis: Chapters 1–17*. New International Commentary on the Old Testament. Grand Rapids: Eerdmans, 1990.

Hamlin, E. John. *Surely There Is a Future: A Commentary on the Book of Ruth*. Grand Rapids: Eerdmans, 1996.

Hancher, Michael. "Performative Utterance, the Word of God, and the Death of the Author." *Semeia* 41 (1988): 27–40.

Harstad, Adolph L. *Joshua*. Concordia Commentary. St. Louis: Concordia, 2004.

Hertzberg, Hans Wilhelm. *Die Bücher Josua, Richter, Ruth*. Das Alte Testament Deutsch 9. Edited by V. Herntrich and A. Weiser. Göttingen: Vandenhoeck & Ruprecht, 1959.

Hubbard, Robert L. *The Book of Ruth*. New International Commentary on the Old Testament. Grand Rapids: Eerdmans, 1988.

———. "Ruth IV 17: A New Solution." *Vetus Testamentum* 38 (1988): 293–301.

Hurvitz Avi. "Ruth 2:7—'A Midrashic Gloss'?" *Zeitschrift für die alttestamentliche Wissenschaft* 95 (1983): 121–23.

Hyman, Ronald T. "Questions and the Book of Ruth." *Hebrew Studies* 24 (1983): 17–25.

Jenni, Ernst. *Lehrbuch der hebräischen Sprache des Alten Testaments.* 2d ed. Basel: Helbing & Lichtenhahn, 1981.

Joüon, Paul. *Ruth: Commentaire philologique et exégétique.* 2d ed. Rome: Pontifical Biblical Institute, 1986.

Keil, Carl Friedrich. *Joshua, Judges, Ruth.* Translated by James Martin. In vol. 2 (2 vols. in 1) of Commentary on the Old Testament in Ten Volumes by C. F. Keil and Franz Delitzsch. Repr., Grand Rapids: Eerdmans, 1978.

Kleinig, John W. *Leviticus.* Concordia Commentary. St. Louis: Concordia, 2003.

Klug, Eugene F. *From Luther to Chemnitz: On Scripture and the Word.* Kampen, Netherlands: J. H. Kok, 1971. Repr., Fort Wayne, Ind.: Concordia Theological Seminary, 1981.

Lacocque, André. *The Feminine Unconventional: Four Subversive Figures in Israel's Tradition.* Minneapolis: Fortress, 1990.

Lambdin, Thomas O. *Introduction to Biblical Hebrew.* New York: Scribner, 1971.

Lawrenz, John C. *Judges, Ruth.* People's Bible Commentary. St. Louis: Concordia, 1999.

Lee, Nancy V. "Choices in the Book of Ruth." *Japan Christian Quarterly* 54 (1988): 234–43.

Linafelt, Tod A. *Ruth.* In *Ruth and Esther* [by Timothy K. Beal]. Berit Olam: Studies in Hebrew Narrative and Poetry. Collegeville, Minn.: Liturgical Press, 1999.

Lipinski, Edward. "Le mariage de Ruth." *Vetus Testamentum* 26 (1976): 124–27.

Luter, A. Boyd, and Barry C. Davis. *God behind the Seen: Expositions of the Books of Ruth and Esther.* Expositor's Guide to the Historical Books. Grand Rapids: Baker, 1995.

Lys, Daniel. "Résidence ou repos? Notule sur Ruth ii 7." *Vetus Testamentum* 21 (1971): 497–501.

Mace, D. *Hebrew Marriage: A Sociological Study.* London: Epworth, 1953.

Matthews, Victor H. *Judges and Ruth.* New Cambridge Bible Commentary. Cambridge: Cambridge University Press, 2004.

Maxey, James. "Oral Evocations of the *Kerygma*: An Orality-Performance Study of 1 Corinthians 15:1–11." Graduate Biblical Seminar, Chicago Lutheran Theological Seminary, 2005.

Mitchell, Christopher W. *The Meaning of* BRK *"To Bless" in the Old Testament.* Atlanta: Scholars Press, 1987.

———. *The Song of Songs.* Concordia Commentary. St. Louis: Concordia, 2003.

Moore, Michael S. "Two Textual Anomalies in Ruth." *Catholic Biblical Quarterly* 59 (1997): 234–43.

Morris, Leon. *Ruth.* In *Judges* [by Arthur E. Cundall], *Ruth.* Tyndale Old Testament Commentaries. Downers Grove, Ill.: Inter-Varsity, 1968.

Myers, Jacob M. *The Linguistic and Literary Form of the Book of Ruth.* Leiden: Brill, 1955.

Nielsen, Kirsten. *Ruth: A Commentary.* Translated by Edward Broadbridge. Old Testament Library. Louisville: Westminster/John Knox 1997.

Noth, Martin. *Die israelitischen Personennamen im Rahmen der gemeinsemitischen Namengebung.* 1928. Repr., Hildesheim: Olms, 1980.

Pfeiffer, Charles F. "Ruth." Pages 267–72 in *The Wycliffe Bible Commentary.* Edited by Charles F. Pfeiffer and Everett F. Harrison. Chicago: Moody, 1962.

Rebera, Basil A. "Translating a Text to Be Spoken and Heard: A Study of Ruth." *The Bible Translator* 43 (1992): 230–36.

———. "Translating Ruth 3:16." *The Bible Translator* 38 (1987): 234–37.

———. "Yahweh or Boaz? Ruth 2:20 Reconsidered." *The Bible Translator* 36 (1985): 317–27.

Rendsburg, Gary. "Dual Personal Pronouns and Dual Verbs in Hebrew." *Jewish Quarterly Review* 73 (1982–1983): 38–58.

Ringgren, Helmer. *Israelite Religion*. Translated by David E. Green. Philadelphia: Fortress, 1966.

Roberts, J. J. M. "The Hand of Yahweh." *Vetus Testamentum* 21 (1971): 244–51.

Roehrs, Walter R. *Concordia Self-Study Commentary* (Old Testament section). St. Louis: Concordia, 1971, 1979.

Rowley, H. H. "The Marriage of Ruth." Pages 171–94 in *The Servant of the Lord and Other Essays on the Old Testament*. 2d ed., rev. Oxford: Blackwell, 1965.

Rudolph, Wilhelm. *Das Buch Ruth, das Hohe Lied, die Klagelieder*. 2d ed. Kommentar zum Alten Testament 17/1–3. Gütersloh: Gerd Mohn. 1962.

Sakenfeld, *The Meaning of Hesed in the Hebrew Bible: A New Inquiry*. Missoula, Mont.: Scholars Press, 1978.

Sasson, *Ruth: A New Translation with a Philological Commentary and a Formalist-Folklorist Interpretation*. Baltimore: Johns Hopkins University Press, 1979.

Seow, C. L. *A Grammar for Biblical Hebrew*. Nashville: Abingdon, 1987.

Slotki, Judah J. "Ruth." Pages 34–65 in *The Five Megilloth*. Edited by A. Cohen. Soncino Books of the Bible. London: Soncino, 1952.

Thompson, Michael E. W. "New Life amid the Alien Corn." *Evangelical Quarterly* 65 (1993): 197–210.

Trible, Phyllis. "A Human Comedy: The Book of Ruth." Pages 161–90 in vol. 2 of *Literary Interpretations of Biblical Narratives*. Edited by Kenneth R. R. Gros Louis and James S. Ackerman. Nashville: Abingdon, 1982.

———. "Two Women in a Man's World: A Reading of the Book of Ruth." *Soundings* 59 (1976): 251–79.

Vuilleumier, René. "Stellung und Bedeutung des Buches Ruth im alttestamentlichen Kanon." *Theologische Zeitschrift* 44 (1988): 193–210.

Waard, Jan de, and Eugene A. Nida. *A Translator's Handbook on the Book of Ruth.* Helps for Translators 15. London: United Bible Societies, 1973.

Weiss, David Halivni. "The Use of קנה in Connection with Marriage." *Harvard Theological Review* 57 (1964): 244–48.

Westbrook, Raymond. *Old Babylonian Marriage Laws.* Horn, Austria: Berger, 1988.

———. *Property and the Family in Biblical Law.* Journal for the Study of the Old Testament: Supplement Series 113. Sheffield: JSOT Press, 1991.

Westermann, Claus. *Genesis 1–11: A Commentary.* Translated by John J. Scullion. Minneapolis: Augsburg, 1984.

Wilch, John R. *Time and Event: An Exegetical Study of the Use of ʿēth in the Old Testament.* Leiden: Brill, 1969.

Wiseman, D. J. *The Alalakh Tablets.* London: British Institute of Archaeology at Ankara, 1953.

Witzenrath, Hagia H. *Das Buch Rut.* Studien zum Alten und Neuen Testament 40. Edited by W. Richter and R. Schnackenburg. Munich: Kösel, 1975.

Wolde, Ellen J. van. "Texts in Dialogue with Texts: Intertextuality in the Ruth and Tamar Narratives." *Biblical Interpretation* 5 (1997): 1–28.

Wright, Charles H. H. *The Book of Ruth in Hebrew.* London: Williams & Norgate, 1864.

Würthwein, Ernst. "Ruth." Pages 1–24 in *Die Fünf Megilloth.* 2d ed. Handbuch zum Alten Testament. Tübingen: Mohr (Siebeck), 1969.

Yeivin, Israel. *Introduction to the Tiberian Masorah.* Translated and edited by E. J. Revell. Masoretic Studies 5. Missoula, Mont.: Scholars Press, 1980.

Text, Translation, and Notes

Chapter 1

Ruth 1:1–5

1:1 וַיְהִ֗י בִּימֵי֙ שְׁפֹ֣ט הַשֹּׁפְטִ֔ים וַיְהִ֥י רָעָ֖ב בָּאָ֑רֶץ וַיֵּ֨לֶךְ אִ֜ישׁ מִבֵּ֧ית לֶ֣חֶם יְהוּדָ֗ה לָגוּר֙ בִּשְׂדֵ֣י מוֹאָ֔ב ה֥וּא וְאִשְׁתּ֖וֹ וּשְׁנֵ֥י בָנָֽיו׃

2 וְשֵׁ֣ם הָאִ֣ישׁ אֱ‍ֽלִימֶ֡לֶךְ וְשֵׁם֩ אִשְׁתּ֨וֹ נָעֳמִ֜י וְשֵׁ֥ם שְׁנֵֽי־בָנָ֣יו ׀ מַחְל֤וֹן וְכִלְיוֹן֙ אֶפְרָתִ֔ים מִבֵּ֥ית לֶ֖חֶם יְהוּדָ֑ה וַיָּבֹ֥אוּ שְׂדֵי־מוֹאָ֖ב וַיִּֽהְיוּ־שָֽׁם׃

3 וַיָּ֥מָת אֱלִימֶ֖לֶךְ אִ֣ישׁ נָעֳמִ֑י וַתִּשָּׁאֵ֥ר הִ֖יא וּשְׁנֵ֥י בָנֶֽיהָ׃

4 וַיִּשְׂא֣וּ לָהֶ֔ם נָשִׁ֖ים מֹֽאֲבִיּ֑וֹת שֵׁ֤ם הָֽאַחַת֙ עָרְפָּ֔ה וְשֵׁ֥ם הַשֵּׁנִ֖ית ר֑וּת וַיֵּ֥שְׁבוּ שָׁ֖ם כְּעֶ֥שֶׂר שָׁנִֽים׃

5 וַיָּמ֥וּתוּ גַם־שְׁנֵיהֶ֖ם מַחְל֣וֹן וְכִלְי֑וֹן וַתִּשָּׁאֵר֙ הָֽאִשָּׁ֔ה מִשְּׁנֵ֥י יְלָדֶ֖יהָ וּמֵאִישָֽׁהּ׃

Note: The vertical rule mark | indicates a point in the translation that corresponds to the end of a Hebrew line.

1 ¹During the days when the judges were judging, there occurred a famine in the land. | So a man went from Bethlehem of Judah to sojourn in the region of Moab— | he, his wife, and his two sons. |
²The man's name was Elimelech, his wife's name was Naomi, | and the names of his two sons were Mahlon and Chilion, Ephrathites from Bethlehem of Judah. | They entered the region of Moab and remained there. |
³But Elimelech, the husband of Naomi, died; so she was left, with her two sons. |
⁴Then they took for themselves Moabite wives; the name of the first was Orpah | and the name of the second was Ruth. They lived there about ten years. |
⁵But also the two of them died—Mahlon and Chilion; | so the woman was left without her two boys and without her husband.

Ruth 1:1–5

1:1 וַיְהִי—The Qal imperfect with *waw* consecutive generally refers to a past, completed action. It is not unusual for a *waw* consecutive to begin a new section (e.g., Gen 11:1, 37:1) or even a book.[1] Indeed, it is the regular formula for opening a new section of a narrative in classical biblical Hebrew, and it is even used at the start of a story to indicate that the account is historical in nature.[2] Although the account of Ruth is related to the well-known events of the book of Judges and the opening clause refers to the judges, וַיְהִי does not imply that the book of Ruth continues or is attached to the book of Judges.[3] Rather, the entire opening clause (וַיְהִי בִּימֵי שְׁפֹט הַשֹּׁפְטִים) is a temporal modifier of the following clause (וַיְהִי רָעָב בָּאָרֶץ), which is the first main clause in the narrative. Thus the opening clause represents the circumstance in which the narrative unfolds.

בִּימֵי שְׁפֹט הַשֹּׁפְטִים—Literally, "in the days of" means "during the time when," indicating an indistinct duration of time.[4] The infinitive construct שְׁפֹט serves as a gerund (verbal noun) and can be translated with a participle, "were judging." It functions in place of a subordinate clause with a conjunction and finite verb.[5] The participle הַשֹּׁפְטִים functions as a substantive noun, "the judges" (see Waltke-O'Connor, § 37.1c, example 9).

---

[1] That is, in Lev 1:1, Num 1:1; Josh 1:1; Judg 1:1; 1 Sam 1:1; 2 Sam 1:1; 2 Ki 1:1; 2 Chr 1:1; Esth 1:1; Ezek 1:1; Jonah 1:1. See Waltke-O'Connor, § 33.2.4a–b; Joüon, § 118 c, footnote 2; Lambdin, *Introduction to Biblical Hebrew*, 123; Campbell, *Ruth*, 49–50; Harstad, *Joshua*, 41.

[2] Thus, the *waw* consecutive does not indicate fiction or a legend (see Sasson, "Ruth," 322).

[3] Keil, *Joshua, Judges, Ruth*, 27, 470; Hubbard, *Ruth*, 84, n. 5. The contrary view was that the *waw* consecutive is comparable to a copulative *waw*: "The fact that whole Books (Lev., Num., Josh., Jud., Sam., 2 Kings, Ezek., Ruth, Esth., Neh., 2 Chron.) begin with the imperfect *consecutive*, and others (Exod., 1 Kings, Ezra) with *waw copulative*, is taken as a sign of their close connection with the historical Books now or originally preceding them" (GKC, § 49 b, footnote 1).

[4] Morris, *Ruth*, 245.

[5] See Jenni, *Lehrbuch der hebräischen Sprache des Alten Testaments*, 119; Waltke-O'Connor, § 36.2.2a–b.

וַיְהִי רָעָב בָּאָרֶץ—This is the main clause after the opening temporal clause.[6] This exact Hebrew ("there occurred a famine in the land") is elsewhere used only in Gen 12:10 and 26:1.[7] "There occurred" is literally "and there was" (וַיְהִי). "The land," as often in the OT, refers to the land of Israel.[8]

וַיֵּלֶךְ אִישׁ—The verb is the Qal imperfect of הָלַךְ with *waw* consecutive. The *waw* consecutive with imperfect frequently refers to logically consequential action (Waltke-O'Connor, § 33.2.1a). Here it has the sense "There occurred a famine. *So* a man went …"

לָגוּר—"To sojourn" (Qal infinitive construct of גּוּר) means to seek refuge or haven as a stranger, a resident alien.

בִּשְׂדֵי מוֹאָב—This is translated "in the region of Moab." שְׂדֵי appears to be the masculine plural (in construct) of שָׂדֶה. See the similar phrases in 1:2, 6a, 22 (without a preposition or with מִן instead of בְּ). The plural could refer to a certain area of Moab, such as the cultivable plateau northeast of the Dead Sea or the strip of well-watered land east of it. However, שְׂדֵי here and in 1:2, 6, 22 may be an archaic singular construct form that indicates the "region" or "territory" of Moab.[9] If so, the phrase is equivalent to the phrase with the singular construct (שְׂדֵה מוֹאָב) in 1:6b; 2:6; 4:3. Apart from those phrases the singular noun שָׂדֶה is common in Ruth meaning an agricultural "field" (e.g., 2:2–3). If it meant "field" in the phrases with "Moab," it could simply refer to open pasture land or an unwalled village surrounded by pasture, indicating that Elimelech's family avoided settling in a walled town, where pagan temptations would be greater.

---

[6] Hubbard, *Ruth*, 84, n. 8; Waltke-O'Connor, § 33.2.4b, example 11.
[7] Cf. Gen 41:54, 56; 42:5; 2 Sam 21:1; 2 Ki 6:25; 8:1; 25:3. Hubbard, *Ruth*, 85.
[8] E.g., Gen 12:7; 2 Sam 21:14; Pss 16:3; 101:6; Is 6:12. Keil, *Joshua, Judges, Ruth*, 470; Slotki, "Ruth," 41; Morris, *Ruth*, 246.
[9] Cf. Keil, *Joshua, Judges, Ruth*, 471; Morris, *Ruth*, 247–48; Campbell, *Ruth*, 50–52; Gray, *Joshua, Judges, Ruth*, 38; Block, *Judges, Ruth*, 626. For Bush (*Ruth, Esther*, 61, 63), both the singular and plural forms refer to the "region" or "territory" of Moab.

Ruth 1:1–5

It is striking that in all seven instances where the author of Ruth refers to "Moab" (מוֹאָב, 1:1, 2, 6 [twice], 22; 2:6; 4:3), it is always preceded by a form of שָׂדֶה, thus referring to "the field(s)/region of Moab." The author studiously avoided the phrase אֶרֶץ מוֹאָב, "the land of Moab," which occurs ten times elsewhere in the OT referring to the country. The terminology chosen by the author of Ruth is appropriate for the era when Moab was dominated by Israel as an occupied territory, from the time of Ehud the Judge (Judg 3:12–30) until the revolt of Moab from Israel's King Joram (2 Ki 3:4–27). Before that era, in the time of Moses, Moab was called a "land" (אֶרֶץ מוֹאָב, Deut 1:5; 28:69 [ET 29:1]; 32:49; 34:5–6). Likewise, Jephthah thrice calls Moab a "land" (אֶרֶץ מוֹאָב, Judg 11:15, 18 [twice]) in his historical summary when referring to Israel during the time of Moses. The phrase "the plains of Moab" is also used in the era of Moses (Numbers 22–36; Deut 34:1, 8) and of Joshua (Josh 13:32), which probably distinguishes that location geographically from the country proper. After Moab's independence from Israel, it is again termed a "land" in Jer 48:24, 33. Otherwise, the OT generally speaks simply of "Moab" or "the Moabites." Moses in the Pentateuch and the Chronicler, who each use "the field of Moab" twice (Gen 36:35, quoted in 1 Chr 1:46; Num 21:20; 1 Chr 8:8), may have understood this term to be interchangeable with "the land of Moab." But the consistent use of "the field(s)/region of Moab" by the author of Ruth leads to the conclusion that, probably at the time both of his writing and of the events of the book of Ruth, Moab was not an independent country but a territory under the control of Israel. This is also an indication that the book of Ruth was written no later than the period of the Israelite monarchy.[10]

הוּא וְאִשְׁתּוֹ וּשְׁנֵי בָנָיו—Previously the subject was the "man" (אִישׁ) alone, but this enlarges it to (literally) "he and his wife and the two of his sons." The resumptive pronoun הוּא is in apposition to the preceding אִישׁ and is needed to add the additional subjects (וּשְׁנֵי בָנָיו וְאִשְׁתּוֹ).[11] The phrase could be rendered in more idiomatic English as "together with his wife and two sons."

---

[10] Cf. Block, *Judges, Ruth*, 626.
[11] Joüon, § 146 c (2).

1:2 וְשֵׁם הָאִישׁ—This is, literally, "and the name of the man." Beginning with a conjunctive *waw* followed by a noun instead of a verb, this is a disjunctive sentence whereby parenthetical information is introduced, namely, the names of the characters (also 1:4) in "a verbless clause of identification" (Waltke-O'Connor, § 8.4.1a). "Man" was anarthrous (אִישׁ) in 1:1, but here it has the anaphoric article, referring to "the" previously mentioned man.[12]

אֱלִימֶלֶךְ—The name "Elimelech" is linguistically typical of the pre-monarchic period. It probably means "my God [אֵלִי] is king [מֶלֶךְ]" (see Judg 8:23). It is one of many ancient names that expressed profound religious conviction.[13]

נָעֳמִי—"Naomi" comes from the verb נָעֵם, "be pleasant, delightful, lovely," which Solomon uses to describe his Shulammite bride in Song 7:7 (ET 7:6),[14] or from a related noun or adjective such as נֹעַם, "delightfulness, pleasantness, grace" (an attribute of the LORD in Pss 27:4; 90:17), or נָעִים, "pleasant, delightful" (applied to the LORD's eternal gifts of grace in this life and after the resurrection in Ps 16:6, 11). The root נעם was widely used in West Semitic names by 1400 B.C. Her name may mean "she of loveliness."[15] The ending

---

[12] Waltke-O'Connor, § 13.5.1d, including example 5; Joüon, § 137 f (3).
[13] Hertzberg, *Die Bücher Josua, Richter, Ruth*, 261; Morris, *Ruth*, 249. Keil renders: "To whom God is king" (*Joshua, Judges, Ruth*, 472). This name occurs only here in the Bible, but also in Ugaritic, Akkadian, and an Amarna letter (Campbell, *Ruth*, 52). For a similar syntax to introduce a story and the names of participants, see 1 Sam 25:2–3 (Hubbard, *Ruth*, 88).
[14] See Mitchell, *The Song of Songs*, 1072, on it in Song 7:7 (ET 7:6), and page 637 on Song 1:16, where the Shulammite applies the adjective נָעִים, "delightful," to Solomon.
[15] See Sasson, *Ruth*, 18; see also Lawrenz, *Judges, Ruth*, 221; Gressmann, "Ruth," 272; Hertzberg, *Die Bücher Josua, Richter, Ruth*, 261; Morris, *Ruth*, 249; Hubbard, *Ruth*, 88–89; Vuilleumier, "Stellung und Bedeutung," 206. Rudolph (*Das Buch Ruth, das Hohe Lied, die Klagelieder*, 38), since the ending can be an endearing form, suggests "darling," and Nielsen (*Ruth*, 42), "my joy." Cf. Abinoam (Judg 4:6) and Elnaam (1 Chr 11:46), both referring to the deity (Campbell, *Ruth*, 53, citing Noth, *Die israelitischen Personennamen im Rahmen der gemeinsemitischen Namengebung*, 166), and Naamah (Gen 4:22; 1 Ki 14:21) and Naaman (2 Ki 5:1). At Ugarit, Naam was an epithet for deities and heroes (Hubbard, *Ruth*, 89, n. 26).

Ruth 1:1–5

(יִ-) is parallel to many Ugaritic female names that end in *y*, and Ugaritic also attests *nʿmy* as a noun, "pleasantness."[16]

וְשֵׁם שְׁנֵי־בָנָיו—Hebrew can use a singular (שֵׁם, "name") instead of an expected plural when the individuals have something in common (Joüon, § 136 l), that is, are members of the same family.

מַחְלוֹן וְכִלְיוֹן—The meanings of the names Mahlon and Chilion are uncertain, although they have the forms of genuine Hebrew names. Each has the ending -וֹן which may form an abstract noun or a diminutive (Joüon, § 88 M b, c, f). Mahlon might be related to מָחוֹל (*maḥol*), "circle dance," for the sense, "little dance." If it derives from חָלָה (*ḥalah*), "be weak, sick," then it could mean "sickly person" (*HALOT*, s.v. מַחְלוֹן; cf. מַחֲלָה, "sickness, disease"). There are several possible derivations for Chilion: from כָּלַל (*kalal*), "to complete, perfect," which has extrabiblical cognates that mean "crown"; כָּלָה (*kalah*), "to be finished, completed; to perish" (cf. כִּלָּיוֹן [*killayon*], "annihilation, extermination"); or כְּלִי (*keli*), "ornament, vessel."[17] The English "Chilion" is from the Vulgate's transliteration of the name as *Chellion*.

Generally, a name that was given because of its actual or supposed meaning described a character or relationship that may have influenced the person's conduct or been fulfilled in his experiences (see, e.g., the names of Jacob and his sons, Gen 25:26; 27:36; 29:32–30:24). The fact that both men quickly die in the narrative (Ruth 1:5)

---

[16] Cyrus H. Gordon, *Ugaritic Textbook: Grammar* (Rome: Pontifical Biblical Institute, 1965), § 8.54.

[17] See the lexicons; Cassel, *Ruth*, 12; Hubbard, *Ruth*, 89–90. Rudolph (*Das Buch Ruth, das Hohe Lied, die Klagelieder*, 38) suggests a derivation for Mahlon from *ḥaliya* in Aramaic and Arabic, meaning "charming." Chilion is attested in Ugaritic. Names related to Mahlon are found in the Bible: Mahalath (Gen 28:9; 2 Chr 11:18), Mahlah (e.g., Num 26:33; 1 Chr 7:18), and Mahli (e.g., Ex 6:19), and they may not be from the same root as חֳלִי (*ḥoli*), "sickness," but from an otherwise unattested root מחל (*mḥl*; Campbell, *Ruth*, 53–54). Thus, Mahlon and Chilion may not originally have meant "weak, sick(ly)" and "wasting/pining away, going extinct," respectively (contra Keil, *Joshua, Judges, Ruth*, 472; Pfeiffer, "Ruth," 269; Gordis, "Personal Names in Ruth," 298; Block, *Judges, Ruth*, 625), although the Hebrew ear may have understood them as such (Hertzberg, *Die Bücher Josua, Richter, Ruth*, 261).

might support negative possible meanings of Mahlon and Chilion (e.g., "sickly" and "extinct," respectively). Because all the names in Ruth have actual Hebrew counterparts, they are not symbolic or fictional but genuine.[18]

אֶפְרָתִים—"Ephrathites" likely indicates the clan of the tribe of Judah to which the family belonged (see 1 Sam 17:12), one of the clans in Bethlehem. The town was already called Ephrath in patriarchal times (Gen 35:19; 48:7). Because of an Akkadian word meaning "place of food," the name, sometimes spelled Ephrathah (אֶפְרָתָה, Ruth 4:11; Ps 132:6; Micah 5:1 [ET 5:2]), may be an equivalent of Bethlehem.[19]

וַיָּבֹאוּ—This is "they entered," Qal imperfect of בוֹא with *waw* consecutive. The *waw* may be rendered consequentially, "so" (as in 1:1b), or omitted as pleonastic (stylistically redundant; Williams, § 435).

וַיִּהְיוּ־שָׁם:—Literally, "and they were there," the verb is translated "remained." This is a legitimate sense of the verb הָיָה, "to be."[20] The clause is similar to וַיֵּשְׁבוּ שָׁם in 1:4.

---

[18] Gressmann, "Ruth," 272; Campbell, *Ruth*, 52–53; Hubbard, *Ruth*, 90.
[19] Hubbard, *Ruth*, 90; see also Gray, *Joshua, Judges, Ruth*, 385; Bush, *Judges, Ruth*, 64–65, 67. Caleb's wife's name was Ephrath (1 Chr 2:19; spelled Ephrathah in 1 Chr 2:50; 4:4), but the clan would not have been named after her; rather, her name, like the place name, is related to the Akkadian cognate. The place name may also refer to the immediate region surrounding the town, as is often the case with towns and cities (Cassel, *Ruth*, 12; Hubbard, *Ruth*, 91, n. 38). Since Ephrath was the ancient name, the original Ephrathite clan members may have been early inhabitants of the tribe of Judah after the conquest, thus the aristocracy of the town; this may be hinted at by "the whole town" being aroused at Naomi's return (Ruth 1:19; Morris, *Ruth*, 249–50). "Ephrathites" from Ephrath should not be confused with members of the tribe of Ephraim, who can be designated by a word with the same spelling (Judg 12:5; 1 Sam 1:1; 1 Ki 11:26; Campbell, *Ruth*, 54–55).
[20] BDB, III 2. 4QRuth^a reads וישבו שם, "and they settled there" (cf. Gray, *Joshua, Judges, Ruth*, 385, who also cites two late Hebrew manuscripts with that verb).

Ruth 1:1–5

1:3 וַתָּ֣מָת—This is the Qal imperfect of מוּת with *waw* consecutive. The *waw* has the adversative sense "but"[21] (also in 1:5a), for it introduces a contrast to living in Moab (1:2).

אִ֣ישׁ נָעֳמִ֑י—The definiteness of a proper name carries over to a noun in construct with it, hence *"the husband* of Naomi."[22]

וַתִּשָּׁאֵ֥ר הִ֖יא וּשְׁנֵ֥י בָנֶֽיהָ׃—Literally, "and she was left, she and the two of her sons," the Niphal imperfect with *waw* consecutive is in logical consequence, hence the *waw* is translated *"so* she was left …" (see also 1:1b, 5b). Naomi with her sons was bereft and remained alone. As also in 1:5, the Niphal of שָׁאַר may indicate bereavement (Gen 7:23; 42:38; Ex 14:28).[23] The singular verb וַתִּשָּׁאֵר and pronoun הִיא indicate that Naomi is "the chief actor among other actors"[24] (the others are "her two sons"). The resumptive pronoun הִיא is needed to add the additional subjects (וּשְׁנֵ֥י בָנֶֽיהָ) to the subject (Naomi) implied by the feminine singular verb.[25] An analogous construction is in 1:6: וַתָּ֤קָם הִיא֙ וְכַלֹּתֶ֔יהָ.

1:4 וַיִּשְׂא֣וּ לָהֶ֗ם נָשִׁים֙ מֹֽאֲבִיּ֔וֹת—The implied subject of the masculine plural verb is the preceding word, בָנֶֽיהָ ("her sons"), at the end of 1:3. The verb is the Qal imperfect of נָשָׂא with *waw* consecutive in the sequential sense: "then[26] they took for themselves wives, Moabitesses." The "textbook" form would be וַיִּשְּׂא֣וּ, with a *daghesh forte* in the *sin* (שּׂ) representing the assimilated נ of the root נשׂא, but that *daghesh* has been lost due to the *shewa* (שְׂ).[27]

---

[21] Waltke-O'Connor, § 33.2.1d.
[22] Waltke-O'Connor, § 13.4c, including example 25.
[23] Block, *Judges, Ruth*, 627.
[24] Waltke-O'Connor, § 16.3.2c.
[25] Joüon, § 146 c (3).
[26] BDB, s.v. וְ, 5 b.
[27] Joüon, § 18 m (3); GKC, § 20 m.

The verb נָשָׂא has the sense of "take (a wife)" (see BDB, 3 d) most often in later OT books (especially 2 Chronicles and Ezra), but it also occurs in Judg 21:23, so it need not indicate a late date for the authorship of Ruth. It is consistently used for exogamous marriages, that is, when Israelites marry non-Israelites.[28] The more common idiom for "take (a wife)" is with לָקַח, as in Ruth 4:13.

עָרְפָּה—It is unlikely that the name Orpah is related to עֹרֶף, "neck." Rather, it may be derived from an Arabic word referring to a woman with a rich growth of hair or from an Akkadian and Ugaritic word meaning "cloud."[29]

רוּת—The Syriac Peshitta renders the name Ruth as equivalent to רְעוּת (with an ע). That would be from the root רעה and mean "companion or friendship,"[30] a synonym cognate to רְעוּת (re'uth), "female companion," and רֵעָה (re'ah), "friend." However, it is almost impossible to explain how the consonant ע would have been omitted in the Hebrew spelling. It is possible that רוּת could be derived from the root ראה (r'h), from which comes the verb רָאָה, "to see," since feminine nouns ending in -וּת are sometimes formed from roots with final ה. If so, רוּת would be contracted from רְאוּת with the middle א omitted after the *shewa* (רְ) and before the long vowel (וּ). It would mean "sight" and perhaps refer to a pleasing appearance.

Yet for "Ruth" the most plausible view is that רוּת is from the root רוה *(rwh)*, "be saturated, drink one's fill" (BDB, Qal), "saturate, water ... cause to drink" (BDB, Hiphil). The feminine nominal ending -וּת was added to produce רְווּת, and then the consonantal ו in the root could easily have disappeared after the *shewa* (רְ) and before

---

[28] See *HALOT*, s.v. נשׂא, Qal, 17; Gow, *The Book of Ruth*, 186–93; Block, *Judges, Ruth*, 628–29.
[29] Campbell, *Ruth*, 55–56; Gray, *Joshua, Judges, Ruth*, 375; Vuilleumier, "Stellung und Bedeutung," 207; see also Hubbard, *Ruth*, 94, n. 14. Sasson (*Ruth*, 20–21) suggests a derivation from the Arabic *gurfa*, "handful of water." The two middle consonants may have been reversed (by metathesis) from the known name Ophrah, "deer" (1 Chr 4:14; Cassel, *Ruth*, 13).
[30] Roehrs, *Concordia Self-Study Commentary*, OT 182. Gordis ("Personal Names in Ruth," 299) derives Ruth from the root רעי ("to wish" in Aramaic and Syriac) for the meaning "willingness, desire."

Ruth 1:1–5

the long vowel (וֹ). Any of the possible meanings of "Ruth," including "saturation," "a drink," "refreshment," "satiety," or "fullness," serve eminently for a name.[31] In fact, "Ruth" may then include a wordplay since Naomi with Ruth returned to Bethlehem after the end of the famine (1:1) when the LORD provided food in Bethlehem (1:6), which he would have accomplished through sending abundant rain; see forms of רָוָה referring to saturating showers in, for example, Is 55:10; Ps 65:11 (ET 65:10) and רְוָיָה ("my cup *overflows*") in Ps 23:5. Moreover, the book includes a dialectical theme between fullness and emptiness, as when Naomi laments, "I went away full, but empty the LORD returned me!" (Ruth 1:21a). But Naomi is not truly empty there because Ruth is with her, and so is the LORD, and Ruth will be the means through whom the LORD will again "fill" Naomi by providing an heir.

וַיֵּשְׁבוּ שָׁם—The Qal imperfect of יָשַׁב with *waw* consecutive introduces a parenthesis with circumstantial information in the form of a sequence.[32]

כְּעֶשֶׂר שָׁנִים:—The preposition כְּ may indicate approximation: "*about* ten years."[33]

---

[31] This solution was first suggested by Rabbi Johanan (died about A.D. 80) and is reflected in the Talmud in the sense of "saturation" (*Baba Bathra*, 14b; *Berakhoth*, 7b). See Bruppacher, "Die Bedeutung des Namens Ruth"; Campbell, *Ruth*, 56; Beattie, "Ruth III," 46; Gray, *Joshua, Judges, Ruth*, 375; Sasson, *Ruth*, 21; Vuilleumier, "Stellung und Bedeutung," 207; Lacocque, *The Feminine Unconventional*, 115; Hubbard, *Ruth*, 94; Block, *Judges, Ruth*, 628. Rudolph (*Das Buch Ruth, das Hohe Lied, die Klagelieder*, 38), rather than trying to derive the names Orpah and Ruth from Hebrew words, regards both as genuine Moabite names. Nevertheless, while only a few texts of ancient Moabite have been preserved, the language was very similar to classical Hebrew, and so it is legitimate to search for cognates of the names in Hebrew.
[32] See Waltke-O'Connor, § 39.2.3c.
[33] Waltke-O'Connor, § 11.2.9b, including example 2 (cf. § 11.2.9e); Joüon, § 133 g.

1:5 וַיָּמוּתוּ גַם־שְׁנֵיהֶם מַחְלוֹן וְכִלְיוֹן—The inclusion of גַם־שְׁנֵיהֶם emphasizes the tragedy of these two additional deaths: literally, "and died *also the two of them*, Mahlon and Chilion." Compare the death of Elimelech in 1:3.

וַתִּשָּׁאֵר הָאִשָּׁה מִשְּׁנֵי יְלָדֶיהָ וּמֵאִישָׁהּ:—The verb וַתִּשָּׁאֵר is repeated from 1:3, and here too it denotes bereavement. Here it takes the preposition מִן (twice) in a privative sense: she "was left *without* her two boys and *without* her husband."[34] Naomi lost her "boys" (plural of יֶלֶד) here at the story's beginning, but she will also gain and hold a "boy" (יֶלֶד) in compensation at the end (4:16). It is unusual for this noun to be used of her grown sons.[35] The author may have selected it to form an inclusio, since the noun occurs in Ruth only in these two verses (1:5; 4:16). Frequently in this narrative, the author makes use of the same word repeatedly for effect. Thus, he used "boys" here unusually so that the readers and hearers would be prepared for "boy" (Obed) at the narrative's conclusion. Because repeating key words is essential for revealing the relationship of parts of a story—or even of different stories—it is important for translators to use the same word in rendering such key Hebrew words.[36]

---

[34] GKC, § 119 w; Williams, § 321; Bush, *Judges, Ruth*, 66. *HALOT*, s.v. שאר, Niphal, 2 b β, gives this for Ruth 1:5: "to be left without (after the loss of) the male members of the family."

[35] Ordinarily used for children, this term otherwise refers to adults only in respect to Rehoboam's young advisers (1 Ki 12:8, 10, 14; 2 Chr 10:8, 10, 14; Morris, *Ruth*, 152; Campbell, *Ruth*, 56; Hubbard, *Ruth*, 96; Nielsen, *Ruth*, 44).

[36] Galli, "Time, Form, and Content," 476. The LXX and most English translations miss the point by rendering the word here in 1:5 as "sons."

Ruth 1:6–22

1:6 וַתָּ֤קָם הִיא֙ וְכַלֹּתֶ֔יהָ וַתָּ֖שָׁב מִשְּׂדֵ֣י מוֹאָ֑ב כִּ֤י שָֽׁמְעָה֙ בִּשְׂדֵ֣ה מוֹאָ֔ב כִּֽי־פָקַ֤ד יְהוָה֙ אֶת־עַמּ֔וֹ לָתֵ֥ת לָהֶ֖ם לָֽחֶם׃
7 וַתֵּצֵ֗א מִן־הַמָּקוֹם֙ אֲשֶׁ֣ר הָיְתָה־שָׁ֔מָּה וּשְׁתֵּ֥י כַלֹּתֶ֖יהָ עִמָּ֑הּ וַתֵּלַ֣כְנָה בַדֶּ֔רֶךְ לָשׁ֖וּב אֶל־אֶ֥רֶץ יְהוּדָֽה׃
8 וַתֹּ֤אמֶר נָעֳמִי֙ לִשְׁתֵּ֣י כַלֹּתֶ֔יהָ לֵ֣כְנָה שֹּׁ֔בְנָה אִשָּׁ֖ה לְבֵ֣ית אִמָּ֑הּ יַ֣עַשׂ יְהוָ֤ה עִמָּכֶם֙ חֶ֔סֶד כַּאֲשֶׁ֧ר עֲשִׂיתֶ֛ם עִם־הַמֵּתִ֖ים וְעִמָּדִֽי׃
9 יִתֵּ֤ן יְהוָה֙ לָכֶ֔ם וּמְצֶ֣אןָ מְנוּחָ֔ה אִשָּׁ֖ה בֵּ֣ית אִישָׁ֑הּ וַתִּשַּׁ֣ק לָהֶ֔ן וַתִּשֶּׂ֥אנָה קוֹלָ֖ן וַתִּבְכֶּֽינָה׃
10 וַתֹּאמַ֖רְנָה־לָּ֑הּ כִּי־אִתָּ֥ךְ נָשׁ֖וּב לְעַמֵּֽךְ׃
11 וַתֹּ֤אמֶר נָעֳמִי֙ שֹׁ֣בְנָה בְנֹתַ֔י לָ֥מָּה תֵלַ֖כְנָה עִמִּ֑י הַֽעֽוֹד־לִ֤י בָנִים֙ בְּֽמֵעַ֔י וְהָי֥וּ לָכֶ֖ם לַאֲנָשִֽׁים׃
12 שֹׁ֤בְנָה בְנֹתַי֙ לֵ֔כְןָ כִּ֥י זָקַ֖נְתִּי מִהְי֣וֹת לְאִ֑ישׁ כִּ֤י אָמַ֙רְתִּי֙ יֶשׁ־לִ֣י תִקְוָ֔ה גַּ֣ם הָיִ֤יתִי הַלַּ֙יְלָה֙ לְאִ֔ישׁ וְגַ֖ם יָלַ֥דְתִּי בָנִֽים׃
13 הֲלָהֵ֣ן ׀ תְּשַׂבֵּ֗רְנָה עַ֚ד אֲשֶׁ֣ר יִגְדָּ֔לוּ הֲלָהֵן֙ תֵּֽעָגֵ֔נָה לְבִלְתִּ֖י הֱי֣וֹת לְאִ֑ישׁ אַ֣ל בְּנֹתַ֗י כִּֽי־מַר־לִ֤י מְאֹד֙ מִכֶּ֔ם כִּֽי־יָצְאָ֥ה בִ֖י יַד־יְהוָֽה׃
14 וַתִּשֶּׂ֣נָה קוֹלָ֔ן וַתִּבְכֶּ֖ינָה ע֑וֹד וַתִּשַּׁ֤ק עָרְפָּה֙ לַחֲמוֹתָ֔הּ וְר֖וּת דָּ֥בְקָה בָּֽהּ׃
15 וַתֹּ֗אמֶר הִנֵּה֙ שָׁ֣בָה יְבִמְתֵּ֔ךְ אֶל־עַמָּ֖הּ וְאֶל־אֱלֹהֶ֑יהָ שׁ֖וּבִי אַחֲרֵ֥י יְבִמְתֵּֽךְ׃
16 וַתֹּ֤אמֶר רוּת֙ אַל־תִּפְגְּעִי־בִ֔י לְעָזְבֵ֖ךְ לָשׁ֣וּב מֵאַחֲרָ֑יִךְ כִּ֠י אֶל־אֲשֶׁ֨ר תֵּלְכִ֜י אֵלֵ֗ךְ וּבַאֲשֶׁ֤ר תָּלִ֙ינִי֙ אָלִ֔ין עַמֵּ֣ךְ עַמִּ֔י וֵאלֹהַ֖יִךְ אֱלֹהָֽי׃
17 בַּאֲשֶׁ֤ר תָּמ֙וּתִי֙ אָמ֔וּת וְשָׁ֖ם אֶקָּבֵ֑ר כֹּה֩ יַעֲשֶׂ֨ה יְהוָ֥ה לִי֙ וְכֹ֣ה יֹסִ֔יף כִּ֣י הַמָּ֔וֶת יַפְרִ֖יד בֵּינִ֥י וּבֵינֵֽךְ׃

1 ⁶Then she [Naomi] arose with her daughters-in-law and returned from the region of Moab, for she had heard in the region of Moab | that the LORD had graciously visited his people to give them food. |

⁷So she left the place where she had been, and her two daughters-in-law [left] with her. | They went on the way to return to the land of Judah. |

⁸But Naomi said to her two daughters-in-law, "Go, return, each to her mother's house! | May the LORD practice faithfulness with you as you have done with the dead and with me! |

⁹May the LORD grant to you that you find security, each in the house of her husband!" | Then she kissed them, and they raised their voices and wept. |

¹⁰But they said to her, "No, with you we shall return to your people!" |

¹¹Then Naomi said, "Return, my daughters! Why should you go with me? | Do I still have sons in my womb that they could become your husbands? |

¹²Return, my daughters; go! For I am too old to belong to a husband. | Suppose I say, 'I have hope, and also I will belong to a husband tonight, and I even will bear sons.' |

¹³But for that would you wait, until they grow up? For that would you deprive yourselves by not belonging to a husband? |

No, my daughters! For it is much more bitter for me than for you, because the hand of the LORD has gone forth against me!" |

¹⁴They raised their voices and wept again. Then Orpah kissed her mother-in-law, but Ruth clung to her. |

¹⁵Then she [Naomi] said, "Look! Your sister-in-law has returned to her people and to her god(s). | Return after your sister-in-law!" |

¹⁶But Ruth said,
   "Do not press me to forsake you,
      to return [turn away] from [following] after you! |
   Because, to wherever you go, I shall go,
      and wherever you lodge, I shall lodge! |
   Your people is my people,
      and your God is my God! |
   ¹⁷Wherever you die, I shall die,
      and there I shall be buried! |
   Thus may the LORD do to me, and do even more so,
      if death will separate me and you!"

Ruth 1:6–22

18 וַתֵּרֶא כִּי־מִתְאַמֶּצֶת הִיא לָלֶכֶת אִתָּהּ וַתֶּחְדַּל לְדַבֵּר אֵלֶיהָ:
19 וַתֵּלַכְנָה שְׁתֵּיהֶם עַד־בֹּאָנָה בֵּית לָחֶם
וַיְהִי כְּבֹאָנָה בֵּית לֶחֶם וַתֵּהֹם כָּל־הָעִיר עֲלֵיהֶן וַתֹּאמַרְנָה הֲזֹאת נָעֳמִי:
20 וַתֹּאמֶר אֲלֵיהֶן אַל־תִּקְרֶאנָה לִי נָעֳמִי קְרֶאןָ לִי מָרָא
כִּי־הֵמַר שַׁדַּי לִי מְאֹד:
21 אֲנִי מְלֵאָה הָלַכְתִּי וְרֵיקָם הֱשִׁיבַנִי יְהוָה
לָמָּה תִקְרֶאנָה לִי נָעֳמִי וַיהוָה עָנָה בִי וְשַׁדַּי הֵרַע לִי:
22 וַתָּשָׁב נָעֳמִי וְרוּת הַמּוֹאֲבִיָּה כַלָּתָהּ עִמָּהּ הַשָּׁבָה מִשְּׂדֵי מוֹאָב
וְהֵמָּה בָּאוּ בֵּית לֶחֶם בִּתְחִלַּת קְצִיר שְׂעֹרִים:

¹⁸When she [Naomi] saw that she [Ruth] was determined to go with her, she stopped urging her. |
¹⁹Then the two of them went on until they entered Bethlehem. | Now, when they entered Bethlehem, the whole town became excited over them. | The women said, "This is Naomi!" |
²⁰But she said to them,
    "Do not call me Naomi ['pleasant']; call me Mara ['bitter'], |
        because the Almighty has made me very bitter! |
    ²¹I went away full, but empty the LORD returned me! |
        Why should you call me Naomi?
    For the LORD has testified against me,
        and the Almighty has afflicted me!" |
²²So Naomi returned, and with her was Ruth the Moabitess, her daughter-in-law, who returned from the region of Moab. | Now they entered Bethlehem at the beginning of barley harvest.

Ruth 1:6–22

1:6 וַתָּ֣קָם—Naomi, last named in 1:3, is the implied subject of this Qal third feminine singular imperfect of קוּם with *waw* consecutive, which resumes the sequence from 1:5a: after her sons died, *"then* she arose." The verb קוּם is frequently employed when commencing an action, especially a journey (e.g., Gen 22:3; 1 Sam 9:3).[37] Here, קוּם also signals the beginning of the main action of the story, as in Gen 23:3 and Ex 1:8 (both times also after a death) and 1 Sam 1:9. One might have expected this verse to begin with a temporal clause indicating that the following narrated events are subsequent to the deaths recorded in 1:3, 5 (cf. the temporal clauses in, e.g., Josh 1:1; Judg 1:1; 2 Sam 1:1), but no such clause introduces this new narrative in Ruth.[38] The three events reported in this verse, "she arose [that she might return] ... for she had heard ... that the LORD had graciously visited," occurred at different times and must have taken place in chronologically reverse order: first "the LORD ... graciously visited his people," then Naomi "heard" about that visitation, and then "she arose." These three events are all presented at the time of Naomi's return because that is the important point here in the story.[39]

הִיא֙ וְכַלֹּתֶ֔יהָ—This is, literally, "she and her daughters-in-law." The resumptive pronoun הִיא is needed to add the additional subjects (plural of כַּלָּה) to the subject (Naomi) implied by the feminine singular verb וַתָּ֣קָם (Joüon, § 146 c (3)). See also the last textual note on 1:3.

וַתָּ֖שָׁב—The singular verb (Qal imperfect of שׁוּב, "return") keeps the focus on Naomi herself. The *waw* consecutive indicates successive action (Waltke-O'Connor, § 33.2.1a; Williams, § 178) and here could be rendered as a purpose clause: "arose ... to return." שׁוּב often means "to turn," "move in the opposite direction," or "go back to the start." Metaphorically, it can mean "to (re)turn to God," "repent" (BDB, 6 d) or *"turn back* to God (= seek penitently)" (BDB, 6 c). In the Hiphil (1:21; 4:15), it often means "to bring back,

---

[37] BDB, s.v. קוּם, Qal, 6 b and c; Morris, *Ruth*, 252; Sasson, "Ruth," 323.
[38] Berlin, Poetics and Interpretation of Biblical Narrative, 104; Hubbard, *Ruth*, 99.
[39] Berlin, Poetics and Interpretation of Biblical Narrative, 96.

restore."⁴⁰ The verb וַתָּ֣שָׁב begins both 1:6 and 1:22 (verses that have other vocabulary in common), and so it brackets this scene (1:6–22) as an inclusio. שׁוּב occurs a total of twelve times in 1:6–22 (see further the textual notes on 1:22), and so "return" gives the main theme to this section. Together with הָלַךְ, which occurs nine times 1:6–22 (see the textual note on וַתֵּלַכְנָה in 1:7), שׁוּב ("return") carries this section's movement and tension.⁴¹

מִשְּׂדֵי מוֹאָב ... בִּשְׂדֵה מוֹאָב—See the textual note on בִּשְׂדֵי מוֹאָב in 1:1.

כִּ֤י שָֽׁמְעָה֙—This כִּי is an explicative conjunction ("because, for") that gives the motivation for the action.⁴²

כִּֽי־פָקַ֤ד יְהוָה֙ אֶת־עַמּ֔וֹ—The verb פָּקַד primarily means to "pay attention to, take note of." With God as subject, it often means to "visit graciously" (BDB, Qal, 2) for salvation and relief, and here takes a direct object (עַמּוֹ), marked with אֶת־. Hubbard paraphrases, "graciously looked after."⁴³ In contrast, when used with the preposition עַל, the verb can denote divine punishment (BDB, Qal, 3).

לָתֵ֥ת לָהֶ֖ם לָֽחֶם׃— The verse ends with three Hebrew words ("to give them food") that have strong alliteration: *latet lahem lahem*. The first word is a Qal infinitive construct from נָתַן, which could be taken as a gerund with a preposition of means: "by giving them food."⁴⁴ The last word (לָחֶם in pause) is the second element in the name Bethlehem, meaning "house of bread/food" (בֵּית לֶחֶם, e.g., 1:1, 2, 19, 22).

---

⁴⁰ *HALOT*, 1429–33; J. A. Soggin, "שׁוב," *TLOT* 3:1313–14.
⁴¹ Campbell, *Ruth*, 63, 79; Hubbard, *Ruth*, 99; Nielsen, *Ruth*, 46.
⁴² Berlin, Poetics and Interpretation of Biblical Narrative, 106.
⁴³ Hubbard, *Ruth*, 97, 100; cf. Gray, *Joshua, Judges, Ruth*, 361, 386; Block, *Judges, Ruth*, 631.
⁴⁴ Sasson, "Ruth," 322; Hubbard, *Ruth*, 97, n. 4; Bush, *Ruth, Esther*, 66.

Ruth 1:6–22

1:7 וַתֵּצֵא מִן־הַמָּקוֹם—Literally, this is "she went forth from the place." The verb is a Qal imperfect from יָצָא with *waw* consecutive as a logical consequence, "so" (as with וַיֵּלֶךְ in 1:1b). The phrase is reminiscent of the exodus from Egypt (מִן יָצָא in, e.g., Ex 13:3, 8; Deut 4:45–46). Like those Israelites, Naomi is returning from foreign exile to the promised land. The same verb will be used to foretell that Israel shall come out of Babylon (the return from exile) and to promise the "new exodus" of all who are called out from spiritual exile to be God's new Israel (the NT church) in the new promised land (Is 48:20; 52:7–12). This promise was fulfilled with the first advent of Jesus Christ and shall be consummated upon his return (Mt 2:13–15; Lk 2:25, 38; 2 Cor 6:17; Rev 18:4).[45]

אֲשֶׁר הָיְתָה־שָּׁמָּה—The relative pronoun אֲשֶׁר, combined with the resumptive element שָׁמָּה ("there"), means "where" (Waltke-O'Connor, § 19.3b). Repetition at long range supplies effect: the sojourn in Moab is bracketed by "there" (1:2) and "where" (1:7); both verses use שָׁם connected to the verb הָיָה. However, variety is achieved with different forms of the words.[46] Ruth 1:2 has שָׁם, while 1:7 has שָׁמָּה with the locative ending (ה־ָ), although that ending has lost its force. Also, 1:2 has וַיִּהְיוּ, while 1:7 has הָיְתָה.

וּשְׁתֵּי כַלֹּתֶיהָ עִמָּהּ—The translation supplies the needed verb, "and her two daughters-in-law [left] with her." The preposition עִם frequently indicates accompaniment, fellowship, and companionship, for example, עִמָּנוּ אֵל, *Immanu-El*, "God is with us" in the Child born of the virgin (Is 7:14). Here the nuance of the preposition is addition, that is, Naomi plus her daughters-in-law (Waltke-O'Connor, § 11.2.14b).

וַתֵּלַכְנָה בַּדֶּרֶךְ—More freely this could be rendered "they took the road." This can be rendered as starting a new sentence and so the *waw* need not be translated (as with וַיָּבֹאוּ in 1:2b). וַתֵּלַכְנָה is the third feminine plural Qal imperfect of הָלַךְ. The previous feminine verbs in 1:6–7 were singular, with Naomi alone as subject, but finally

---

[45] Cf. Hamlin, *Surely There Is a Future*, 14. The Christian church traditionally has included readings from Isaiah 52 at Christmas.
[46] Campbell, *Ruth*, 63; Hubbard, *Ruth*, 98, n. 5.

Ruth 1:6–22

here the verbal action becomes plural: all three women set out decisively together.⁴⁷ The verb הָלַךְ occurs ten times in Ruth 1, and so it, together with שׁוּב (see the textual note on it in 1:6), carries the movement in the first chapter.⁴⁸

לָשׁוּב אֶל־אֶרֶץ יְהוּדָה:—This purpose clause with the infinitive of שׁוּב ("to return") seems to say that all three were "returning" to Judah, although only Naomi had previously been there (see 1:10, 22).⁴⁹

1:8 וַתֹּאמֶר נָעֳמִי לִשְׁתֵּי כַלֹּתֶיהָ—The *waw* consecutive has contrastive force: "*But* Naomi said …" (as also with וַיָּמָת in 1:3a).

לֵכְנָה שֹּׁבְנָה—Both are Qal feminine plural imperatives, from הָלַךְ and שׁוּב, respectively. Naomi will repeat שֹׁבְנָה in 1:11–12. The imperative of הָלַךְ ("go!") is often used in Hebrew as an emphatic opener followed by another imperative (BDB, Qal, I 5 f (1) and (2)). It can thus be understood as adding stress to the second imperative, "return!" The storyteller employs variety by reversing the order of these commands in 1:12. Although the double command in Hebrew conveys urgency, here the imperatives are followed by a blessing, so the listener hears them as a loving exhortation.⁵⁰

אִשָּׁה לְבֵית אִמָּהּ—This is, literally, "a woman to the house of her mother." In this context, אִשָּׁה means "each (woman)," as also in 1:9, corresponding to the frequent use of אִישׁ to mean "each (man)."

יַעַשׂ יְהוָה עִמָּכֶם חֶסֶד—The verb עָשָׂה, "to do, practice," is often used with abstract concepts, and frequently, as here, with חֶסֶד, "faithfulness," especially in Genesis through 1 Kings (see *DCH*, s.v. חֶסֶד, when used as the object of עשׂה). When used with the verb עָשָׂה

---

⁴⁷ Hubbard, *Ruth*, 101.
⁴⁸ Hubbard, *Ruth*, 101; Linafelt, *Ruth*, 8.
⁴⁹ Bush, *Ruth, Esther*, 74.
⁵⁰ Campbell, *Ruth*, 64; Rebera, "Translating a Text to Be Spoken and Heard," 234; Hubbard, *Ruth*, 98, n. 9; 102; Bush, *Ruth, Esther*, 74–75.

("practice, do") and the noun חֶסֶד ("faithfulness"), the preposition עִם ("with") marks a personal complement, and the phrase (literally, "practice faithfulness with") could be rendered as "show kindness to" someone (Waltke-O'Connor, § 11.2.14b, example 5) or "faithfully treat/deal with someone." The Kethib (consonantal text) is the Qal imperfect יַעֲשֶׂה, while the Qere (the preferred text, to be read aloud) is the jussive יַעַשׂ, which has a modal (optative) meaning, as often in prayer: "May the LORD ..." However, the imperfect form can have the same modal meaning as a jussive and be used in prayer.[51] (יִתֵּן beginning 1:9 could be an imperfect or a jussive and expresses a prayer.)

The pronominal suffix on עִמָּכֶם ("with you") and also the verb עֲשִׂיתֶם (Qal perfect of עָשָׂה, "you have done") in the following clause are masculine plural, even though in the context they clearly refer to the daughters-in-law. This phenomenon of using masculine verbs and pronouns that refer to women is repeated six more times in Ruth (1:9, 11, 13, 19, 22; 4:11). Biblical Hebrew frequently uses the more common masculine forms in place of feminine ones, especially in the second person plural (Joüon, §§ 149 b; 150 a). Some believe these masculine-looking forms represent an archaic feminine dual suffix,[52] which would support an early date for the composition of the book of Ruth.

---

[51] Joüon, § 113 l; Waltke-O'Connor, § 31.5b; Steenstra in Cassel, *Ruth*, 16; Campbell, *Ruth*, 65.

[52] Rendsburg, "Dual Personal Pronouns and Dual Verbs in Hebrew," 38–44, 52; Myers, *The Linguistic and Literary Form of the Book of Ruth*, 20; Aistleitner, *Wörterbuch der ugaritischen Sprache*, § 838 (Ugaritic has such a dual pronoun); Andersen, *The Sentence in Biblical Hebrew*, 118, n. 2, on Gen 18:20; Campbell, *Ruth*, 65 (who proposes twelve other instances in Gen 19:9; 31:9; Ex 1:21; Judg 16:13 [sic; probably Judg 16:3]; 19:24aα, aβ, b; 1 Sam 6:7a, bα, bβ, 10a, b); Gray, *Joshua, Judges, Ruth*, 386; Sasson, *Ruth*, 23; Bush, *Ruth, Esther*, 75–76.

1:9 יִתֵּן֩ יְהוָ֨ה לָכֶ֜ם וּמְצֶ֣אןָ מְנוּחָ֗ה—This is, literally, "may the LORD grant to you, and find rest!" The form of the third masculine singular Qal verb יִתֵּן (from נָתַן) is either imperfect or jussive, but in either case it has the jussive meaning, "grant that …"[53] With God as subject and closely connected with an object like "rest," it petitions that God will bring about or furnish what the prayer requests. Here יִתֵּן has an indirect object (לָכֶם, "grant *to you*," with a masculine suffix in place of a feminine), but it lacks a direct object.

The exclamation point at the end of the translated sentence reflects the imperative וּמְצֶאןָ (feminine plural, from מָצָא, "find," with *waw*). It serves as an object clause (Joüon, § 177 h). It lacks the expected final ה as a vowel letter, as also do the feminine plural imperatives לֵכְןָ in 1:12 and קְרֶאןָ in 1:20 (GKC, §§ 46 f, 74 h). Following a jussive (יִתֵּן), an imperative (וּמְצֶאןָ) is frequently used to express an intended consequence or result (as also in 4:11).[54] Therefore the imperative is not to be translated as a command, but as a result clause that is part of the prayer request: "May the LORD grant … *that you find* security." The direct object of the imperative ("find") is מְנוּחָה, literally, "a resting place," but translated as "security."

אִשָּׁה בֵּית אִישָׁהּ—As in 1:8, אִשָּׁה means "each (woman)." The phrase "house of her husband" is an accusative of place without a preposition,[55] and so the translation supplies "in." "Her husband" refers to a new husband that Naomi prays each woman would find. It does not mean that either woman now has a new husband, nor does it refer to the deceased Israelite husbands.

וַתִּשַּׁק לָהֶן—The *waw* consecutive (Qal imperfect of נָשַׁק) resumes the sequence: "then she kissed them" (as with וַיִּשְׂאוּ in 1:4a).

וַתִּשֶּׂאנָה קוֹלָן וַתִּבְכֶּינָה׃—This is, literally, "and they raised their voice and they wept," but the two verbs form a hendiadys, meaning "they raised their voices as they wept" or "they wept loudly" (cf. *HALOT*, s.v. נשׂא, Qal, 8). Since Naomi meant her speech and

---

[53] Cf. C. J. Labuschagne, "נתן," *TLOT* 2:782–83; Hubbard, *Ruth*, 98, n. 11; 105; Bush, *Ruth, Esther*, 76.
[54] GKC, § 110 i; Steenstra in Cassel, *Ruth*, 16; Campbell, *Ruth*, 65–66. Ruth 4:11 too has the jussive יִתֵּן, which is followed by the imperative וַעֲשֵׂה.
[55] Waltke-O'Connor, § 10.2.2b; Joüon, § 126 h; Bush, *Ruth, Esther*, 76.

Ruth 1:6–22

kiss as a final parting, all three women will have wept aloud. Both verbs are third feminine plural Qal imperfects (of נָשָׂא and בָּכָה, respectively) with *waw* consecutive, and both recur in 1:14. The singular קוֹל, "voice," has a collective sense, also in 1:14. The recurrence of the expression in 1:14 forms an inclusio or bracket for this dialogue section.[56]

The wording in Ruth 1:9b–10a, including a series of feminine verbs, displays alliteration:

וַתִּשַּׂק לָהֶן וַתִּשֶּׂאנָה קוֹלָן וַתִּבְכֶּינָה: וַתֹּאמַרְנָה־לָּהּ
Wattishshaq   lahen,   wattisse'nah   qolan,   wattivkeynah. Watto'marnah-lah.[57]

1:10 וַתֹּאמַרְנָה־לָּהּ—The *waw* introduces a contrast: "*But* they said to her" (as does *waw* in 1:3a, 8a).

כִּי־אִתָּךְ נָשׁוּב לְעַמֵּךְ:—Here כִּי could be used as a conjunction introducing a direct quotation ("they said *that* …"), or it could be asseverative, strengthening the following statement ("they said, "*Surely* with you …"). But here the context implies that the daughters-in-law are replying negatively, and so כִּי means "no, on the contrary" (*HALOT*, s.v. כִּי II, 3 c, citing Ruth 1:10 and also Gen 31:16; Ps 44:23 [ET 44:22]). The young women's objection serves a retarding role in the story.[58] The preposition (with suffix) אִתָּךְ ("*with you*") comes first in the quotation, and hence it is in the emphatic position of the energetic declaration. This preposition may mean accompaniment for the purpose of helping (Num 14:9; 2 Ki 9:32).[59] Instead of returning to their Moabite homes as Naomi commanded (שֹׁבְנָה, 1:8), they use the same verb (שׁוּב; see the textual notes on it in 1:7, 22) in the imperfect (נָשׁוּב) to declare that they intend to "return" with Naomi.[60]

---

[56] Hubbard, *Ruth*, 106; Bush, *Ruth, Esther*, 77.
[57] Rebera, "Translating a Text to Be Spoken and Heard," 234.
[58] Gressmann, "Ruth," 277.
[59] Waltke-O'Connor, § 11.2.4a; Bush, *Ruth, Esther*, 77.
[60] Hubbard, *Ruth*, 106.

1:11 שֹׁ֣בְנָה בְנֹתַ֔י—Naomi uses the feminine plural imperative of שׁוּב from 1:8 a second time ("return, go back"). Coming before her series of rhetorical questions and statements that are designed to persuade her daughters-in-law, the imperative itself has the character of persuasion.[61]

לָ֥מָּה תֵלַ֖כְנָה עִמִּ֑י—This interrogative (לָ֫מָּה, "why"), if accompanied with an imperative or rhetorical yes/no question, introduces a question that is not seeking information but is really making a statement.[62] For the sense of the preposition עִם, see the textual note on it in 1:8.

הַֽעֽוֹד־לִ֤י בָנִים֙ בְּמֵעַ֔י—This is a nominal clause. The preposition לְ is used here to denote possession (BDB, s.v. לְ, 5 a; *HALOT*, s.v. לְ I, 10, 11): "Are there still belonging to me sons in my womb?" that is, "Do I still have sons in my womb?" Similar is the use of לְ for possession in the next clause (לָכֶם) and with לְאִישׁ ("belong to a husband") thrice in 1:12–13.

וְהָי֥וּ לָכֶ֖ם לַאֲנָשִֽׁים׃—A verb with *waw* conjunctive may introduce a purpose clause in a consequent situation after a nominal clause: "that they could become husbands for/belonging to you" (see Waltke-O'Connor, § 32.2.4a, example 2). "For you [לָכֶם] as husbands [לַאֲנָשִׁים]" is rendered simply as "your husbands."

1:12 שֹׁ֤בְנָה בְנֹתַי֙ לֵ֔כְןָ—Naomi repeats the same two imperatives that she used in 1:8 (לֵ֣כְנָה שֹּׁ֔בְנָה), but in reverse order for variety or emphasis.[63] She also used שֹׁבְנָה בְנֹתַי in 1:11. Hence this is now Naomi's third use of the feminine plural imperative of שׁוּב, "return!" In the midst of her rhetorical questions and statements, it has the character of persuasion.[64] לֵ֔כְןָ is the feminine plural imperative of הָלַךְ without the expected final ה as vowel letter (GKC, § 46 f).

---

[61] Rebera, "Translating a Text to Be Spoken and Heard," 235.
[62] Hyman, "Questions and the Book of Ruth," 19–21; Bush, *Ruth, Esther*, 77.
[63] Hubbard, *Ruth*, 110.
[64] Rebera, "Translating a Text to Be Spoken and Heard," 235.

Ruth 1:6–22

כִּי זָקַנְתִּי מִהְיוֹת לְאִישׁ—The stative verb with the perfect tense indicates an adjectival present condition: "for *I am too old* to belong to a husband." With the preposition מִן and הָיָה, it indicates a comparison of capability ("too old").[65] The verb הָיָה (Qal infinitive construct: הֱיוֹת) followed by the preposition לְ indicates belonging to (or being possessed by) someone (here: אִישׁ, "a husband"), as in 1:13 (הֱיוֹת לְאִישׁ). Compare the לְ of possession in לִי in 1:11 and later with יֵשׁ in 1:12 ("I have hope").

כִּי אָמַרְתִּי—Here כִּי has the sense of "if" introducing a conditional protasis, "If I would say ..." or "Suppose I say ..." See *HALOT*, s.v. כִּי II, 11; Waltke-O'Connor, § 38.2d, including example 4 (2 Ki 4:29) and example 5 (Lev 1:2). All the rest of this verse is part of the hypothetical protasis, and so all three perfect verbs (אָמַרְתִּי ... הָיִיתִי ... יָלַדְתִּי) in the second half of the verse are part of the condition.[66] The apodosis comes in 1:13, but for clarity the translation ends this sentence at the end of 1:12 and begins 1:13 with another sentence.

יֶשׁ־לִי תִקְוָה—This is, literally, "there belongs to me hope," that is, "I have hope." Again לְ is used for possession (BDB, s.v. לְ, 5 a; *HALOT*, s.v. לְ I, 10, 11). The context would allow the expression to be rendered in the progressive present, "I'm still hoping."

גַּם ... וְגַם—This construction usually means "both ... and," but גַּם has an emphatic role here: "also ... and even."[67] The two clauses introduced by גַּם are epexegetical in that they explain the preceding clause (what her hope would be): first, that she would belong to a husband tonight, and second, that she would even have sons. (The LXX omits a rendering of הַלַּיְלָה, "tonight," and the omission exemplifies its tendency to tone down an impossibility.)

---

[65] Brockelmann, § 111g; Gerleman, *Ruth, Das Hohelied*, 19; Waltke-O'Connor, §§ 11.2.11e; 14.4f; Bush, *Ruth, Esther*, 78.
[66] Cf. GKC, § 106 p; Keil, *Joshua, Judges, Ruth*, 473; Steenstra in Cassel, *Ruth*, 16–17; Brockelmann, § 164cβ; Hubbard, *Ruth*, 107, n. 5; Bush, *Ruth, Esther*, 78–79.
[67] Cf. Williams, §§ 378–79; Waltke-O'Connor, § 39.3.4d.

1:13 הֲלָהֵן ... הֲלָהֵן—This unusual repeated form begins with the interrogative particle (־הֲ). The first and most likely explanation is that לָהֵן is the preposition לְ and the third person feminine plural pronoun (הֵן) in a neuter sense, referring to the previously mentioned hypothetical conditions (1:12).[68] Thus הֲלָהֵן literally means "for those things ...?" but is translated "for that ...?" In each clause this prepositional phrase is in the first, emphatic position: "*For that* would you ... ?"

A second view is that לָהֵן is a conjunction meaning "on this account, therefore," equivalent to the Aramaic לָהֵן in Dan 2:6, 9; 4:24 (ET 4:27; see BDB and *HALOT*, s.v. לָהֵן).

A third view is that הֵן- is a masculine dual absolute ending, which appears in Moabite.[69] It would mean "for them" and refer to Naomi's hypothetical new "sons" (בָנִים, the last word of 1:12). That understanding fits well with the clause following the first occurrence and is plausible with the clause following the second occurrence. The two clauses would then mean this: "But for them would you wait, until they grow up? For them [i.e., while waiting for them] would you deprive yourselves by not belonging to a husband?" This third view is supported by the LXX, which translates each הֲלָהֵן with a masculine plural form of the personal pronoun (αὐτοὺς ... αὐτοῖς). It is also supported by the Targum for both occurrences and by the Vulgate and Peshitta for the first occurrence.[70] According to this third view, the form is equivalent in meaning to הֲלָהֶם ("for them ... ?") with the regular Hebrew form of the masculine plural suffix (הֶם-). However, we might have expected the narrator (if not Naomi herself) to have used the normal Hebrew form instead of a Moabite form that is not

---

[68] Gerleman, Ruth, Das Hohelied, 19.
[69] Fontinoy, *Le duël dans les langues semitiques*, 61–68, 81–90; see also Hubbard, *Ruth*, 111, n. 31.
[70] The Targum's translation of each occurrence includes a form of the masculine pronoun "them." The Vulgate's translation of the first clause (*si eos expectare velitis*) is similar to that of the LXX (μὴ αὐτοὺς προσδέξεσθε). The Peshitta apparently translates the first occurrence as "for them", although it places that prepositional phrase after the verb ("would you wait?") even though in the Hebrew הֲלָהֵן precedes תְּשַׂבֵּרְנָה.

used anywhere else in the book or the OT. Some have suggested that הָלָהֵן is simply a misspelling for הָלָהֶם,[71] but that is unlikely since הָלָהֵן is repeated.

תְּשַׂבֵּ֔רְנָה עַ֚ד אֲשֶׁ֣ר יִגְדָּ֔לוּ—The Piel of שָׂבַר, to "*wait* for" or "*hope* for" (see BDB, Piel, 1 and 2, respectively), usually takes the preposition לְ ("for"). Probably it does so here too since the preceding הָלָהֵן likely is some form of the preposition (see the preceding textual note). Whether הָלָהֵן means "for that" or "for them," it is clarified by עַ֚ד אֲשֶׁ֣ר יִגְדָּ֔לוּ ("until they grow up," referring to the "sons" at the end of 1:12).

תֵּעָגֵ֔נָה—This ("deprive yourselves") is the second feminine plural Niphal imperfect of עָגַן. The expected form would be תֵּעָגֶ֫נָּה, with the *daghesh* (-ּנ-) marking the second, assimilated נ from תֵּעָגֵנְנָה, but the *daghesh* has been lost (GKC, § 51 m). The verb עָגַן occurs only here in Scripture, but in rabbinic Hebrew and Aramaic it means "to bind, tie," and passive forms mean "be secluded, be prevented from marrying" and often refer to women who remain unmarried or are deserted by their husbands and ordinarily are not free to remarry (see Jastrow, s.vv. עָגַן and עֲגַן). So it here refers to a woman refraining from marriage and living without a husband,[72] as confirmed by the following clause.

לְבִלְתִּ֥י הֱי֖וֹת לְאִ֑ישׁ—This epexegetical clause (literally, "to not belong to a husband") explains the preceding verb (see the previous textual note). בִּלְתִּי (with לְ) is a negative particle used with infinitives. As in 1:12 (מִהְי֣וֹת לְאִ֔ישׁ), here too הָיָה (in Qal infinitive construct) followed by לְ indicates "belonging to" (married to) "a husband" (אִישׁ).

---

[71] This is suggested as a possibility by Morris, *Ruth*, 258; Rudolph, *Das Buch Ruth, das Hohe Lied, die Klagelieder*, 40; Campbell, *Ruth*, 68–69; Bush, *Ruth, Esther*, 79.

[72] Keil, *Joshua, Judges, Ruth*, 473; Hubbard, *Ruth*, 112. עָגַן and the previous verb (Piel of שָׂבַר) are the only alleged Aramaisms in Ruth identified by M. Wagner (*Die lexikalischen und grammatikalischen Aramaismen im alttestamentlichen Hebräisch* [Berlin: Töpelmann, 1966]). However, שָׂבַר is more likely an archaic Hebrew word (Campbell, *Ruth*, 69), and עָגַן is attested in rabbinic Hebrew as well as Aramaic.

אַל בְּנֹתַי—Without a verb, אַל ("no") may function elliptically as an emphatic, independent negative to reject a demand in the discourse of a narrative (see Gen 19:17–18; Judg 19:22–23).[73] A jussive verb may be implied (Joüon, § 160 j), such as יְהִי (GKC, § 152 g): "May it not be!"

כִּי־מַר־לִי מְאֹד מִכֶּם—Alliteration is created by three of these short Hebrew words beginning with the letter מ, which also ends the last word (*mar, me'od, mikkem*).[74] A first possibility for מַר is that it is the adjective, "bitter," used as a noun, "bitterness" (*HALOT*, s.v. מַר I, 4). If so, then לְ would denote possession: מַר־לִי, "bitterness to me," means "I have bitterness." The preposition מִן (מִכֶּם, with second masculine plural suffix in place of feminine; see the last textual note on 1:8) would indicate comparison, and the whole clause would mean, "I have much more bitterness than you" (cf. Waltke-O'Connor, § 14.4f, example 32).

A second possibility, reflected in the translation above, is that מַר could be the third masculine singular Qal perfect of מָרַר, "to be bitter" (so BDB, s.v. מָרַר I, Qal, 2, and *HALOT*, s.v. מרר I, Qal, 1). The verb is impersonal, with no expressed subject ("*It* is bitter ...") but with Naomi as the indirect object (לִי, "... to me"). The prepositional phrase מִכֶּם likely denotes comparison, strengthened by מְאֹד, "much, very": "It is much more bitter for me than for you."[75]

---

[73] *HALOT*, s.v. אַל I, 1 a; Joüon, § 161 l 4; Morris, *Ruth*, 255; Würthwein, "Ruth," 8–9; Campbell, *Ruth*, 66, 70; Gerleman, *Ruth, Das Hohelied*, 19; Williams, § 403; Gray, *Joshua, Judges, Ruth*, 386–87; Hubbard, *Ruth*, 99; Bush, *Ruth, Esther*, 80.

[74] Hubbard, *Ruth*, 112, n. 37. Instead of the comparative, ESV interprets: "It is exceedingly bitter to me for your sake."

[75] The context makes it unlikely that the preposition מִן would indicate source or cause, in which case the construction with the impersonal verb would mean "it is very bitter to me on your account" (BDB, s.v. מָרַר I, Qal, 2), or more freely, "I am very bitter because of you." Also less likely is the view that the preposition מִן could form an elliptical comparison; the clause would then mean "I am much too unhappy [bitter] for you" (Joüon, § 141 i; § 152 d says מַר is the impersonal verb; cf. Waltke-O'Connor, § 14.4f, example 32).

Ruth 1:6–22

Even though the form of the verb מָרַר is impersonal here, the following reference to "the hand of the LORD" (see the next textual note) hints that Naomi considers the LORD to be the cause of her bitterness. Her milder lament here prepares the reader for 1:20, where she will state this openly. She will use the noun מָרָא (*Mara,* related to the verb מָרַר here) to describe herself in 1:20. Then she will use a Hiphil form (הֵמַר) of the same verb here (מָרַר) with "the Almighty" as subject to state that "the Almighty has made me very bitter!" (1:20). For other embittered lives of Israelites, see Ex 1:14; 1 Sam 30:6.

Other verses in Ruth (see 1:16–17, 20–21; 4:11–12, 14–15) have obvious poetic parallelism. The last two clauses of 1:13 may be a poetic couplet in synonymous parallelism:[76]

כִּי־מַר־לִי מְאֹד מִכֶּם
כִּי־יָצְאָה בִי יַד־יְהוָה׃

For it is much more bitter for me than for you,
because the hand of the LORD has gone forth against me!

יָצְאָה בִי יַד־יְהוָה׃—The noun יָד is feminine and so it takes a feminine verb, יָצְאָה, literally, "the hand of the LORD has gone forth against me" (cf. BDB, s.v. יָצָא, Qal, 2 c). It can be compared to passages where the LORD stretches out his hand (שָׁלַח יָד) against someone in judgment or punishment (e.g., Ex 3:20; 9:15; Job 1:11; 2:5). In such passages, God's "hand" refers to the working of his irresistible power.[77] Here, the adversative בְּ expresses disadvantage: "against" (Williams, § 242).

---

[76] Campbell, *Ruth,* 70.
[77] Ex 7:4; 1 Sam 5:6; Job 12:9–10; Ps 39:11 (ET 39:10); Heb 10:31; A. S. van der Woude, "יָד," *TLOT* 2:501–2; Roberts, "The Hand of Yahweh"; Hubbard, *Ruth,* 113.

1:14 וַתִּשֶּׂנָה קוֹלָן וַתִּבְכֶּינָה עוֹד—The first three words are repeated from the end of 1:9 (see the textual note there), but here the א in וַתִּשֶּׂאנָה (the form in 1:9) has elided to make וַתִּשֶּׂנָה (see GKC, §§ 23 f; 76 b; Joüon, § 78 f; cf. וְצָמֵת in 2:9). The repetition of "they raised their voice and wept" conveys the emotion of the final parting of the women. It also suggests that the adverb עוֹד has the sense "again" (*HALOT*, 3), which modifies the combined action of the two verbs as a unit (a hendiadys). However, עוֹד could mean "a long time" (cf. BDB, 1 a; see Gen 46:29).[78]

וַתִּשַּׁק עָרְפָּה לַחֲמוֹתָהּ—The verb form of נָשַׁק is the same as in 1:9, where Naomi kissed her daughters-in-law. The feminine noun חָמוֹת refers specifically to the "husband's mother" (BDB) even though it usually is translated more generally as "mother-in-law." The Semitic languages have many specific terms for relatives because matters of kinship were so important in the ancient Near East. In contrast, English has no separate terms to distinguish between a husband's mother or siblings and those of the wife. חָמוֹת occurs ten times in Ruth, always referring to Naomi. Elsewhere in the OT it occurs only in Micah 7:6, to which Jesus alludes in Mt 10:35–36 and Lk 12:53.

In order to clarify the result of Orpah kissing Naomi here, the LXX adds "and she [Orpah] returned to her people"; the Peshitta adds "she turned and went"; and NIV adds "kissed her ... *good-by*."[79]

וְרוּת דָּבְקָה בָּהּ:—The *waw* on וְרוּת has an adversative meaning: "*but* Ruth ..."[80] This clause inverts the usual verb-subject word order and forms a chiasm with the previous clause; the Hebrew word order is "kissed Orpah ... Ruth clung."). This structure, with Ruth's name first in this clause, heightens the contrast between her and Orpah. This clause also provides a second attributive for Naomi in a kind of parallelism, as she is first kissed (by Orpah) and then embraced (by Ruth).[81]

---

[78] Bush, *Ruth, Esther*, 81.
[79] Cf. Campbell, *Ruth*, 61, 72.
[80] Campbell, *Ruth*, 72; cf. BDB, s.v. וְ, 1 e.
[81] Berlin, Poetics and Interpretation of Biblical Narrative, 106; Hubbard, *Ruth*, 115.

Ruth 1:6–22

The verb דָּבַק, "to cling, cleave, stick to" someone, usually takes the preposition בְּ with the object and "signifies the formation of a new unity binding both sides together."⁸² It is used in Gen 2:24 (in contrast with עָזַב): in the commitment of affection and loyalty, a husband forsakes (עָזַב) his parents to cling to (דָּבַק בְּ) his wife and become one flesh with her—a new unity. Similarly, Ruth forsook her father and mother (עָזַב, 2:11) but refused to forsake Naomi (עָזַב, 1:16) and instead clung to her; thus she was united with Naomi in life and in faith.⁸³ Indeed, in a number of other passages דָּבַק בְּ is used for "clinging to" to the LORD in love and faith. The repetition of דָּבַק in 2:8, 21, 23, though in the weaker sense that Ruth "clings to" Boaz's young women working in the field, serves to remind the hearers of Ruth's commitment to Naomi.

1:15 הִנֵּה שָׁבָה יְבִמְתֵּךְ—The interjection הִנֵּה ("look!"; traditionally rendered as "behold!") functions to attract attention. Here it introduces an announcement by Naomi with emphasis to convince Ruth to leave her (also used in 2:4; 3:2, 8; 4:1).⁸⁴ שָׁבָה is the third feminine singular Qal perfect (while שָׁבָה would have been the participle, "returning"). The perfect indicates that Orpah had already "returned" in the sense of having made the firm decision. The noun יְבָמָה (with second feminine singular suffix, יְבִמְתֵּךְ), "sister-in-law," is evidently a feminine cognate of Old Babylonian *yabamum*, "brother-in-law."⁸⁵ יְבָמָה occurs in the OT only here and in Deut 25:7, 9, where it refers to the wife of a husband's brother in the

---

⁸² Hamlin, Surely There Is a Future, 19.
⁸³ Keil, *Joshua, Judges, Ruth*, 474; E. S. Kalland, "דָּבַק," *TWOT* 1:177-78; Luter and Davis, *God Behind the Seen*, 39; Nielsen, *Ruth*, 48.
⁸⁴ Andersen, The Sentence in Biblical Hebrew, 94; Berlin, Poetics and Interpretation of Biblical Narrative, 91.
⁸⁵ Bush, *Ruth, Esther*, 81–82. Cf. Campbell, *Ruth*, 72–73 and Hubbard, *Ruth*, 114, n. 5.

context of the levirate marriage. In rabbinic Hebrew יְבָמָה often refers specifically to "the widow of a brother who died without issue [children]" (Jastrow), which is appropriate here. For it the LXX coined the word σύννυμφος, "the wife of one's husband's brother" (LEH), used only in LXX Ruth 1:15.

אֶל־עַמָּהּ וְאֶל־אֱלֹהֶיהָ—"People" (עַם) refers to a national group of blood relatives.[86] אֱלֹהִים can refer to "God," a "god," or (plural) "gods," depending on the context. Here אֱלֹהֶיהָ likely has the singular meaning "her god" (so Luther [WA DB 9/1.172]). In 1:16 וֵאלֹהַיִךְ אֱלֹהָי are singular in meaning because they refer to the God of Israel, so אֱלֹהֶיהָ here is likely also singular in meaning for an appropriate parallel: "her god ... your God ... my God" (1:15–16).

שׁוּבִי אַחֲרֵי יְבִמְתֵּךְ—This is Naomi's fourth use of the feminine imperative of שׁוּב, "return"; those in 1:8, 11, 12 were plural (שֹׁבְנָה). Here it takes the preposition אַחֲרֵי in the pregnant sense, "return [by following] after your sister-in-law" (see *HALOT*, s.v. שׁוּב, Qal, 1 a β). Similarly, in 1:16 שׁוּב takes מֵאַחֲרֵי ("return/turn back from [following] after ..."). After her prodding statement about Orpah, this imperative addressed to Ruth has the character of a plea.[87]

1:16 וַתֹּאמֶר רוּת—Because of Ruth's responding protest, the *waw* has the adversative force of "but" (as in 1:3a, 8a).

אַל־תִּפְגְּעִי־בִי—This Qal imperfect with the negative אַל functions as a negative imperative. פָּגַע generally means "meet, encounter" someone (see 2:22) or in a hostile sense, "fall upon, attack." But in this kind of context, it has the sense of "urge, pressure, force" (see Gen 23:8),[88] "request, *entreat*" (BDB, Qal, 4), "press" or

---

[86] A. R. Hulst, "גּוּר/עַם," *TLOT* 2:896–97; Hubbard, *Ruth*, 116, n. 18.
[87] Rebera, "Translating a Text to Be Spoken and Heard," 235.
[88] See Campbell, *Ruth*, 61; Hubbard, *Ruth*, 114, n. 9.

Ruth 1:6–22

"plead with someone" (*HALOT*, Qal, 3 a), and usually takes the preposition בְּ attached to the person (hence בִּי).

לְעָזְבֵךְ—This is the Qal infinitive construct of עָזַב with the preposition לְ and the second feminine singular suffix: "to forsake you."

לָשׁוּב מֵאַחֲרָיִךְ—This is, literally, "to return from after you," that is, to turn back or turn away from following after her. Ruth repeats Naomi's wording (שׁוּב with אַחֲרֵי in a pregnant sense in 1:15b) but adds מִן to form מֵאַחֲרָיִךְ, which could be reflected by translating "turn *away from* [following] after you" or just "turn away from you" (*HALOT*, s.v. שׁוּב, Qal, 1 a β),[89] although that would lose the connection to the motif of returning expressed by the frequent repetition of שׁוּב in chapter 1.

אֶל־אֲשֶׁר תֵּלְכִי אֵלֵךְ וּבַאֲשֶׁר תָּלִינִי אָלִין—The relative pronoun אֲשֶׁר with the preposition אֶל has the sense "to whatever place; wherever." Likewise, בַּאֲשֶׁר (also in 1:17) has the sense "in whatever place; wherever" (see BDB, s.v. אֲשֶׁר, 4 b (γ)). The two verbs תֵּלְכִי אֵלֵךְ are both Qal imperfects (second feminine singular and first common singular, respectively) from הָלַךְ ("you go, I shall go"). The first refers to the indefinite future, while the second is a promissory declaration. Likewise, תָּלִינִי אָלִין ("you lodge, I shall lodge") are both Qal imperfects of לִין, "to lodge, spend the night." That verb fits in reference to the longer journey on to Bethlehem (rather than the shorter one back to Moab), and in Ruth's determination to stay with Naomi wherever she goes.[90] Several months later, Ruth, following Naomi's instructions, will journey to the threshing floor, where Boaz will use this same verb to command her to "spend the night [here]" (3:13).

By repeating her verbs and nouns, the middle section of Ruth's vow is in alliteration (1:16c–17a): *ʾAsher teleki ʾelek, uvaʾasher talini ʾalin. ʿAmmek ʿammi, weʾlohayik ʾelohay. Baʾasher tamuti ʾamut.*[91]

---

[89] See Campbell, *Ruth*, 73. Bush renders: "from following you" (*Ruth, Esther*, 70).
[90] Campbell, *Ruth*, 73–74; Sasson, *Ruth*, 30; Gray, *Joshua, Judges, Ruth*, 388.
[91] Rebera, "Translating a Text to Be Spoken and Heard," 234.

Ruth 1:6–22

עַמֵּךְ עַמִּי וֵאלֹהַיִךְ אֱלֹהָי:—Again, Ruth's words to Naomi have the same vocabulary Naomi used about Orpah ("her people and … her god[s]," 1:15). The nominal sentences are declarations in the present tense: "Your people *is* my people, and your God *is* my God." Although the Hebrew word for "God" is plural in form (אֱלֹהִים), as it was in 1:15, where it referred to a Moabite god or gods, here it must be singular in sense, as it always is when referring to the God of Israel. In the next verse Ruth will clarify that Naomi's "God," who is now also Ruth's "God" (1:16), is "the LORD" (1:17).

1:17 בַּאֲשֶׁר תָּמוּתִי אָמוּת וְשָׁם אֶקָּבֵר—On בַּאֲשֶׁר, "wherever," see the fifth textual note on 1:16. After the present-tense declarations in 1:16b, these imperfects, like those earlier in 1:16 ("I shall go … I shall lodge"), must be rendered in the future tense ("I shall …") to convey the sense of Ruth's unyielding determination. The adverb (with conjunction) וְשָׁם, "and there," is in the emphatic position preceding the verb it modifies (אֶקָּבֵר).[92]

כֹּה יַעֲשֶׂה יְהוָה לִי וְכֹה יֹסִיף—This oath formula is, literally, "Thus may the LORD do to me, and thus may he increase." The verbs are imperfect in form (יַעֲשֶׂה, Qal of עָשָׂה, and יֹסִיף, Hiphil of יָסַף) but clearly jussive in meaning (Joüon, § 165 a). This imprecatory oath leaves unstated the form of punishment that God would inflict if the oath is violated. The origin of this oath may have been in covenant ceremonies, and the oath originally may have called for the LORD to slaughter anyone who violated it, just as a covenant could be ratified by a solemn oath with the slaughter of an animal as a sign of the penalty for violating the covenant (Gen 15:7–17; Jer 34:18–20). Some commentators suppose that the person, while uttering the oath "Thus may the LORD do to me," would have made some symbolic gesture comparable to the modern practice of drawing a finger across the throat to represent the penalty of death for violating it. The next

---

[92] Hubbard, *Ruth*, 118.

Ruth 1:6–22

idiom, וְכֹה יֹסִיף, "and thus may he do even more so," invokes God to impose an additional punishment of his choice (cf. 2 Sam 24:13).[93] This basic oath form (כֹּה עָשָׂה יהוה/אֱלֹהִים) appears eleven other times in the OT, all in the books of Samuel and Kings. In most of those passages, Israelites invoke "God" (אֱלֹהִים), but in 1 Ki 19:2 and 20:10 pagans invoke "gods" (also אֱלֹהִים). Only in 1 Sam 20:13 and Ruth 1:17 does the speaker invoke "the LORD" (יהוה), and this is the only place in the book where Ruth invokes "the LORD," so Ruth is here uttering a powerful confession of faith in the personal name of Israel's covenant God.[94] In Samuel and Kings the oath often concerns weighty matters of state, but Jonathan uses it to swear his enduring loyalty to David (1 Sam 20:13). Here Ruth uses it to swear her enduring loyalty to Naomi and her resolve to accompany Naomi even as far as burial (1:17a), so that not even death should separate them. The oath marks the preceding vow (1:16b–17a) as a sworn promise before the LORD. The invocations of the name of the LORD in Naomi's blessing (1:8–9) and Ruth's oath (1:17) form an inclusio around the intervening speeches (1:10–16).[95]

כִּי הַמָּוֶת יַפְרִיד בֵּינִי וּבֵינֵךְ:—The preceding oath formula is often followed by a clause beginning with כִּי, which then usually serves as an asseverative conjunction, "surely … !"[96] If that were the case here, this clause would, literally, be "surely death *will* separate between me and you." However, Ruth has just declared, "Wherever you die, I shall die, and there I shall be buried!" (1:17a). She has stated that even death *shall not* separate her from Naomi, because she shall die and be buried in the same place as Naomi. Therefore many

---

[93] For discussions of the oath formula, see GKC, § 149 d; Joüon, § 165 a–b; Campbell, *Ruth*, 74; Morris, *Ruth*, 261, who notes, citing D. J. Wiseman, that the same formula was found at Mari and Alalakh (eighteenth century B.C.); de Waard and Nida, *A Translator's Handbook on the Book of Ruth*, 19; Berlin, *Poetics and Interpretation of Biblical Narrative*, 106; Gray, *Joshua, Judges, Ruth*, 388; Bush, *Ruth, Esther*, 82–83; Block, *Judges, Ruth*, 642–43; Hubbard, *Ruth*, 118–20.
[94] Campbell, *Ruth*, 74–75.
[95] Hubbard, *Ruth*, 119.
[96] 1 Sam 14:44; 20:13; 2 Sam 3:9, 35; 1 Ki 2:23; 19:2. See BDB, s.v. כִּי, 1 c; GKC, § 149 d; Joüon, § 165 a–b.

commentaries and English translations consider כִּי to be conditional ("if"). Ruth says, "Thus may the LORD do to me ... *if* death will separate me and you!" and the clause is a declaration that death *will not* separate her from Naomi. For example, Campbell analyzes the conjunctions that can be used with the oath formula (אִם, אִם לֹא, כִּי אִם, and כִּי אִם) and, citing 1:17a, concludes that the clause here means "*if* even death ..." (so also RSV) and is a strong affirmation that "promises loyalty to death and to the grave, including the adoption of Israelite burial custom."[97]

That view is preferable to the expedient taken by other translations that add qualifiers, for example, "if *ought but* death" (KJV), "if *anything but* death" (NIV, ESV), or "death *alone*," since even with those additions Ruth would still be saying that death *would* separate her from Naomi.

"Death" (הַמָּוֶת) stands in the emphatic position, since it is the subject and it precedes the verb (יַפְרִיד). Normal Hebrew word order is verb-subject.[98] The generic article may be used in Hebrew with abstract terms denoting states (Waltke-O'Connor, § 13.5.1g), but here it may be demonstrative or emphatic, even personifying "the death" as a force to be reckoned with (cf. הַמָּוֶת in Deut 30:15, 19; Is 25:8; Ps 116:15).[99]

The verb יַפְרִיד ("separate," Hiphil imperfect of פָּרַד) recalls Abraham's separation (Niphal of פָּרַד in Gen 13:9, 11, 14) from Lot, the father of Moab (Gen 19:36–37). That the verb here is negated in the context of the oath may imply a reunion of the two lines through Ruth the Moabitess.[100]

---

[97] Campbell, *Ruth*, 74–75. Unfortunately, Campbell denies that it has "the sense of a blessed reunion after death" (p. 75).
[98] Morris, *Ruth*, 261; Hubbard, *Ruth*, 119.
[99] See John R. Wilch, "Sermon: Psalm 116," *Lutheran Theological Review* 16 (2003–2004): 59–61 (a sermon on Ps 116:15).
[100] Hubbard, *Ruth*, 120, n. 34.

Ruth 1:6–22

1:18 וַתֵּ֕רֶא—With this Qal imperfect (third feminine singular of רָאָה) the *waw* consecutive indicates consequence with the resumptive clause: "*When* she saw …"[101]

כִּי־מִתְאַמֶּצֶת הִיא—In Qal אָמַץ means "be strong, brave." The Hithpael, which occurs elsewhere only in 1 Ki 12:18; 2 Chr 10:18; 13:7, here has a direct reflexive meaning (Waltke-O'Connor, § 26.2c), literally, "make oneself strong," that is, "summon one's courage," or be "determined" (RSV). Gray renders: "having rallied herself."[102] The (feminine singular) participle expresses durative action: she remained "firmly resolved, determined"[103] "to go with her" (לָלֶכֶת אִתָּהּ).

וַתֶּחְדַּל לְדַבֵּר אֵלֶיהָ:—After the protasis that indicated simultaneity ("*When* she saw …"), the Qal imperfect with *waw* consecutive (of חָדַל, "cease, stop") is resumptive and the *waw* need not be translated ("When … [then] …").[104] The following phrase with infinitive construct is, literally, "to speak to her," but דִּבֶּר can bear a stronger sense, for example, "threaten, promise, order, propose" (see *HALOT*, 5–7), so that "urging" is appropriate here.

To the end of 1:18 the LXX adds ἔτι ("further"), and the Syriac adds "to turn away." Such is not needed, though, because the narrator's style changes pace and becomes more concise when the story makes a transition, as here.[105] The short report in 1:18 forms an inclusio with the report preceding the dialogue (1:6–7).[106]

---

[101] See Bush on 3:7a (*Ruth, Esther*, 159, n. 7a).
[102] Gray, Joshua, Judges, Ruth, 388.
[103] See Enns, *Ruth*, 28; Bush, *Ruth, Esther*, 83.
[104] Williams, §§ 440, 496; Bush, Ruth, Esther, 83; cf. Berlin, Poetics and Interpretation of Biblical Narrative, 106.
[105] Campbell, *Ruth*, 62.
[106] Hubbard, *Ruth*, 121.

1:19 וַתֵּלַכְנָה שְׁתֵּיהֶם—Masculine forms of שְׁנַיִם ("two") occurred five times in 1:1–5. Feminine forms (of שְׁתַּיִם) occurred in 1:7–8. Here שְׁתֵּיהֶם appears to have a masculine (third person plural) suffix, even though the preceding verb (וַתֵּלַכְנָה) is feminine (third person plural imperfect, from הָלַךְ). Many manuscripts have the feminine suffix (שְׁתֵּיהֶן). The suffix on שְׁתֵּיהֶם may be an archaic feminine dual; see the last textual note on 1:8.

עַד־בֹּאָנָה בֵּית לָחֶם—The preposition עַד is followed by a Qal infinitive construct of בּוֹא with third feminine plural suffix (GKC, § 91 f; Joüon, § 94 h), literally, "until their entering Bethlehem." The place name is a local accusative (Waltke-O'Connor, § 10.2.2b), not a direct object of the infinitive. Instead of meaning "come to," בּוֹא with such a local accusative can mean "to enter" a place (Joüon, § 125 n), as also in 1:2, 19b, 22; 2:18; 3:15. Perhaps the preposition בְּ is not used with בֵּית by haplology (not haplography), that is, to avoid the repetition of bilabial stops in בְּבֵית (Waltke-O'Connor, § 10.2.2, footnotes 14 and 15).

וַיְהִי כְּבֹאָנָה בֵּית לֶחֶם—This temporal clause is, literally, "and it was as their entering Bethlehem." The *waw* consecutive introduces a new development: "Now, when …" This clause is omitted in the LXX as if redundant. However, it is not, for וַיְהִי, as a temporal clause, signals that the next episode (the women in Bethlehem, 1:19b–22) really begins here (1:19b).[107] The repetition of בֹּאָנָה בֵּית לֶחֶם ("their entering Bethlehem") from the preceding clause serves to slow the pace and build suspense. The preposition כְּ used temporally can indicate that two things occur at the same time (correspondence), or, as is the case here, when the second (the city's excitement) is the immediate result of the first (their entrance).[108]

וַתֵּהֹם כָּל־הָעִיר עֲלֵיהֶן—The verb is a Niphal imperfect with *waw* consecutive from הוּם, "murmur, roar, be excited," which is onomatopoeic (as is "hum" in English). The Niphal occurs in only two other passages: for the positive excitement caused by the arrival

---

[107] Campbell, *Ruth*, 75; Hubbard, *Ruth*, 123; Bush, *Ruth, Esther*, 89.
[108] Cf. Hubbard, *Ruth*, 121; Waltke-O'Connor, § 11.2.9e, including example 17.

of the ark in Israel's military camp (1 Sam 4:5) and Jerusalem's excitement at Solomon's coronation (1 Ki 1:45), though there it might also involve consternation since Adonijah had already exalted himself as king (1 Ki 1:5–10).[109] The verb is a by-form of הָמָה, "roar, be boisterous, in commotion," and of הָמַם, "make a noise." The noun עִיר, usually rendered "city," can refer to an inhabited walled town of any size. Here כָּל־הָעִיר is translated "the whole town." The expression is a synecdoche: "the whole town" stands for a major part of the population.[110]

וַתֹּאמַרְנָה—The verb is feminine plural, hence "the women said ... ," but there is no clearly defined subject (cf. Joüon, § 155 b, footnote 1). It must refer to the women of the town, who would have been present there during the day at their household duties, while the men were in the fields tending to the harvest (1:22).[111]

הֲזֹאת נָעֳמִי—The interrogative particle -הֲ can have an exclamatory meaning, *"this is indeed Naomi!"* (Joüon, § 161 b).

1:20 וַתֹּאמֶר—Because Naomi opposes the women's use of her name, the *waw* is adversative: "But she said ..." (as in 1:3a, 8a).

קְרֶאןָ לִי מָרָא—The Qal feminine plural imperative (of קָרָא, "call") lacks the final ה as a vowel letter (GKC, §§ 46 f, 74 h), as did imperatives in 1:9, 12. The adjective מַר, "bitter," is from מָרַר "be bitter." The normal Hebrew feminine form is מָרָה, which is the reading in many Hebrew manuscripts. The form מָרָא may be an Aramaized spelling (GKC, § 80 h; Joüon, § 89 k), but if so, it does not mean that the date of writing is late. The form could also be a diminutive or hypocoristicon indicating familiarity or fondness, since

---

[109] Cf. Sasson, "Ruth," 323; Bush, *Ruth, Esther*, 91; Block, *Judges, Ruth*, 645.
[110] Bush, *Ruth, Esther*, 91.
[111] Morris, *Ruth*, 262.

Ruth 1:6–22

such an ending is found in West Semitic onomastica (א-) and appended to feminine names at Mari (-a).[112]

הֵמַר שַׁדַּי לִי מְאֹד:—The Hiphil third masculine singular perfect verb, from מָרַר, has a causative meaning, "to make bitter," and the form and sound of הֵמַר make a wordplay with מָרָא.[113] Job uses the same verb in a similar context: וְשַׁדַּי הֵמַר נַפְשִׁי, "and Shaddai [the Almighty] has made my soul bitter" (Job 27:2; cf. his use of a cognate noun in Job 13:26). There the verb takes a direct object, whereas here it takes a prepositional phrase: הֵמַר שַׁדַּי לִי could be rendered literally as "the Almighty caused bitterness for me" or "made things bitter for me." The wording here recalls the similar phrase מַר־לִי in 1:13. The rendering "the Almighty has dealt very bitterly with me" (NASB, RSV, and ESV, following KJV) is both grammatically and theologically suspect because it could suggest that God was embittered against Naomi. The divine epithet שַׁדַּי is usually translated "the Almighty," following the LXX, which usually uses παντοκράτωρ, but here the LXX has ὁ ἱκανός, "the (All-)Sufficient One." The Vulgate's *Omnipotens* is probably closest to the sense of שַׁדַּי according to its usage in the OT.[114]

---

[112] Sasson, *Ruth*, 32–34; Hubbard, *Ruth*, 122, n. 9; cf. Campbell, *Ruth*, 76; Bush, *Ruth, Esther*, 92; Gray, *Joshua, Judges, Ruth*, 389.
[113] De Waard and Nida, A Translator's Handbook on the Book of Ruth, 20.
[114] Scholars have suggested that שַׁדַּי may originally have meant "the Mountain One," based on Akkadian *shadu* (see *HALOT*, 4; cf. *shdyn* in a seventh-century B.C. text as an epithet of *ʾlhn*; Jo Ann Hackett, *The Balaam Text from Deir ʿAllā* [Chico, Calif.; Scholars Press, 1980], 86–87). Other suggestions include "strong," from Arabic *shadda,* and "Overpowerer," from שָׁדַד (*shadad*). See Cassel, *Ruth*, 23–24; Rudolph, *Das Buch Ruth, das Hohe Lied, die Klagelieder*, 45; V. P. Hamilton, "שַׁדַּי," *TWOT* 2:907; M. Weippert, "שַׁדַּי," *TLOT* 3:1304–10; Ringgren, *Israelite Religion*, 22; Pfeiffer, "Ruth," 269; Morris, *Ruth*, 263–68; Campbell, *Ruth*, 76–77; Gray, *Joshua, Judges, Ruth*, 389; Hubbard, *Ruth*, 124–25; Bush, *Ruth, Esther*, 92–93; Lawrenz, *Judges, Ruth*, 228; Block, *Judges, Ruth*, 646.

Ruth 1:6–22

1:21 אֲנִי מְלֵאָה הָלַכְתִּי—The superfluous pronoun אֲנִי is for emphasis in order to contrast chiastically with יְהוָה: this clause begins with "I," and the next one ends with "the LORD."[115] The lack of a *waw* on אֲנִי makes this declaration terser. The feminine adjective מְלֵאָה ("full") is an adverbial accusative of state, modifying the verb הָלַכְתִּי (Qal perfect first common singular from הָלַךְ), and it is in the emphatic position before the verb.[116] The sense allows rendering the verb "went *away*" from the point of reference, Bethlehem.

וְרֵיקָם הֱשִׁיבַנִי יְהוָה—The adverb רֵיקָם ("emptily, empty-handed") is in the emphatic position before the verb it modifies, הֱשִׁיבַנִי.[117] The adjective רֵיק means "empty," and the addition of ־ָם forms one of the few true adverbs in Hebrew (cf. also יוֹמָם). The narrator ties the story together by repeating words even at long range; רֵיקָם reappears in 3:17.[118] The verb הֱשִׁיבַנִי is a Hiphil third masculine singular perfect from שׁוּב with first common singular suffix: "he brought me back" or "he returned me." In another long-range repetition, the Hiphil of שׁוּב (מֵשִׁיב, participle) serves in a contrasting context in 4:15, meaning "*restore* your soul."

Ruth 1:21a thus has two parallel clauses, and the three members of each stand in contrast: "I ... the LORD," "full ... empty," "went away ... brought back."[119]

לָמָּה תִקְרֶאנָה לִי נָעֳמִי—The interrogative ("Why ...?") is not looking for an answer, but calls into question their use of "Naomi" for her, and carries a corrective meaning, as does לָמָּה also in Gen 42:1 and Ruth 1:11.[120]

(וְשַׁדַּי הֵרַע לִי) וַיהוָה עָנָה בִי—This and the following clause (וְשַׁדַּי הֵרַע לִי) stand in synonymous poetic parallelism; both have the same word order (subject, verb, prepositional phrase). After the preceding rhetorical question, the *waw* on וַיהוָה has a causal, disjunctive sense:

---

[115] Morris, *Ruth*, 263; Hubbard, *Ruth*, 126; but see Bush, *Ruth, Esther*, 93.
[116] GKC, § 118 n; Joüon, § 126 a; Hubbard, *Ruth*, 122, n. 13, 125; Linafelt, *Ruth*, 20.
[117] Hubbard, *Ruth*, 126; Linafelt, *Ruth*, 20.
[118] Campbell, *Ruth*, 77.
[119] Hubbard, *Ruth*, 126, n. 29.
[120] Hyman, "Questions and the Book of Ruth," 19.

"*for* the LORD ..." explains why she should not be called "Naomi."[121] The idiom עָנָה בְּ usually means "to testify against" someone (BDB, s.v. עָנָה I, 3 a; *HALOT*, s.v. עָנָה I, 2), as also in the Eighth Commandment. עָנָה בִּי is in alliteration or a paronomasia with נָעֳמִי. The general motif of testifying occurs again with the noun עֵדִים, "witnesses," in 4:10–11.[122]

The LXX, Syriac, Vulgate, and Luther (WA DB 9/1.172) all translated as if the verb were a homograph meaning "humiliate, afflict." However, that verb has that meaning in the Piel, which would be עִנָּה (see BDB, s.v. עָנָה III, and *HALOT*, s.v. עָנָה II), and it never appears in the MT in that sense with the preposition בְּ. Michael Moore argues that the artistic author may have chosen עָנָה for a deliberate wordplay: although in context here it means "testify," it sounds similar to עִנָּה, "humiliate," and thus implies that Naomi suffered in different ways.[123]

וְשַׁדַּי הֵרַע לִי:—The verb is the Hiphil third masculine singular perfect of רָעַע, meaning "do an injury, hurt" someone, and it often takes the preposition לְ with the object (BDB, s.v. רָעַע, Hiphil, 1; *HALOT*, s.v. רעע I, Hiphil, 2 a, gives "to do something bad to someone"). In a legal context it may have a juridical sense, "pronounce a guilty sentence upon someone," as it does in Ex 5:22; Num 11:11; and 1 Ki 17:20, where (in all three verses) God's presumed verdict and punishment is also questioned.[124] If so here, it would be parallel to the previous verb, "*testified* against." The whole clause (וְשַׁדַּי הֵרַע לִי) is very similar to הֵמַר שַׁדַּי לִי at the end of 1:20. The similarity suggests that 1:20b–21 may have chiastic parallelism:

---

[121] BDB, s.v. וְ, 1 k; Waltke-O'Connor, § 39.2.3b; see Gen 24:56.
[122] Keil, *Joshua, Judges, Ruth*, 476; C. J. Labuschagne, "ענה,"*TLOT* 2:929–30; Campbell, *Ruth*, 77, 83; Witzenrath, *Das Buch Rut*, 20; Sasson, *Ruth*, 31, 35; Hubbard, *Ruth*, 122, n. 14, 126–27, including n. 31, who says that this verb is used in this way only here with God as subject; Collins, "Ambiguity and Theology in Ruth," 99; Lawrenz, *Judges, Ruth*, 228.
[123] Moore, "Two Textual Anomalies in Ruth"; also Sasson, *Ruth*, 36.
[124] Campbell, *Ruth*, 77; Bush, *Ruth, Esther*, 93.

Ruth 1:6–22

A   The Almighty has made me very bitter!
B   I went away full, but empty the Lord returned me!
B' Why should you call me Naomi?
    For the Lord has testified against me,
A' and the Almighty has afflicted me!

A and A' express the suffering caused by Shaddai, while B and B' contrast what she once had and was with what the LORD has done to her.[125]

1:22 וַתָּ֤שָׁב נָעֳמִי֙—The *waw* consecutive (with third feminine singular imperfect of שׁוּב) here introduces recapitulation: "so Naomi returned."[126] As in 1:7a, Naomi alone is the subject of the singular verb, showing that she is the main actor, even though she is accompanied (see the next textual note).

וְר֨וּת הַמּוֹאֲבִיָּ֤ה כַלָּתָהּ֙ עִמָּ֔הּ—As in 1:7a, a prepositional phrase with עִמָּהּ ("with her") adds another participant in Naomi's action. In the translation, "with her" comes first so that the clause ends with a reference to Ruth, since the following clause probably refers to Ruth (even though it is true of Naomi too).

הַשָּׁ֖בָה מִשְּׂדֵ֣י מוֹאָ֑ב—The syntax prominently highlights that Ruth "returned" from Moab,[127] just as the start of the verse highlights Naomi's return. The accent on the penultimate syllable of הַשָּׁ֖בָה indicates that the verb is the Qal third feminine singular perfect (of שׁוּב), emphasizing the past, accomplished act. It has the definite article (-הַ), which serves as a relative pronoun: "(she) *who* returned."

---

[125] Trible, "A Human Comedy, 169.
[126] As also in Gen 2:1; 23:20; Josh 10:40; 1 Sam 17:50; 31:6. Joüon, § 118 i, cites Ruth 1:22 as a passage where a *waw* consecutive with imperfect is used "for a **conclusion** or a **summing up**." See also Cassel, *Ruth*, 23; Williams, § 178; Waltke-O'Connor, § 33.2.1a; Hubbard, *Ruth*, 128, n. 1; Bush, *Ruth, Esther*, 93–94.
[127] Cf. Campbell, *Ruth*, 79–80; Sasson, *Ruth*, 36–37; Hubbard, *Ruth*, 129; Bush, *Ruth, Esther*, 94.

The identical form with penultimate accent and the article occurs again in 2:6 (referring to Ruth) and 4:3 (referring to Naomi). Similar constructions where a perfect verb has the article serving as a relative pronoun appear occasionally elsewhere in the OT (e.g., הַבָּאָה in Gen 18:21; 46:27).[128] If the accent were on the last syllable (הַשָּׁבָה, like הַבָּאָה in Ruth 4:11), the verb would be the Qal feminine singular participle with the article ("the one returning").[129] In either case, this is the twelfth time that the verb שׁוב ("return") appears in 1:6–22. Six times it points to Moab (1:8, 11, 12, 15a, b, 16) and six times to Judah (1:6, 7, 10, 21, 22aα, aβ).[130]

וְהֵמָּה בָּאוּ בֵּית לֶחֶם—Normally in Hebrew narrative such a sentence would begin with וַיָּבֹאוּ, as does 1:2b. But here a pronoun (grammatically unnecessary) with *waw* precedes a perfect verb. This structure signals that the narrator is inserting a parenthetical, explanatory comment about the season when the women arrived.[131] This serves to highlight the time of the harvest in respect to their return. The form of the pronoun (הֵמָּה) is masculine plural, even though it refers to Naomi and Ruth. Hebrew often uses masculine forms in place of feminine ones, and this pronoun is so used here and also in Song 6:8 and Zech 5:10 (GKC, § 32 n; Joüon, § 149 c). Some argue that it is an old feminine dual form.[132] The name of

---

[128] Other examples are cited in Williams, § 91; GKC, § 138 k; Joüon, § 145 e; Waltke-O'Connor, § 19.7d.

[129] GKC, § 138 k, Joüon, § 145 e, and Waltke-O'Connor, § 19.7d, example 7, argue that despite the accent, the form here is probably a participle because the article is rarely used with perfect verbs in early Hebrew texts; it is more common later. However, such an argument based on the dating of texts is circular. Gen 18:21 and 46:27 are early (Mosaic) texts, and Ruth 1:22; 2:6; and 4:3 are fairly early (united monarchy) texts, all of which have a perfect verb with the article.

[130] Cf. Sasson, *Ruth*, 36; Hubbard, *Ruth*, 128, n. 1, 129; Bush, *Ruth, Esther*, 94.

[131] Compare how the parenthetical comment in 1:2 begins with a noun with *waw* (… וְשֵׁם הָאִישׁ).Compare also the chronological note in 1:4b, which begins in the usual way with וַיֵּשְׁבוּ.

[132] E.g., Fontinoy, *Le duël dans les langues semitiques*, 59–60; Hubbard, *Ruth*, 130; Bush, *Ruth, Esther*, 94. See also the last textual note on 1:8.

Ruth 1:6–22

"Bethlehem" is an accusative of place after the verb בּוֹא, meaning "to enter"; see the second textual note on 1:19.

בִּתְחִלַּת קְצִיר שְׂעֹרִים:—The temporal בְּ used with the noun תְּחִלָּה in construct indicates a point in time (Williams, § 241): "at the beginning of [the] harvest of barley."

Excursus: Faithfulness

When the Israelites put into practice their faith in the LORD, the God of life now and forever, they were faithful to his covenant with them, worshiping him alone (Ex 14:31; 19:3–8; 23:32; Deut 6:4–6). Willful, unrepentant violation of the covenant—in essence idolatry—which would include rejecting their duties pertaining to their ancestral land, meant that they were canceling their participation in the covenant and therefore in everlasting life with the LORD (Ex 32:33; Deut 19:14; 27:17; 29:9–19 [ET 29:10–20]).

It is not that assurance of life after death was absolutely tied to the land inheritance remaining in one's family. Likewise, there is no hint that the burial of Elimelech and his sons in Moab, of the exiles in Babylonia (see Jer 29:4–14), or of Jeremiah and Baruch in Egypt (Jer 43:5–7; 45:2–5), meant forfeiting the life after death that God promised his faithful people. This depended ultimately on the LORD's grace, which they received through faith (see Gen 5:22–24; 15:6; Is 7:9; Hab 2:4).

That Naomi as the family's matriarch lost her children was critical. It was essential that the family name be continued because this was inextricably linked with the inheritance, for the LORD had provided the land of Israel for his people to use and parcel out among the tribes, clans, and families by his own direction (Num 26:55–56). God remained the true owner of the land, his royal estate (Lev 25:23; see also, e.g., Ex 9:29; 19:5; Deut 10:14), and the Israelites were his royal servants, thus, not landowners but tenants. The tithe was the annual lease payment to the LORD (Lev 27:30–33).

The Israelites were forbidden to sell their inheritance; it could only be leased (Lev 25:23–28; Num 36:7). What they privately owned was only the harvests from the land, so that, if a purchase or repurchase ("redemption") came into question, it concerned the value of the remaining harvests until the next Jubilee Year, when the land was to be returned to its inheritor as an emancipation (Lev 25:8–17). If at all possible, a family's inherited land should remain within that family throughout all generations as the down payment or deposit of the LORD's covenant faithfulness to them personally.

Naomi's hope to provide an heir was the objective of her daring plan for Ruth with Boaz (3:1–4). And, true to her complete commitment to Naomi (1:16–17), Ruth fully obeyed her in fulfilling her instructions (3:5–6). There is no indication by the author that Ruth went beyond strict obedience to Naomi when she not only requested Boaz to marry her ("spread out your 'wing' over your handmaid," 3:9), but also added her reason for choosing him ("because you are a redeemer [גֹּאֵל, *go'el*]"). It was the responsibility of a family's redeemer, that is, the closest paternal male relative, to keep the inheritance within the family (Lev 25:25). However, it was not the redeemer's express duty by law or custom to produce an heir through the family's childless widow by levirate marriage. That duty was only incumbent upon the deceased man's unmarried brother, and "brother" there cannot be meant in the extended sense, but must refer to a son of the same father (Deut 25:5–6).[133]

Now, it was Naomi's gamble with Boaz that this ideally upright, pious, and influential "honorable gentleman" (אִישׁ גִּבּוֹר חַיִל, Ruth 2:1),[134] who had been favorably impressed by Ruth's "faithfulness" (חֶסֶד, *ḥesed*, 3:10; see 1:8) and was fully informed about her family's predicament (2:11–12), would acquiesce; and he did. In their request to Boaz, Naomi and Ruth therefore combined marriage with redemption (3:9), and Boaz duly understood their objective as such, namely, "to perpetuate the name of the deceased on his inheritance" (4:5, 10).

---

[133] The above is borne out by the only other relevant biblical case (Gen 38:6–26). See Naomi's arguments (Ruth 1:11–13) and the Sadducees' hypothesis (Mt 22:23–28); R. L. Harris, "גָּאַל," *TWOT* 1:144; H. Ringgren, "גָּאַל," *TDOT* 2:351–52.

[134] See the textual notes on 2:1 and 2:4, 8–12; 4:1–2. In 3:11 Boaz will use a corresponding phrase when he calls Ruth an "honorable woman" (אֵשֶׁת חַיִל).

Ruth 1:6–22

True fidelity (חֶסֶד, *ḥesed*, 1:8; 2:20; 3:10) to the LORD and his covenant with Israel—not personal satisfaction—was the highest priority of Naomi, Ruth, and Boaz. The solemn oaths of Ruth and Boaz (1:16; 3:13) confirmed their fidelity. In recognizing Ruth's "faithfulness" (3:10), Boaz praised her as an "honorable woman" (אֵשֶׁת חַיִל, 3:11), thus sufficiently virtuous to be worthy of marriage to such an exemplary Israelite as he who was characterized as an "honorable gentleman" (אִישׁ גִּבּוֹר חַיִל, 2:1). That was Naomi's hope and goal, Ruth's commitment, and Boaz's sacrifice—all for the sake of fidelity to the LORD and his covenant. And God fully rewarded them by working out his plan of salvation through them, for all three became ancestors not only of King David but also of Jesus the Christ (4:17; Mt 1:5–17; Lk 3:23–32).

In contrast, Orpah (Ruth 1:14–15) and the primary "redeemer" (4:1–8, the closest male relative of Elimelech) both refused to make a self-sacrifice, for they were more concerned about their own personal situation and their own inheritance than about another person's critical situation or inheritance. By thus failing to act in love for their neighbor as for themselves (Lev 19:18), they failed to reflect the LORD's own holiness in the way he had commanded for his holy people (Lev 19:2). They did not trust him to take care of them if they would make a sacrifice (Deut 11:13–15). It seems likely that this Israelite redeemer had faith in the LORD, especially since he initially agreed to redeem (Ruth 4:4), but his faith was weak. Orpah, on the other hand, apparently abandoned any faith in the LORD that she may have had when she "returned to her people and to her [Moabite] god(s)" (1:15). These actions by Orpah and the redeemer as reported in Ruth amount to loving themselves more than God (see Deut 6:5), in effect making an idol of themselves (see Deut 5:7–9). The redeemer's decision excluded him from the role in salvation history of being an ancestor of David and of Christ—a role that Boaz instead received. By returning to "her god(s)," Orpah chose everlasting death as she selfishly sought to insure a better life in this world (see Deut 11:16–17, 21; 30:15–20).

Text, Translation, and Notes

Chapter 2

Ruth 2:1–17

2:1 וּֽלְנׇעֳמִ֞י מוֹדָ֣ע לְאִישָׁ֗הּ אִ֚ישׁ גִּבּ֣וֹר חַ֔יִל מִמִּשְׁפַּ֖חַת אֱלִימֶ֑לֶךְ
וּשְׁמ֖וֹ בֹּֽעַז׃

2 וַתֹּאמֶר֩ ר֨וּת הַמּוֹאֲבִיָּ֜ה אֶֽל־נׇעֳמִ֗י אֵֽלְכָה־נָּ֤א הַשָּׂדֶה֙
וַאֲלַקֳטָ֣ה בַשִּׁבֳּלִ֔ים אַחַ֕ר אֲשֶׁ֥ר אֶמְצָא־חֵ֖ן בְּעֵינָ֑יו
וַתֹּ֥אמֶר לָ֖הּ לְכִ֥י בִתִּֽי׃

3 וַתֵּ֤לֶךְ וַתָּבוֹא֙ וַתְּלַקֵּ֣ט בַּשָּׂדֶ֔ה אַחֲרֵ֖י הַקֹּצְרִ֑ים
וַיִּ֣קֶר מִקְרֶ֔הָ חֶלְקַ֤ת הַשָּׂדֶה֙ לְבֹ֔עַז אֲשֶׁ֖ר מִמִּשְׁפַּ֥חַת אֱלִימֶֽלֶךְ׃

4 וְהִנֵּה־בֹ֗עַז בָּ֚א מִבֵּ֣ית לֶ֔חֶם
וַיֹּ֥אמֶר לַקּוֹצְרִ֖ים יְהוָ֣ה עִמָּכֶ֑ם וַיֹּ֥אמְרוּ ל֖וֹ יְבָרֶכְךָ֥ יְהוָֽה׃

5 וַיֹּ֤אמֶר בֹּ֙עַז֙ לְנַעֲר֔וֹ הַנִּצָּ֖ב עַל־הַקּוֹצְרִ֑ים לְמִ֖י הַנַּעֲרָ֥ה הַזֹּֽאת׃

6 וַיַּ֗עַן הַנַּ֛עַר הַנִּצָּ֥ב עַל־הַקּוֹצְרִ֖ים וַיֹּאמַ֑ר
נַעֲרָ֤ה מֽוֹאֲבִיָּה֙ הִ֔יא הַשָּׁ֥בָה עִֽם־נׇעֳמִ֖י מִשְּׂדֵ֥ה מוֹאָֽב׃

7 וַתֹּ֗אמֶר אֲלַקֳטָה־נָּא֙ וְאָסַפְתִּ֣י בׇעֳמָרִ֔ים אַחֲרֵ֖י הַקּוֹצְרִ֑ים
וַתָּב֣וֹא וַֽתַּעֲמ֗וֹד מֵאָ֤ז הַבֹּ֙קֶר֙ וְעַד־עַ֔תָּה זֶ֛ה שִׁבְתָּ֥הּ הַבַּ֖יִת מְעָֽט׃

8 וַיֹּאמֶר֩ בֹּ֨עַז אֶל־ר֜וּת הֲל֧וֹא שָׁמַ֣עַתְּ בִּתִּ֗י אַל־תֵּלְכִי֙ לִלְקֹט֙
בְּשָׂדֶ֣ה אַחֵ֔ר וְגַ֛ם לֹ֥א תַעֲבוּרִ֖י מִזֶּ֑ה וְכֹ֥ה תִדְבָּקִ֖ין עִם־נַעֲרֹתָֽי׃

9 עֵינַ֜יִךְ בַּשָּׂדֶ֤ה אֲשֶׁר־יִקְצֹרוּן֙ וְהָלַ֣כְתְּ אַחֲרֵיהֶ֔ן
הֲל֥וֹא צִוִּ֛יתִי אֶת־הַנְּעָרִ֖ים לְבִלְתִּ֣י נׇגְעֵ֑ךְ
וְצָמִ֗ת וְהָלַכְתְּ֙ אֶל־הַכֵּלִ֔ים וְשָׁתִ֕ית מֵאֲשֶׁ֥ר יִשְׁאֲב֖וּן הַנְּעָרִֽים׃

10 וַתִּפֹּל֙ עַל־פָּנֶ֔יהָ וַתִּשְׁתַּ֖חוּ אָ֑רְצָה
וַתֹּ֣אמֶר אֵלָ֗יו מַדּוּעַ֩ מָצָ֨אתִי חֵ֤ן בְּעֵינֶ֙יךָ֙ לְהַכִּירֵ֔נִי וְאָנֹכִ֖י נׇכְרִיָּֽה׃

11 וַיַּ֤עַן בֹּ֙עַז֙ וַיֹּ֣אמֶר לָ֔הּ הֻגֵּ֨ד הֻגַּ֜ד לִ֗י כֹּ֤ל אֲשֶׁר־עָשִׂית֙ אֶת־חֲמוֹתֵ֔ךְ
אַחֲרֵ֖י מ֣וֹת אִישֵׁ֑ךְ וַתַּֽעַזְבִ֞י אָבִ֣יךְ וְאִמֵּ֗ךְ וְאֶ֙רֶץ֙ מֽוֹלַדְתֵּ֔ךְ
וַתֵּ֣לְכִ֔י אֶל־עַ֕ם אֲשֶׁ֥ר לֹא־יָדַ֖עַתְּ תְּמ֥וֹל שִׁלְשֽׁוֹם׃

12 יְשַׁלֵּ֥ם יְהוָ֖ה פָּעֳלֵ֑ךְ וּתְהִ֨י מַשְׂכֻּרְתֵּ֜ךְ שְׁלֵמָ֗ה מֵעִ֤ם יְהוָה֙
אֱלֹהֵ֣י יִשְׂרָאֵ֔ל אֲשֶׁר־בָּ֖את לַחֲס֥וֹת תַּֽחַת־כְּנָפָֽיו׃

2 ¹Now Naomi had an acquaintance of her husband, an honorable gentleman from the clan of Elimelech, | and his name was Boaz. |
²Ruth the Moabitess said to Naomi, "Please let me go out to the field | so I can glean ears of grain after whomever I may find favor in his eyes." | And she said to her, "Do go, my daughter!" |
³So she went out, and she came and gleaned in the field after the reapers. | It so happened that this was the portion of the field belonging to Boaz, who was from the clan of Elimelech. |
⁴And behold, Boaz indeed was arriving from Bethlehem. |
He said to the reapers, "The LORD be with you!" And they said to him, "The LORD bless you!" |
⁵Then Boaz said to his servant who was stationed over the reapers, "Who is this young woman?" |
⁶The servant who was stationed over the reapers answered, |
"She is a Moabite young woman, the one who returned with Naomi from the region of Moab. |
⁷She said, 'Please let me glean and gather into sheaves after the reapers.' | So she came and has remained since early morning until now—[except for] this, her sitting in the house a little while." |
⁸Then Boaz said to Ruth, "Pay attention, my daughter: Do not go off to glean | in another field! Yes, never depart from this one! But here cling closely to my young women. |
⁹Keep your eyes on the field they are reaping so that you follow the women. | Have I not commanded the young men not to touch you? | When you are thirsty, you may go to the jars and drink from what the young men draw." |
¹⁰Then she fell face down and bowed to the ground. |
She said to him, "Why have I found favor in your eyes for [you] to acknowledge me even though I am a foreigner?" |
¹¹Then Boaz replied to her, "It has surely been told me all that you did for your mother-in-law | after the death of your husband and how you abandoned your father and mother and the country of your relatives | and came to a people whom you did not know previously. |
¹²May the LORD fulfill your deed and may your reward be full from the LORD, | the God of Israel, to whom you have come to seek refuge under his wings!"

Ruth 2:1–17

13 וַתֹּ֣אמֶר אֶמְצָא־חֵ֤ן בְּעֵינֶ֙יךָ֙ אֲדֹנִ֔י
כִּ֣י נִֽחַמְתָּ֔נִי וְכִ֥י דִבַּ֖רְתָּ עַל־לֵ֣ב שִׁפְחָתֶ֑ךָ
וְאָנֹכִי֙ לֹ֣א אֶֽהְיֶ֔ה כְּאַחַ֖ת שִׁפְחֹתֶֽיךָ׃
14 וַיֹּאמֶר֩ לָ֨ה בֹ֜עַז לְעֵ֣ת הָאֹ֗כֶל גֹּ֤שִֽׁי הֲלֹם֙
וְאָכַ֣לְתְּ מִן־הַלֶּ֔חֶם וְטָבַ֥לְתְּ פִּתֵּ֖ךְ בַּחֹ֑מֶץ
וַתֵּ֙שֶׁב֙ מִצַּ֣ד הַקּוֹצְרִ֔ים וַיִּצְבָּט־לָ֣הּ קָלִ֔י וַתֹּ֥אכַל וַתִּשְׂבַּ֖ע וַתֹּתַֽר׃
15 וַתָּ֖קָם לְלַקֵּ֑ט וַיְצַו֩ בֹּ֨עַז אֶת־נְעָרָ֜יו לֵאמֹ֗ר
גַּ֣ם בֵּ֧ין הָעֳמָרִ֛ים תְּלַקֵּ֖ט וְלֹ֥א תַכְלִימֽוּהָ׃
16 וְגַ֛ם שֹׁל־תָּשֹׁ֥לּוּ לָ֖הּ מִן־הַצְּבָתִ֑ים
וַעֲזַבְתֶּ֥ם וְלִקְּטָ֖ה וְלֹ֥א תִגְעֲרוּ־בָֽהּ׃
17 וַתְּלַקֵּ֥ט בַּשָּׂדֶ֖ה עַד־הָעָ֑רֶב
וַתַּחְבֹּט֙ אֵ֣ת אֲשֶׁר־לִקֵּ֔טָה וַיְהִ֖י כְּאֵיפָ֥ה שְׂעֹרִֽים׃

¹³Then she said, "I find such favor in your eyes, my lord, | for you have comforted me and you have spoken to the heart of your maidservant | —although as for me, I am not comparable to one of your maidservants."

¹⁴Boaz said to her at the time of the meal, "Come here | and eat some of the food, and dip your piece [of bread] in the vinegar!" | So she sat down beside the reapers, and he heaped up for her parched grain. She ate, was full, and had some left over. |

¹⁵When she got up to glean, Boaz ordered his workers, | "Even among the sheaves she may glean, and you shall in no way humiliate her! |

¹⁶Yes, you shall surely pull out for her [some stalks] from the piles, | and you shall leave [them] so she can glean [them], and do not at all rebuke her!" |

¹⁷So she gleaned in the field until the evening. | Then she beat out what she had gleaned; it amounted to about a bushel of barley.

Ruth 2:1–17

2:1 וּֽלְנָעֳמִ֞י מוֹדַ֣ע לְאִישָׁ֗הּ—The opening sentence of this chapter begins with a disjunctive *waw* clause (וְ attached to a noun rather than a verb), which can indicate that the narrator is presenting parenthetical, explanatory information that is essential for full appreciation of the following new episode, namely, the proleptic introduction of a major new character.[135] This clause is, literally, "and (belonging) to Naomi was an acquaintance (belonging) to her husband." Hebrew normally employs the preposition לְ (rather than a verb) to indicate possession: "(belonging) to Naomi …" means "Naomi had …" (see BDB, s.v. לְ, 5 a, and לְ also in 1:11–12). A construct phrase can also indicate possession, but instead a second לְ is used (לְאִישָׁהּ) to keep the referent indefinite ("*an* acquaintance").[136]

The consonants of the Kethib are to be vocalized מְיֻדָּע, "acquaintance, close friend," the Pual participle of יָדַע, "to know," which is one of the narrator's key terms. The verb יָדַע occurs seven other times (2:11; 3:3–4, 11, 14, 18; 4:4), and other words from this root occur in 2:10 and 3:2. The Qere is מוֹדָע, a noun meaning "kinsman, relative" (elsewhere in the OT only in Prov 7:4, parallel to "sister"), which would indicate a close blood relative. However, the following phrase "from the clan of Elimelech" would be too redundant after "relative," so the Kethib is preferable. The Pual participle may well be a somewhat antiquated one for a covenant partner, that is, someone "known" as such. In Job 19:14 it is parallel to קְרוֹבַי, "my close ones," and in Ruth 2:20 קָרוֹב ("related, close") is parallel to the covenant term גֹּאֲלֵנוּ, "our redeemers." Thus, while מוֹדָע ("relative") would emphasize the man's close blood relationship, מְיֻדָּע ("an acquaintance") stresses his covenant

---

[135] Waltke-O'Connor, § 39.2.3c, including example 11. Similar disjunctive waw clauses begin Ruth 1:2 and also Gen 3:1; Ex 3:1; Josh 6:1; Judg 11:1; 1 Sam 3:1. See Hubbard, *Ruth*, 132, n. 4; Bush, *Ruth, Esther*, 101.

[136] Waltke-O'Connor, § 11.2.10f, including example 46. Since לְאִישָׁהּ is definite (because of the suffix), the construct phrase מְיֻדַּע־אִישָׁהּ would mean "*the* acquaintance of her husband."

Ruth 2:1–17

responsibility within the clan.[137] This indefinite term in a circumstantial verbless clause identifies the class membership of a new character now being introduced.[138]

אִישׁ גִּבּוֹר חַיִל—"An honorable gentleman."

מִמִּשְׁפַּחַת אֱלִימֶלֶךְ—While מִשְׁפָּחָה (here in construct) is often rendered "family," it refers to the greater family of relatives: a grouping of families or a clan (or phratry) that set the bounds of kinship. There were a number of clans in each Israelite tribe (Deut 29:17 [ET 29:18]; Josh 7:14).[139] The name of this particular clan was evidently Ephrath, since Elimelech and his sons were identified as "Ephrathites" in Ruth 1:2. What we call "family" (or "extended family") was indicated by "house" or "father's house" (Gen 12:1; 24:40; cf. "mother's house," Ruth 1:8; "house of her husband," 1:9; and "your household/house," 4:11–12).[140]

וּשְׁמוֹ בֹעַז:—The name בֹּעַז ("Boaz") may mean "in him [בּוֹ] is strength [עֹז]," which is supported by the way the LXX (Βοος) and the Vulgate (Booz) vocalize the consonants (as if בֹּעֹז, boʿoz). The name would refer to God, to whom "strength" (עֹז) is attributed in, for example, Ex 15:2 (עָזִּי, "my strength"), 13; Pss 29:1; 63:3 (ET 63:2). Or it may mean "in [בְּ] the strength [עֹז] of" (בְּעֹז, beʿoz), a hypocoristicon or shortened form of the phrase "in the strength of the LORD" (בְּעֹז־יהוה, as in Micah 5:3), but this is uncertain and debated. בֹּעַז ("Boaz") was also the name of one of the two pillars before the Solomonic temple (1 Ki 7:21); the other was named יָכִין (yakin, Jachin), meaning "he [God] establishes." Although a Hebrew speaker would associate the name Boaz with "strength," it may be an authentic name whose meaning has been lost.[141]

---

[137] See Campbell's thorough discussion (*Ruth*, 88–90); see also Keil, *Joshua, Judges, Ruth*, 477; Sasson, *Ruth*, 39; Gray, *Joshua, Judges, Ruth*, 390; Hubbard, *Ruth*, 132–33; but cf. Bush, *Ruth, Esther*, 100–101.
[138] Andersen, The Sentence in Biblical Hebrew, 31–32.
[139] C. U. Wolf, "Tribe," *IDB* 4:698–99; Sasson, *Ruth*, 40.
[140] Campbell, *Ruth*, 90; Hubbard, *Ruth*, 133–34; Bush, *Ruth, Esther*, 101.
[141] See the discussions by Campbell (*Ruth*, 90–91), Hubbard (*Ruth*, 134–35), and Vuilleumier ("Stellung und Bedeutung," 207). Keil (*Joshua, Judges, Ruth*, 477), Noth (*Die israelitischen Personennamen*, 228), Rudolph (*Das Buch Ruth, das Hohe Lied, die Klagelieder*, 48), Beattie ("Ruth III,"

Ruth 2:1–17

2:2 וַתֹּאמֶר רוּת—The sequential *waw* consecutive may be pleonastic and need not be translated literally (see 1:2b).

אֵלְכָה־נָּא ... וַאֲלַקֳטָה—The verbs are first common singular cohortatives: the Qal of הָלַךְ and the Piel of לָקַט. The first has the nuance of seeking permission: "Please let me go out ..." Since the sense is that Ruth would go out of the village to the cultivated fields, it is fitting here to render הָלַךְ as "go out, forth" (BDB, s.v. הָלַךְ, Qal, I 1 b). The particle of entreaty, נָּא, is regularly a precative, "please," and often follows a cohortative when requesting permission.[142] The second cohortative (וַאֲלַקֳטָה) expresses desire in a purpose clause: "... so I can glean."[143] The *daghesh forte* normally in the middle radical of a Piel verb (־קֵּ־) is omitted because of the (composite) *shewa* (־קֳ־).[144] That Ruth requests permission from Naomi, who will respond by granting it (2:2b), further indicates Ruth's submissive role in relation to Naomi (see also 3:5). The verb לָקַט, "to glean," occurs twelve times in Ruth, all in 2:2–23, and so it is a prominent thematic term in chapter 2.[145]

הַשָּׂדֶה—The translation supplies "*to* the field" because this is an accusative of place[146] after a verb of motion. Referring collectively to the arable land of the town's farmers, it is in the singular, for the individual tracts of the owners were not fenced off but only identified with markers.[147]

---

46), and Enns (*Ruth*, 34) derive the meanings "lively," "alacrity," or "sharp-witted" from an Arabic root *bġz*.

[142] Joüon, § 114 d; GKC, § 108 c; Bush, *Ruth, Esther*, 102; Lawrenz, *Judges, Ruth*, 231; Lambdin, *Introduction to Biblical Hebrew*, 170; Campbell, *Ruth*, 91–92; Hubbard, *Ruth*, 136, n. 1.

[143] See Waltke-O'Connor, § 34.5.2b; Hubbard, *Ruth*, 136, n. 3; Bush, *Ruth, Esther*, 102. Joüon interprets the second cohortative as successive: "I want to go and (then) I shall glean" (§ 122 c (2); see also § 119 j).

[144] GKC (§§ 10 h; 64 i) explains the composite *shewa* but follows manuscripts that have the *daghesh*.

[145] Campbell, *Ruth*, 109; Hamlin, *Surely There Is a Future*, 27; cf. Nielsen, *Ruth*, 53.

[146] Williams, § 54; Waltke-O'Connor, § 10.2.2b.

[147] Deut 19:14; 27:17; Job 24:2; Prov 15:25; 22:28; Campbell, *Ruth*, 92; Barber, *Ruth: An Expositional Commentary*, 145–46, n. 9; Gray, *Joshua, Judges, Ruth*, 391; Hubbard, *Ruth*, 138; Bush, *Ruth, Esther*, 102.

בַּשִׁבֳּלִים—This plural of שִׁבֹּלֶת is rendered "ears of grain." The article (in בַּ-) is used here because there would definitely be ears in the field. The preposition בְּ probably is used here to introduce the object of the verb, so it is not translated (though that use of בְּ is not otherwise attested with the Piel of לָקַט). The preposition could have the locative sense, "at, in, among"; compare "glean(ed) in the field [בַּשָּׂדֶה]" (2:3, 8, 17).[148] Elsewhere in Ruth לָקַט is used without a direct object, and so "ears of grain" is implied as its direct object. (The verb takes בֵּין in 2:15b and is preceded by אֵת אֲשֶׁר in 2:17b, 18; see the textual notes on those verses.)

אַחַר אֲשֶׁר אֶמְצָא־חֵן בְּעֵינָיו—Literally, "after whomever I may find favor in his eyes," this is equivalent to "wherever someone is favorable to me." The Piel of לָקַט earlier in the verse takes this prepositional phrase with אַחַר because a gleaner follows "after" the reapers and collects whatever grain is left. (Normally a gleaner also follows "after" the women who gather the cut stalks into sheaves, and collects only those stalks or ears not gathered by the other women, but Boaz will grant an extraordinary favor to Ruth in 2:15–16.) See 2:3, where the Piel of לָקַט takes אַחֲרֵי ("she gleaned … after the reapers") and 2:7, 9, which have אַחֲרֵי.

The relative pronoun אֲשֶׁר here means "whomever" since it refers to a person who is hypothetical or unknown at this point in the story. In Hebrew אֲשֶׁר regularly takes a pronoun complement (here on בְּעֵינָיו) that is redundant in English ("whomever … in *his* eyes").

The idiom מָצָא חֵן בְּעֵינֵי ("find favor in the eyes of" someone) is common in the OT. It can be used for a subordinate seeking or receiving a request or privilege granted by a superior person[149] (see BDB, s.v. חֵן, 2 b (1)), and with that same sense, as here, it will recur in Ruth 2:10, 13. It can also be a formula for addressing God (see BDB, s.v. חֵן, 2 b (2)). The imperfect אֶמְצָא (Qal

---

[148] See Bush, *Ruth, Esther*, 102–3. Gerleman (*Ruth, Das Hohelied*, 23) understands the בְּ as participatory, that is, that Ruth wanted to "participate in gleaning ears"; בְּ is used in this way, for example, with אָחַז, אָכַל, נָגַע, and שָׁתָה.

[149] Campbell, *Ruth*, 92; Hubbard, *Ruth*, 139; see also Bush, *Ruth, Esther*, 103.

Ruth 2:1–17

first common singular of מָצָא) has a modal nuance, "I *may/might* find," expressing Ruth's hope that someone would look upon her with favor.

לְכִי בִתִּי:—This is, literally, "go, my daughter!" The Qal feminine singular imperative of הָלַךְ has a permissive sense (thus, "do go!") in response to Ruth's cohortative petition.[150] In the sense "go ahead," this contrasts with Naomi's earlier repeated commands to Ruth (and Orpah) with שׁוּב, "return, go back!" (1:8, 11, 12, 15). Earlier Naomi had called Ruth and Orpah "my daughters" (1:11, 12, 13). Starting here, Ruth will be called "my daughter" (בַּת with first common singular suffix) by Naomi (also in 2:22; 3:1, 16, 18) and by Boaz (2:8; 3:10, 11). This address expresses close familiarity and affection besides age seniority.[151]

2:3 וַתֵּלֶךְ וַתָּבוֹא וַתְּלַקֵּט—"So she went (out), and she came and gleaned": the first *waw* consecutive indicates consequence or result: "so ..." (as in 1:1b). On הָלַךְ meaning "go out," see the second textual note on 2:2. These three brief verbs quickly change the scene from the town to the country. Although the verbs themselves are in chronological order, the second summarizes activity that is explained more fully in what follows, so the whole verse is not strictly in chronological order. "She came" will be explained as coming upon Boaz's field (2:3b) and that must have taken place before she "gleaned."[152]

וַיִּקֶר מִקְרֶהָ—This is not a consecutive clause reporting another incident that took place after the preceding (2:3a). Rather, 2:3b is an epexegetical conjunctive clause, elaborating the preceding וַתָּבוֹא, "she came."[153] This is, literally, "and her happenstance

---

[150] Joüon, § 114 n; Hubbard, *Ruth*, 136, n. 4; Bush, *Ruth, Esther*, 98.
[151] See Hubbard, *Ruth*, 108.
[152] Campbell, *Ruth*, 92; Hubbard, *Ruth*, 140.
[153] Waltke-O'Connor, § 33.2.2a, including example 2; Joüon, § 118 k; Andersen, *The Sentence in Biblical Hebrew*, 99; Hubbard, *Ruth*, 140, n. 2.

happened (upon) ..." The same combination of verb and noun occurs elsewhere only in Eccl 2:14–15.

The verb וַיִּקֶר is the Qal imperfect with *waw* consecutive of קָרָה, "to happen, occur" (cf. the by-form קָרָא II, "encounter, happen"). It can be used in a clause such as this without any explicit identification of the agent, cause, or purpose. The cognate noun מִקְרֶה (here with third feminine singular suffix) in narrative is usually taken to mean "accident, chance" (BDB) or "happenstance" (1 Sam 6:9; 20:26),[154] that is, peripety (turn of fortune). Besides Ruth 2:3; 1 Sam 6:9; 20:26, the only other occurrences of the noun in the OT are in verses in Ecclesiastes where Solomon laments that suffering and death happen to all alike; some translate it "fate" (so NASB and NIV in Eccl 2:14, 15; 3:19) or "destiny" (so NIV in Eccl 9:2–3) but ESV renders it as "event" in Eccl 2:14; 9:2–3. Ecclesiastes does not portray the world as governed by chance, fate, or unknown causes. Rather, God has authority over all things and will judge everyone, so that the eternal outcome will *not* be the same for all people (see Eccl 2:24–26; 3:17–18; 9:1; 11:9; 12:14). Some render the clause here in Ruth 2:3 with "chance," for example, "by chance she came" (*HALOT*, s.v קרה I, Qal, c) or "she chanced upon" (*HALOT*, s.v מִקְרֶה, 1). However, the literal overstatement, "her happenstance happened ..." may be the clue that it was precisely not by chance, but by God's guidance.[155]

חֶלְקַת הַשָּׂדֶה לְבֹעַז—The construct phrase is followed by the לְ of possession, "the portion of the field belonging to Boaz," instead of having a three-word construct chain (see Waltke-O'Connor, § 9.7b, example 10; GKC, § 129 d).

---

[154] Bush, *Ruth, Esther*, 104.
[155] See Gerleman, *Ruth, Das Hohelied*, 25; Hubbard, *Ruth*, 140–41. That the sense is similar to that in of Solomon in Ecclesiastes may be a hint that Ruth too was authored by a wise man.

Ruth 2:1–17

2:4 וְהִנֵּה־בֹ֗עַז בָּ֚א מִבֵּ֣ית לֶ֔חֶם—The demonstrative הִנֵּה, "behold," can announce the arrival of a new actor after that of a main actor (as in 2 Sam 13:36; 1 Ki 20:13). When introducing a "surprise clause" (thus: "behold, Boaz indeed ..."), הִנֵּה can refer to the characters in the story being surprised (as in Judg 3:25). But if that were the case here for Ruth, the narrator would have reported, "Behold, the owner of the field came" (since Ruth had not yet met Boaz). Rather, here the narrator uses הִנֵּה to elicit surprise in the hearers or readers of the account, since we have already been introduced to Boaz (2:1). When just the right thing occurs after the scene has been set (2:3), הִנֵּה may be followed by a participle (Gen 24:15; Ruth 4:1; 1 Ki 1:22). Thus, while the form of בָּא could be either the Qal perfect or participle, it is more likely a participle: "Boaz was arriving." The construction with הִנֵּה does not mean that only a brief amount of time elapsed; Ruth 2:7b indicates that the better part of the morning (see 2:14a) elapsed between Ruth's arrival and Boaz's. Emphasis is also added by alliteration: *Boʿaz baʾ mibbet leḥem*.[156] While "from Bethlehem" may appear superfluous after 1:22, naming the town again here is a clue to how Boaz heard about Ruth (from the townspeople, 2:11).[157]

יְהוָ֣ה עִמָּכֶ֑ם ... יְבָרֶכְךָ֖ יְהוָֽה׃—The greetings "The LORD be with you" and "The LORD bless you" are chiastic in Hebrew with God's covenant name (יהוה) at the beginning of the first one and the end of the second. The first salutation is a Hebrew nominal sentence, which can have an optative mood; many blessings are optative nominal sentences (Joüon, § 163 b). Its basis is the LORD's frequent promise "I am/will be with you!" The preposition עִם ("with") can indicate "fellowship and companionship" (BDB, 1) or advantage (Williams, § 331).

The second greeting uses the Piel jussive of בָּרַךְ, "to bless," and it is identical to the first clause of the Aaronic Benediction (Num 6:24a). The Piel of בָּרַךְ often refers to a person speaking a benediction as a greeting, and it is also employed with many other kinds of spoken blessings.

---

[156] See Campbell, *Ruth*, 92–93; Hubbard, *Ruth*, 143; Lacocque, *The Feminine Unconventional*, 88; Bush, *Ruth, Esther*, 111.
[157] Andersen, The Sentence in Biblical Hebrew, 94; Berlin, Poetics and Interpretation of Biblical Narrative, 92–94; Bush, Ruth, Esther, 112.

2:5 וַיֹּ֤אמֶר בֹּ֙עַז֙—The *waw* is sequential: "*then* Boaz said" (see also 1:4a; 2:11).

לְנַעֲר֔וֹ הַנִּצָּ֖ב עַל־הַקּֽוֹצְרִ֑ים—The noun נַעַר ("servant") denotes a subordinate, here a trusted manager (probably not a slave). We might say "employee." Often נַעַר implies relatively young age, but sometimes it refers to older subordinate men (e.g., 2 Sam 9:9; 1 Ki 20:14; 2 Ki 5:20). It recurs five more times in Ruth, all in this chapter ("servant" also in 2:6; "young men" in 2:9 [twice]; "workers" in 2:15, 21; cf. הַבַּחוּרִים, "young men," in 3:10). The corresponding feminine נַעֲרָה, "young woman," refers to Ruth (2:5–6; 4:12) and Boaz's female workers (2:8, 22–23; 3:2). The eleven instances of these two nouns in this chapter stress youth, in contrast to Naomi and Boaz.[158] Elsewhere in the OT, when the terms mean "young woman" (Gen 24:16; 34:12; Judg 21:12) or "young man" (Gen 34:19) they can denote marriageability. See also the last textual note on 2:8.

Boaz had elevated this subordinate. הַנִּצָּב is the Niphal participle (with article) of נָצַב, "*be stationed = appointed* over (עַל)" (BDB, Niphal, 2). Thus this "servant" was the foreman or overseer, while the "reapers" (הַקּוֹצְרִים, participle of קָצַר) were hired hands, that is, day laborers.

לְמִ֥י הַנַּעֲרָ֖ה הַזֹּֽאת:—Literally, Boaz asks, "Belonging to whom is this young woman?" (on this use of לְ, see the first textual note on 2:1). The question is not strictly about ownership, but, judging by the answer, probes the situation, both identity (family, people) and relevant circumstances—an appropriate question to or about a stranger (see Gen 32:18–19 [ET 32:17–18]; 1 Sam 30:13–14). The translation "Who is this young woman?" implies all that and is preferable to "Whose is … ?" It was appropriate for Boaz to question his foreman first about any stranger in his field.[159]

---

[158] Campbell, *Ruth*, 93; Hubbard, *Ruth*, 145.
[159] Campbell, *Ruth*, 93–94; Hubbard, *Ruth*, 145–46; Bush, *Ruth, Esther*, 113.

Ruth 2:1–17

2:6 וַיַּעַן ׃ ׃ ׃ וַיֹּאמֶר—After "he answered" (Qal imperfect of עָנָה with *waw* consecutive), the Hebrew adds "and he said" immediately before the quotation. The latter verb is omitted in the translation (also in 2:11) but is reflected by the English quotation marks. Hebrew narrative is characteristically repetitious and so repeats the subject from 2:5 ("the servant who was stationed over the reapers"), which slows the pace for effect.

נַעֲרָה מוֹאֲבִיָּה הִיא—The narrator keeps reminding his audience of Ruth's foreign background ("Moabite," 1:22; 2:2, 21; 4:5, 10; see also 1:15; 2:10).[160] Here the special emphasis is by the foreman, who also refers to "Moab" at the end of the verse.

הַשָּׁבָה עִם־נָעֳמִי—The verb ("who returned") is the Qal third feminine singular perfect of שׁוּב with the article, as also in 1:22; 4:3. See the third textual note on 1:22.

מִשְּׂדֵה מוֹאָב—This is, literally, "from the field of Moab," see the textual note on בִּשְׂדֵי מוֹאָב in 1:1.

2:7 אֲלַקֳטָה־נָּא—This ("please let me glean") is the same polite Piel cohortative, requesting permission, that Ruth used earlier, here with נָא (see the second textual note on 2:2).

וְאָסַפְתִּי בָעֳמָרִים—After a cohortative, a perfect verb with *waw* consecutive (Qal of אָסַף, "to gather") may indicate simple sequence or consequent action.[161] The plural of עֹמֶר, "sheaf," has the preposition בְּ. The form בָעֳמָרִים could be definite or indefinite. Most translations understand it to have the article (hence בָ before the guttural ע) and thus translate "among the sheaves"[162] (a proper translation for בֵּין הָעֳמָרִים in 2:15). However, it is better to

---

[160] Hubbard, *Ruth*, 147.
[161] Joüon, §§ 119 j; 122 c (2); Waltke-O'Connor, § 32.2.2b, example 5; Bush, *Ruth, Esther*, 113.
[162] So RSV, NASB, NIV, ESV.

understand בָּעֳמָרִים as indefinite: the preposition has the short vowel (-בָּ with *qamets chatuph*) corresponding to that in the composite *shewa* (-עֳ- with *chateph qamets*); see GKC, § 9 v. The verb לְקַט, "glean," that began the verse lacks an object and implies "ears of grain" as its natural object (see the textual note on בַשִׁבֳּלִים in 2:2). So אָסַף will refer to gathering the ears "into sheaves" or "into bundles,"[163] indicated by בָּעֳמָרִים. The preposition בְּ can mean "into" with verbs of motion (BDB, s.v. בְּ, I 4). The term עֹמֶר occurs in other OT books only in the singular, where it makes good sense as a collective noun, that is, a certain amount or a pile of cut ears.[164] Thus, it is not necessary to speculate that Ruth made a bold request to "glean and gather among the sheaves," that is, to take ears that the harvesters had already bound together but had not yet removed. Gleaners were only permitted to gather leftover, unbound ears after the workers had completed their harvest, and that is all that Ruth requests. However, in 2:15–16 Boaz grants far more than she had requested.

וַתָּבוֹא וַתַּעֲמוֹד—The first *waw* consecutive (with the Qal imperfect of בּוֹא) indicates consequential action of result (as in 1:1b): she received permission, "*so* she came." עָמַד (usually "stand") can mean "remain" (Ex 9:28; Deut 5:31; 2 Ki 15:20). Thus, Ruth persisted in gleaning there rather than going elsewhere to glean.[165] She would have been on her feet the whole time she was working. וַתַּעֲמוֹד is written plene with וֹ. Such plene forms are frequent in Ruth (e.g., הֲלוֹא in 2:8–9).[166]

מֵאָז הַבֹּקֶר וְעַד־עָתָּה—This phrase is, literally, "from then the morning and until now." מֵאָז (the preposition מִן plus the adverb אָז) can be used as a compound preposition meaning "from time of,

---

[163] Bush, *Ruth, Esther*, 117, considers the phrase an adverbial expression of manner and translates, "gather them in bundles." Block, *Judges, Ruth*, 656, advocates the same understanding.
[164] Lev 23:10, 11, 12, 15; Deut 24:19; Job 24:10. For the singular, *HALOT*, s.v. עֹמֶר I, gives "small heap of cut corn [that is, grain]."
[165] Hubbard, *Ruth*, 149; Bush, *Ruth, Esther*, 118; Block, *Judges, Ruth*, 657.
[166] Myers, The Linguistic and Literary Form of the Book of Ruth, 10.

Ruth 2:1–17

since" (BDB, s.v. מֵאָז [under אָז], b; cf. *HALOT*, s.v. אָז, 4 b). The context here favors "since early morning until now."[167]

זֶה שִׁבְתָּהּ הַבַּיִת מְעָט:—These last four Hebrew words of 2:7 are the most difficult to render in the whole book. The demonstrative זֶה ("this") can mean "here" when it refers to a place (as does מִזֶּה, "from this [field]," in 2:8), but it could also refer to an action (Ruth's "sitting" or "resting"). The most natural way to take שִׁבְתָּהּ is as the Qal infinitive of יָשַׁב with third feminine singular suffix. Since יָשַׁב can mean to "sit, sit down" (BDB, 1 b), this literally seems to say, "this, her sitting [in] the house a little while." Or if שִׁבְתָּהּ is the noun שֶׁבֶת (with third feminine singular suffix) that is derived from יָשַׁב, the phrase would mean "this, her sitting place [was] the house for a little while." Or שִׁבְתָּהּ could be the noun שַׁבָּת (with third feminine singular suffix) that is derived from שָׁבַת, "to cease, stop," in which case the phrase would mean "this, her cessation [of work] at the house [was/is] short."

As an accusative of place (Waltke-O'Connor, § 10.2.2b), הַבַּיִת probably should be rendered "*in/at* the house." Ruth could hardly have gone to her own home and then returned; she goes home for the first time in 2:18. Some have suggested that הַבַּיִת ("the house") refers to a shelter of some sort in the field,[168] although the narrative does not otherwise refer to it (cf. especially 2:14).[169] If there were a

---

[167] Cf. Gerleman, *Ruth, Das Hohelied*, 23; Bush, *Ruth, Esther*, 118.
[168] Is 1:8 (cf. Is 4:5–6) refers to a "booth" or "hut" in a vineyard with סֻכָּה.
[169] Moore explains that the author used שִׁבְתָּהּ, which implies several possible interpretations, as an intentional wordplay ("Two Textual Anomalies in Ruth," 239–43). Some regard הַבַּיִת as a scribal addition that should be deleted (so Gerleman, *Ruth, Das Hohelied*, 23; Hertzberg, *Die Bücher Josua, Richter, Ruth*, 266, 269; Rudolph, *Das Buch Ruth, das Hohe Lied, die Klagelieder*, 47; Würthwein, "Ruth," 14). Bush, *Ruth, Esther*, 119, also advocates dropping the word from the text, but calls "the reason usually given," that is, dittography (a repetition of the consonants הבת from שִׁבְתָּהּ), "forced and improbable." If הַבַּיִת is deleted, the speech that remains is somewhat chopped. Some who advocate the emendation suppose that the foreman was uneasy toward his boss, perhaps partly because he realized that Boaz was related to Ruth's mother-in-law, but that is quite speculative.

verb of motion, הַבַּיִת could mean "*to* the house" (cf. the textual note on הַשָּׂדֶה in 2:2).

Here מְעָט is a temporal adverb: "a little while" (cf. BDB, 1 d; as also in Job 10:20b; 24:24). Thus, some render: "she rested here just a little while."[170]

The ancient versions offer divergent translations. The LXX has "she did not rest in the field [even] a little" (οὐ κατέπαυσεν ἐν τῷ ἀγρῷ μικρόν) and the Vulgate, "not even for a moment did she return home" (*et ne ad momentum quidem domum reversa est*). The Syriac has a much shorter text: "… from early morning until descending/stooping."

One of the less radical proposed emendations is that the verb שִׁבְתָּהּ could be repointed שָׁבְתָה (Qal perfect, third feminine singular of שָׁבַת), "she stopped, rested." Some interpreters attempt to construct a scenario that would explain why the foreman's utterance is almost unintelligible.[171]

2:8 הֲלוֹא שָׁמַעַתְּ בִּתִּי—This negative rhetorical question, literally, "Have you not heard, my daughter?" seeks not an answer but signifies a strong affirmative declaration (GKC, § 150 e; see הֲלוֹא also in Gen 27:36; Josh 10:13; Ruth 2:9; 3:1, 2). Since שָׁמַע often has the meaning "heed, listen" and the perfect can refer to the present (like a stative verb), the force in this context is an imperative:

---

[170] See Lys, "Residence ou repos?" 497–99, who identified nineteen different renderings; Hurvitz, "Ruth 2:7—'A Midrashic Gloss'?"; Bush, *Ruth, Esther*, 118–19.

[171] Campbell, *Ruth*, 94, suggests that these last words of 2:7 "provide the transition" to the following verses. Carasik, "Ruth 2,7: Why the Overseer Was Embarrassed," speculates that the young men had harassed Ruth when she tried to get a drink from their water; when Boaz arrived, Ruth was leaving his field, and the embarrassed overseer offered a lame explanation.

Ruth 2:1–17

"pay attention" to my benevolent instructions.[172] Naomi showed familiarity and age seniority by addressing Ruth as "my daughter" (2:2), but by Boaz, this can express his superiority in status as well as in age. These uses of the term thus imply that Naomi and Boaz were much closer to each other in age than Boaz and Ruth.[173]

אַל־תֵּלְכִי לִלְקֹט בְּשָׂדֶה אַחֵר—This is, literally, "Do not go to glean in another field." הָלַךְ (Qal second feminine singular imperfect) in this context means "go away" (it meant "go out" in 2:2). The Qal infinitive construct לְקֹט expresses purpose (Joüon, § 168 c) and is the only instance in Ruth of the Qal of לָקַט (the Piel is common). Elsewhere in the OT the Qal is not used in a context of gleaning grain (the usual Piel meaning); instead, the Qal means "to pick up, gather" in a general sense. Since Boaz evidently had gleaning in mind (see 2:15–16), the Qal is only a variation on the part of Boaz or the narrator.[174]

וְגַם לֹא תַעֲבוּרִי מִזֶּה—Literally, this is "And also you shall not pass away from this [field]." גַּם is emphatic.[175] In contrast to אַל in the previous command, which can be used for specific, temporary injunctions, לֹא is stronger and ordinarily indicates an absolute, permanent command (as in the Ten Commandments)[176] and so is translated, "Yes, *never* depart from this one!" תַעֲבוּרִי (Qal second feminine singular imperfect of עָבַר) is written with a *shureq* (וּ) instead of the expected תַעֲבְרִי (which in pause could be תַּעֲבֹרִי). The form with *shureq* could be archaic, in which case Boaz may be using a somewhat staid speech. Other Qal imperfects with *shureq* (וּ) are in Ex 18:26 and Prov 14:3.[177] With the preposition מִן, עָבַר can

---

[172] See Joüon, § 112 a; Campbell, *Ruth*, 96; Hyman, "Questions and the Book of Ruth," 17–18; Hubbard, *Ruth*, 154; Bush, *Ruth, Esther*, 119; Harstad, *Joshua*, 420. The negative הֲלוֹא is written plene with וֹ, as also in 2:9 (see also וַתַּעֲמֹוד in 2:7).
[173] See Hubbard, *Ruth*, 154.
[174] See Campbell, *Ruth*, 96–97; Hubbard, *Ruth*, 154.
[175] Williams, § 379; Hubbard, *Ruth*, 152, n. 3.
[176] GKC, § 109 d; Morris, *Ruth*, 274; Hubbard, *Ruth*, 155.
[177] Cf. Joüon, § 44 c; GKC, § 47 g; Campbell, *Ruth*, 85, n. *h*; Hubbard, *Ruth*, 155.

mean "go beyond the limits of" (2 Sam 15:24; 16:1), which expresses the general command more specifically.[178]

וְכֹה תִדְבָּקִין עִם־נַעֲרֹתָי—The *waw* on the locative adverb (וְכֹה) is adversative, presenting a contrast to the preceding, hence "*but* here …"[179] The verb דָּבַק, used emphatically when Ruth "clung" to Naomi in 1:14, is more general here: literally, "cling with my young women" (similarly in 2:21, 23). A more congenial rendering could be given in English, but consistently translating it as "cling" is important for the story. The narrator repeats the verb to connect Ruth's clinging to Naomi (1:14) to her faithful clinging to Boaz's women workers (2:8), which leads toward Ruth's union with Boaz himself; she proposes marriage to him in chapter 3, and he marries her in chapter 4.

Another example of archaic speech in Boaz's mouth is the paragogic *nun* at the end of תִדְבָּקִין.[180] The paragogic *nun* appears in Ruth only in speech by the older adults Boaz (whose words Ruth quotes in 2:21) and Naomi (3:4, 18). Other examples spoken by Boaz are יִקְצֹרוּן and יִשְׁאָבוּן in 2:9. In the OT דָּבַק takes the preposition עִם only here and in 2:21. It takes בְּ in 1:14; 2:23; and often elsewhere in the OT.

The plural of the feminine noun נַעֲרָה, the "young women" to whom she is to cling, contrasts with the "young men" whom Boaz orders not to touch her (הַנְּעָרִים, 2:9a) and not to humiliate her (נְעָרָיו, 2:15). Naomi later refers to these same "young women" (2:22; 3:2; they are also mentioned in 2:23). But when Ruth quotes Boaz in 2:21, she says that he told her to cling to הַנְּעָרִים, literally, "the young men," but it will be translated "the workers" because there it must be a more general term for the workers of both sexes, including the "young women" here (2:8). Likewise, the masculine term "the reapers" (הַקּוֹצְרִים, 2:3–7, 14) includes both the young men who cut the handfuls of stalks and the young women who followed and gathered the sheaves.[181]

---

[178] Bush, *Ruth, Esther*, 120.
[179] Campbell, *Ruth*, 97; Hubbard, *Ruth*, 155.
[180] Waltke-O'Connor, §§ 20.2f; 31.7.1a, example 2d; Joüon, § 44 f; Sasson, *Ruth*, 245.
[181] Campbell, *Ruth*, 97; Hubbard, *Ruth*, 155–56.

Ruth 2:1–17

2:9 עֵינַיִךְ בַּשָּׂדֶה—Literally, "your eyes on the field," this nominal sentence is unusual for an implied jussive: "Let your eyes be on the field," rendered "Keep your eyes on the field" for an English idiom. (A nominal sentence is common for a jussive blessing, for example, יְהוָה עִמָּכֶם, "The LORD be with you!" 2:4.) In the OT, the eyes are the sense organ for attention before activity ("eyes ... on [בְּ, as in Ruth 2:9]," Deut 11:12; "eyes ... toward [עַל]," 1 Ki 1:20; cf. 1 Ki 9:3).[182]

אֲשֶׁר־יִקְצֹרוּן—The imperfect verb (Qal of קָצַר) is rendered as a present, "(which) they are reaping." It is masculine plural (with paragogic *nun*[183]), for it evidently refers specifically to the men, who are grasping the stalks and cutting off the ears of grain. The women come after the men and gather the bunches of ears; hence in the next clause Ruth is to follow after the women (אַחֲרֵיהֶן, literally, "after them [feminine]").[184] The change in gender is obscured in a literal English translation but would have been obvious to Ruth and Israelites; the language mirrors the reality of ancient practice.

וְהָלַכְתְּ אַחֲרֵיהֶן—Following a jussive (see the first textual note on this verse), a perfect (Qal perfect second feminine singular of הָלַךְ) with *waw* consecutive, referring to a consequent situation (Waltke-O'Connor, § 32.2.2a), may introduce a purpose clause: literally, "*so that* you follow after them." The third plural suffix (יְ־הֶן) is feminine; "after them" specifically means "after the women."

הֲלוֹא צִוִּיתִי אֶת־הַנְּעָרִים לְבִלְתִּי נָגְעֵךְ—"Have I not commanded the young men not to touch you?" is another negative rhetorical question indicating a strong positive declaration (as 2:8a; see also Jonah 4:2). Boaz was here in effect issuing a command to his workers; they surely paid attention to this important interview. The perfect in such a case may be used for an act accomplished at the moment of its utterance, so that it could be rendered: "Do I not hereby

---

[182] Hubbard, *Ruth*, 157.
[183] Waltke-O'Connor, §§ 20.2f; 31.7.1a; Joüon, § 44 f.
[184] Campbell, *Ruth*, 98; Gerleman, *Ruth, Das Hohelied*, 23; Hubbard, *Ruth*, 157–58.

command ... ?"[185] As in 1:13, לְבִלְתִּי is the negative used with an infinitive construct: here נָגְעֵךְ, Qal infinitive construct with object suffix from נָגַע, "*touch* = harm" (BDB, 3).[186] הַנְּעָרִים probably refers specifically to "the young men" (not all "the workers," as it does in 2:21) since the verb ("touch") refers to physical contact, even possibly sexual contact, as in Gen 20:6 and Prov 6:29. The women would resort only to verbal abuse.

וְצָמִת וְהָלַכְתְּ אֶל־הַכֵּלִים—Both verbs are Qal perfect second feminine singular with *waw* consecutive. וְצָמִת (defectively written for וְצָמִית) is from צָמָא, inflected as if the א were ה (GKC, § 75 qq; Joüon, § 78 f; see also וַתִּשֶּׁנָה in 1:14). The two verbs form a temporal clause denoting successive actions: "and when you are thirsty, you may go." The force of וְהָלַכְתְּ (like that of וְשָׁתִית in the next clause) is to grant permission: "you may go."[187] הַכֵּלִים, literally, "the vessels," refers here to "the [water] jars" (see *HALOT*, s.v. כְּלִי, 1; 1 Ki 10:21).

וְשָׁתִית מֵאֲשֶׁר יִשְׁאֲבוּן הַנְּעָרִים:—The perfect with *waw* consecutive (Qal second feminine singular of שָׁתָה) grants permission: "and you may drink." Boaz would have had his employees draw water for the use of them all from the town well that was probably near the gate. This was women's work for households,[188] but it appears that men provided for field workers, hence the verb (יִשְׁאֲבוּן, Qal imperfect of שָׁאַב with paragogic *nun*[189]) is masculine and its subject, הַנְּעָרִים, refers to "the young men" rather than all "the workers" (as it does in 2:21).

---

[185] See Joüon, § 112 g; de Waard and Nida, *A Translator's Handbook on the Book of Ruth*, 32; cf. Hyman, "Questions and the Book of Ruth," 17–18; Hubbard, *Ruth*, 158.
[186] Only here and in Gen 26:29 and Is 52:11 does נָגַע occur without a preposition with its object (Joüon, § 125 b; Campbell, *Ruth*, 98).
[187] Joüon, § 166 b, says it is preferable to take the clause as temporal, "when you are thirsty ... ," rather than as conditional, "if ..." Cf. Joüon, § 167 b; GKC, §§ 112 kk and 164 b 4; Brockelmann, § 164a; Gerleman, *Ruth, Das Hohelied*, 24; Bush, *Ruth, Esther*, 122.
[188] Hubbard, *Ruth*, 160. It was thus striking for a man to be seen carrying water (Mk 14:13).
[189] Waltke-O'Connor, §§ 20.2f; 31.7.1a; Joüon, § 44 f.

Ruth 2:1–17

2:10 וַתִּפֹּל עַל־פָּנֶיהָ וַתִּשְׁתַּחוּ אָרְצָה—The *waw* consecutive (on the imperfect of נָפַל) is sequential: literally, "*then* she fell upon her face and she bowed to the ground." Ruth's response exhibits not only humility and appreciation but also consternation over Boaz's generosity. She probably fell to her knees and bowed her head to the ground, as King Jehu is portrayed on the Black Obelisk of Shalmaneser III. This was the typical Near Eastern expression of submission to a superior (cf. 1 Sam 25:23; 2 Sam 1:2).[190] וַתִּשְׁתַּחוּ (third feminine singular imperfect with *waw* consecutive, contracted from וַתִּשְׁתַּחֲוָה) is the Hishtaphel of חָוָה ("bow down; worship"), the only verb to occur in that conjugation in the OT.[191] אָרְצָה ("to the ground") has the final *he* directive.

מַדּוּעַ—"Why?" does not introduce a rhetorical question (as did לָמָּה in 1:11, 21), but one seeking a response (forthcoming in 2:11–12), as is regularly the case with מַדּוּעַ (e.g., Gen 40:7; 1 Sam 20:27).[192]

... מָצָאתִי חֵן בְּעֵינֶיךָ—Ruth expresses her deep gratitude: (literally) "Why have I found favor in your eyes to acknowledge me and I am a foreigner?" For the idiom "find favor in" someone's "eyes," see the textual note on it in 2:2. Here the verb מָצָאתִי is perfect because Ruth has indeed "found" what she hoped for in 2:2 with the imperfect אֶמְצָא, "I may find."

לְהַכִּירֵנִי וְאָנֹכִי נָכְרִיָּה—The verb is the Hiphil infinitive construct of נָכַר with object suffix; the infinitive forms a result clause.[193] The Hiphil can mean "recognize, acknowledge" or "be partial" toward, "regard favorably" (see *HALOT*). Compare Ps 142:5 (ET 142:4), where it means "take notice of, be concerned about" someone. Ruth, as a "foreigner," enjoyed no covenant privileges (cf.

---

[190] *ANEP*, §§ 351, 355; Hubbard, *Ruth*, 161.
[191] This verb was formerly thought to have been the Hithpael of the root שׁחה, but evidence from Ugarit indicates otherwise (Waltke-O'Connor, § 21.2.3d; Seow, *A Grammar for Biblical Hebrew*, 230–32; *HALOT*, s.v. חוה II).
[192] Hyman, "Questions and the Book of Ruth," 19–20.
[193] "Why have I found favour in your eyes, as a result of which you have been interested in me?" (Joüon, § 124 l). See also Joüon, § 124 s, and Waltke-O'Connor, § 36.2.3d, example 19.

Deut 14:21; 23:21 [ET 23:20]), and Israelites should avoid contact with her (see Judg 19:12 and above on Ruth 1:15).[194] Ruth's words here imply that Boaz had prior knowledge that she was a foreigner, that is, a stranger from another ethnic people; she had a lower status than the native Israelites and than a resident alien or sojourner (גֵּר; cf. גּוּר, "sojourn," in 1:1). The *waw* on וְאָנֹכִי is emphatic: "*even* a foreigner" (see *HALOT*, s.v. וְ, 3). But Boaz, by granting her permission to glean beside his own female workers, who presumably were Israelites, "acknowledge[d]" Ruth as a legitimate gleaner, as if she were a resident alien, if not a full Israelite. (He will treat her as an Israelite relative in 2:14–16.) The verb has been somewhat stretched semantically for the sake of a wordplay, for this verb has the same root, נכר, as נָכְרִיָּה, the feminine of נָכְרִי, "foreigner"—someone conspicuous as a stranger. The wordplay creates alliteration: *lehakkireni we'anoki nokriyyah*. This is the only occurrence of נָכְרִי in the book, but it conveys the same point about Ruth as "Moabitess."

2:11 וַיַּעַן בֹּעַז וַיֹּאמֶר לָהּ—Literally, "And Boaz answered and he said to her," this double expression, which is common in Hebrew, is translated, "Then Boaz replied to her." For this sequential use of וְ, see the first textual note on 2:5. For עָנָה ... אָמַר, see the first textual note on 2:6; as there, "and he said" is omitted in our rendering.

הֻגֵּד הֻגַּד לִי—For emphasis the Hophal infinitive absolute of נגד precedes the Hophal perfect: "It has surely been told to me" (see also Josh 9:24). The construction is a mark of classical Hebrew prose. Boaz had been well-informed about Ruth's reputation.[195]

כֹּל אֲשֶׁר־עָשִׂית אֶת־חֲמוֹתֵךְ—This phrase is the subject of the passive verb הֻגַּד, "has been told." Here עָשָׂה (עָשִׂית is Qal perfect second feminine singular) takes the preposition אֶת ("did *with*")

---

[194] Campbell, *Ruth*, 98; Hubbard, *Ruth*, 162–63.
[195] Campbell, *Ruth*, 99; Hubbard, *Ruth*, 153, n. 6; 163.

Ruth 2:1–17

instead of the more common לְ ("did *to*"), but עָשָׂה in this sense takes אֵת also in, for example, Ezek 22:14 and עִם in Ruth 1:8; 2:19.[196]

וַתַּעַזְבִי אָבִיךְ וְאִמֵּךְ—Literally, "and you abandoned your father and your mother," the *waw* has the explicative sense, "and *how* you ..." (as in 1 Ki 18:13), as the LXX recognized (πῶς).[197] Like Ruth 1:14, this clause recalls Gen 2:24, where God calls a man to sacrifice his closest family circle to marry and cling to his wife. With the rest of the verse, it also recalls the call and response of Abraham (Gen 12:1, 4; see also Ruth 1:16–17).[198]

וְאֶרֶץ מוֹלַדְתֵּךְ—The noun מוֹלֶדֶת (from יָלַד, "give birth") means "kindred, relatives."

תְּמוֹל שִׁלְשׁוֹם:—This pair of nouns, literally, "yesterday, third [prior] day," serves as an adverbial idiom, "previously, formerly."[199]

2:12 יְשַׁלֵּם יְהוָה פָּעֳלֵךְ—The Piel of שָׁלֵם has a causative meaning, "to fulfill, recompense, complete," and looks forward to the adjective of the same root in the next clause (שְׁלֵמָה, "full, complete"). The form of יְשַׁלֵּם could be imperfect or jussive, but the context of prayer indicates the latter: "May the LORD fulfill your deed." The syntax is uniquely terse here, with no sign (אֶת־) before the direct object (פָּעֳלֵךְ). Similar clauses elsewhere in the OT usually include an indirect object, "to/for (them/him)," and the preposition "according to" before "deed." The noun פֹּעַל, "deed, thing done" (BDB, 1), refers to the actions by Ruth that Boaz recounted in 2:11.

וּתְהִי מַשְׂכֻּרְתֵּךְ שְׁלֵמָה—The noun מַשְׂכֹּרֶת means "wages" in its other OT occurrences (Gen 29:15; 31:7, 41), but the closely related noun שָׂכָר can mean "*reward*, for work done, faithfulness" (BDB, 2),

---

[196] Rudolph, *Das Buch Ruth, das Hohe Lied, die Klagelieder*, 47; Brockelmann, § 117b; Gerleman, *Ruth, Das Hohelied*, 24; Hubbard, *Ruth*, 163.
[197] Joüon, § 118 j; Campbell, *Ruth*, 99.
[198] Hubbard, *Ruth*, 164.
[199] Campbell, *Ruth*, 99.

as in Gen 15:1; 30:18; 2 Chr 15:7 (cf. 1 Sam 26:23). Especially in Gen 15:1 the "reward" clearly is an unearned, unmerited gift by God's grace, and at the end of Ruth 2:13, Ruth will emphasize her unworthiness. The adjective שָׁלֵם (feminine שְׁלֵמָה to agree with מַשְׂכֹּרֶת), "whole, complete, full," is from the same root as the opening verb in 2:12, יְשַׁלֵּם, and the noun שָׁלוֹם, shalom, "peace."

מֵעִם יְהוָה אֱלֹהֵי יִשְׂרָאֵל—The combination of the prepositions מִן and עִם (literally, "*from with* the LORD") stresses that the source of the reward is the LORD, Israel's covenant God, whose personal name is explicated with his well-known title, "the God of Israel."[200] Contrast "her god(s)" in 1:15, referring to Orpah's Moabite god(s).

אֲשֶׁר־בָּאת לַחֲסוֹת תַּחַת־כְּנָפָיו—Such a Hebrew relative clause uses a relative pronoun (אֲשֶׁר) followed by a prepositional phrase with the repetition of the referent as a pronominal suffix, literally, "the LORD ... *who* you have come to take refuge under *his* wings."[201] The verb בָּאת ("you came/have come") is Qal perfect second feminine singular of בּוֹא. The Qal infinitive construct of חָסָה with לְ (לַחֲסוֹת) forms a purpose clause: "to seek refuge."

2:13 אֶמְצָא־חֵן בְּעֵינֶיךָ אֲדֹנִי—Ruth had used this Hebrew idiom ("find favor in the eyes of") twice before: in her initial quest to glean wherever she would "find favor" (2:2) and in her rhetorical question affirming that she had indeed "found favor" in the eyes of Boaz (2:10). Here she is not requesting additional favor. Rather, she uses the expression as an exclamation to express gratitude to a superior (as in Gen 47:25; 2 Sam 16:4, which also have מָצָא in the imperfect) after Boaz had explained his beneficence (2:11)[202] and had prayed for her (2:12). Thus, literally, "I find such favor in your

---

[200] Hubbard, *Ruth*, 167.
[201] See Waltke-O'Connor, § 19.3b.
[202] Bush, *Ruth, Esther*, 124; Block, *Judges, Ruth*, 664.

eyes, my lord," it might be rendered, "You give me such favor, my lord!" The expression may also affirm her desire that she receive the fulfillment of his prayer for her in 2:12, as Hannah uses the idiom in 1 Sam 1:18 (also with מָצָא in the imperfect) to express her gratitude for and her hope for the fulfillment of the prayer Eli spoke over her.

אֲדֹנִי (*ʾadoni*, "my lord") occurs only here in Ruth and is an address of courteous respect by an inferior that keeps the proper distance from the superior by refraining from naming him.[203] It is similar to English "sir." The singular form of the suffix (־ִי) distinguishes this term, used in the OT to refer to a person, from אֲדֹנָי (*ʾadonai*), which refers to God (but is absent from Ruth).

The following two כִּי clauses explain the reasons for Ruth's gratitude ("for you ... and [for] you ..."), though the second כִּי is not translated for the sake of English idiom. See BDB, s.v. כִּי, 3 c.

כִּי נִחַמְתָּנִי—The Piel (second masculine singular perfect with first common singular object suffix) of נָחַם, "to comfort," is used for consoling the distressed and grieving (e.g., Pss 23:4; 69:21 [ET 69:20]; Is 40:1).[204]

וְכִי דִבַּרְתָּ עַל־לֵב שִׁפְחָתֶךָ—The idiom "speak to/upon the heart of" someone (e.g., Gen 50:21; 2 Sam 19:8 [ET 19:7]; Is 40:2) can mean to "speak kindly, comfort" (BDB, s.v. דָּבַר, Piel, 5), reassure, or encourage. The noun שִׁפְחָה, "maidservant," is from the same root as מִשְׁפָּחָה, "clan," an important word in this chapter (2:1, 3). In some contexts שִׁפְחָה appears to be synonymous with אָמָה, "maiden" (see 3:9), but in others, a distinction is evident: שִׁפְחָה denotes the lowest level of menial servant or slave, usually in service to the housewife, though a woman could use it self-deprecatingly, that is, humbly placing herself on a lower social level than is justified (1 Sam 1:18; 25:27, 41; 28:21–22).[205] An אָמָה was socially higher

---

[203] Hubbard, *Ruth*, 169. Similarly, Sarah, as well as Abraham's servant, so spoke of Abraham (Gen 18:12; 24:27) and Jacob of Esau (Gen 32:5, 6, 19 [ET 32:4, 5, 18]; cf. Ps 45:12 [ET 45:11]), and Rachel so addressed Laban (Gen 31:35) and Abigail, David (1 Sam 25:24–25).
[204] Campbell, *Ruth*, 100; Hubbard paraphrases: "You have allayed my fears" (*Ruth*, 153; see also p. 169).
[205] Sasson, *Ruth*, 53; *HALOT*.

because she was eligible to become a concubine of the master and thus a member of the family (Ex 11:5; Judg 9:18; 19:19).[206] Ruth, having been encouraged by Boaz's favor, realized that Boaz seemed to elevate her from a foreigner without any privileges (Ruth 2:10) to the lowliest "maidservant," who at least had minimal advantages over a foreigner. Her next statement acknowledges that she had not deserved this; it was a gracious gift of favor.

וְאָנֹכִי לֹא אֶהְיֶה כְּאַחַת שִׁפְחֹתֶיךָ:—With proper humility Ruth uses a concessive clause with an emphatic pronoun (וְאָנֹכִי) as a *casus pendens*: "as for me, I should not be like one of your maidservants."[207] She states that she does not deserve to be treated or considered to be like (כְּ) a maidservant, who was part of the household. However, the point that Boaz had accepted her in some small way[208] stands emphatically as the last word in this conversation: though unworthy, she acknowledges that he deems her to be one of his "maidservants" (שִׁפְחֹתֶיךָ:).

2:14 וַיֹּאמֶר לָה בֹעַז—The *mappiq* (ה-) is omitted in לָה ("to her") because the following word has the accent on the first syllable (see Num 32:42).[209]

לְעֵת הָאֹכֶל—Literally, this is "at the time of the food." For farmers during the harvest this was not the main daily meal (see 3:3, 7) but only an uncooked lunch as a mid-day work break. עֵת indicates here an occasion "for appropriate activity according to the social order,"[210] thus, the normal time for eating.[211]

---

[206] Campbell, *Ruth*, 101; Hubbard, *Ruth*, 169–70; Block, *Judges, Ruth*, 665.
[207] See Williams, § 528. For the use of אַחַת as a substantive, see Waltke-O'Connor, § 15.2.1f, including example 20.
[208] Cf. Campbell, *Ruth*, 101–2; Hubbard, *Ruth*, 170–71.
[209] GKC, § 103 g; cf. Joüon, §§ 25 a and 103 f; Keil, *Joshua, Judges, Ruth*, 479; Hubbard, *Ruth*, 171, n. 1.
[210] Wilch, *Time and Event*, 28.

Ruth 2:1–17

גֹּ֤שִֽׁי הֲלֹם֙—Literally, "draw near here," the verb is the Qal feminine singular imperative of נָגַשׁ. The *holem* is unusual (one would expect גְּשִׁי), but almost the same clause (גֹּ֤שׁוּ הֲלֹם֙) is in 1 Sam 14:38.[212] Boaz called Ruth, who was busy gleaning but not far off, to share the reapers' lunch. By implication, this invitation raised her status from a poor gleaner to the level of his company of workers, the status that Ruth had just mentioned ("one of your maidservants," 2:13).

וְאָכַ֣לְתְּ מִן־הַלֶּ֔חֶם—After an imperative (גֹּ֤שִֽׁי), a perfect with *waw* consecutive often follows and has the same force as an imperative.[213] Hence the following two perfects are translated as imperatives: "Come here and *eat* ... *dip* ..." The preposition מִן is partitive ("*some of* the food").[214] לֶחֶם often means "food" in general (e.g., Gen 3:19).

וְטָבַ֥לְתְּ פִּתֵּ֖ךְ בַּחֹֽמֶץ—The noun פַּת often is in construct with לֶחֶם (e.g., Judg 19:5), but even when not (as here), it usually refers to a "piece, morsel" of bread, probably of barley for a poor person.[215] Since the pronominal suffix makes the noun definite (פִּתֵּךְ, "your piece") and it is the direct object of the verb (טָבַל, "dip"), we would expect the accusative marker אֵת, normal in prose (e.g., in 2:11). But the usage of אֵת is irregular, and it may be explained as an emphatic particle that can be omitted (as here; Waltke-O'Connor, § 10.3b). חֹמֶץ probably was strong "vinegar" made from wine (Num 6:3), or a by-product of wine-making, used sparingly to soften the hard bread. Ordinarily חֹמֶץ was too acrid to drink (Ps 69:22 [ET 69:21]; Prov 10:26; 25:20), but could be refreshing for relieving the heat (Talmud, *Shabbat*, 113b). For the dipping of a piece of bread in a bowl, see Jn 13:26. According to *Midrash Rabbah Ruth*, § 5.6, on Ruth 2:14, dipping the bread in vinegar could symbolize the Messiah's suffering

---

[211] See Dalman, *Arbeit und Sitte in Palästina*, 1^II:612–13; Hubbard, *Ruth*, 171, n. 2.
[212] Cf. GKC, § 66 c; Waltke-O'Connor, § 34.4a, example 1; Gerleman, *Ruth, Das Hohelied*, 24; Hubbard, *Ruth*, 171, n. 3.
[213] Waltke-O'Connor, § 32.2.2b; Joüon, § 119 l, footnote 2.
[214] Williams, § 324; Waltke-O'Connor, § 11.2.11e.
[215] Dalman, *Arbeit und Sitte in Palästina*, 4:71–72; Hubbard, *Ruth*, 172.

(cf. Is 53:5).²¹⁶ "Vinegar" may have been the ὄξος offered to Jesus on the cross (Mt 27:48 and parallels), since the LXX translates חֹמֶץ in Ps 69:22 as ὄξος (LXX Ps 68:22; ET 69:21).²¹⁷

וַתֵּ֤שֶׁב מִצַּד֙ הַקּוֹצְרִ֔ים—After Boaz's gracious invitation, the Qal imperfect (third feminine singular) of יָשַׁב with *waw* consecutive is consequential: "*so she sat down.*" It may mean "sit down" to eat at a table (1 Ki 13:20; cf. Gen 27:19) or simply "to sit" (cf. *HALOT*, Qal, 1 and 2). Since Ruth and the reapers were in the field, they probably sat on their heels or on the ground. מִצַּד (the preposition מִן and צַד, "side") means "at the side of, next to" (*HALOT*, s.v. צַד, 3). Ruth humbly did not sit among the reapers, but near them. Here הַקּוֹצְרִים probably includes the workers of both sexes: both the men who reaped and the women who followed and gathered the sheaves (2:7–9).²¹⁸

וַיִּצְבָּט־לָ֥הּ קָלִ֖י—The verb צָבַט occurs only here in the OT. In rabbinic Hebrew and Aramaic it means "seize, grasp, hold," as do cognates in Ugaritic, Akkadian, and Arabic, and so BDB gives "hold out" to someone, and *HALOT* explains it as "to **pick up** and offer to someone."²¹⁹ However, the LXX coined βουνίζω (from βουνός, "mound") to translate it here, thus "to heap up," and used the same verb (perfect passive participle, βεβουνισμένων) for the "piles" of cut ears of grain in 2:16. The context supports "and he *heaped up* for her parched grain" since Ruth, after satisfying herself, had enough left over to offer it to Naomi (2:18). קָלִי, "roasted/parched grain," very common in the Near East for at least the poor, was likely recently

---

²¹⁶ Dalman, *Arbeit und Sitte in Palästina*, 4:403.
²¹⁷ Keil, Joshua, Judges, Ruth, 479; Dalman, *Arbeit und Sitte in Palästina*, 2:157; 3:18; 4:380, 403; Rudolph, *Das Buch Ruth, das Hohe Lied, die Klagelieder*, 49; Hertzberg, *Die Bücher Josua, Richter, Ruth*, 270; de Waard and Nida, *A Translator's Handbook on the Book of Ruth*, 36; Campbell, *Ruth*, 102; Enns, *Ruth*, 39–40; Hubbard, *Ruth*, 173; Bush, *Ruth*, Esther, 125; Block, *Judges, Ruth*, 666–67. Or the ὄξος in Mt 27:48 and parallels may have been sour wine mixed with water (Erich H. Kiehl, *The Passion of Our Lord* [Grand Rapids: Baker, 1990], 137).
²¹⁸ Campbell, *Ruth*, 102; Hubbard, *Ruth*, 173.
²¹⁹ Block derives the sense " 'to hand,' that is, 'to give with the hand' " (*Judges, Ruth*, 667).

Ruth 2:1–17

harvested barley. At harvest time it served as a substitute for wheat bread (cf. 1 Sam 17:17; 25:18; 2 Sam 17:28).[220]

וַתֹּאכַל וַתִּשְׂבַּע וַתֹּתַר—The three verbs are, literally, "And she ate and she was satiated/full and she had left over." שָׂבַע usually means "*be sated* (with food)" or with drink (BDB Qal 1). The cognate noun שֹׂבַע in 2:18 will refer to the "fullness" of food she had left over from this verse. וַתֹּתַר is the Hiphil imperfect of יָתַר with *waw* consecutive, "to have left over ... more than enough" (*HALOT*, Hiphil, 2). The *holem* is spelled defectively, and the verb is in pause (GKC, § 69 v); otherwise the expected form would be וַתּוֹתֵר. The verb implies an internal pronominal object, "to keep/have *some of it* left over" (see also, e.g., 2 Ki 4:43–44; Waltke-O'Connor, § 10.2.1a).

2:15 וַתָּקָם לְלַקֵּט וַיְצַו בֹּעַז אֶת־נְעָרָיו לֵאמֹר—The first imperfect with *waw* consecutive (וַתָּקָם, Qal of קוּם) forms a temporal clause indicating simultaneous occurrence with the second one (וַיְצַו, Piel of צָוָה), which is resumptive: "*When* she got up ... Boaz ordered ..." After "she sat down" (2:14), קוּם here has its literal meaning, "arise, get up," but it may serve double purpose by also signaling the beginning of new action and a new episode of the scene (see the textual note on וַתָּקָם at the start of 1:6). נְעָרָיו here likely refers to "his workers" of both sexes; even though the forms of כָּלַם ("humiliate") later in 2:15 and גָּעַר ("rebuke") in 2:16 are masculine, the actions they are to prohibit include verbal abuse, which the women could inflict, but not necessarily physical abuse, which the

---

[220] Dalman, *Arbeit und Sitte in Palästina*, 2:253–54, states that, if necessary, bread could be made from barley; see Ruth 3:15; 2 Sam 17:27–29; 2 Ki 7:18; 2 Chr 2:14 (ET 2:15). See also Keil, *Joshua, Judges, Ruth*, 479; Rudolph, *Das Buch Ruth, das Hohe Lied, die Klagelieder*, 47; Gerleman, *Ruth, Das Hohelied*, 27; de Waard and Nida, *A Translator's Handbook on the Book of Ruth*, 37; Campbell, *Ruth*, 102–3; Gray, *Joshua, Judges, Ruth*, 379, 392; Joüon, *Ruth*, 59–60; Hubbard, *Ruth*, 174–75; Bush, *Ruth, Esther*, 127.

men could inflict (see 2:9: "Have I not commanded the young men not to touch [נָגַע] you?"). לֵאמֹר (Qal infinitive construct with לְ, literally, "to say") serves simply to introduce direct speech, thus translated by a comma and quotation marks.

גַּם בֵּין הָעֳמָרִים תְּלַקֵּט—Boaz's command is emphatic, for it begins with גַּם, "even … ," and a prepositional phrase before the verb ("*among the sheaves* she may glean"). As shown by the plural verbs that follow in 2:15 through 2:16, the command is addressed directly to the workers, not to the (singular) foreman.[221] The preposition בֵּין here definitely means "*among* the sheaves," in contrast to Ruth's use of בְּ in 2:2 (בַּשִׁבֳּלִים, "ears of grain") and in 2:7 (בָעֳמָרִים, "*into* sheaves"). For עֹמֶר, "sheaf," see the textual note on it in 2:7. For the vowel of the article (-הָעֳ), see GKC, § 35 k. Thus Ruth is not required to wait until after the female workers had gathered up the piles and bound the ears; she is thus permitted to glean among the cut stalks at the same time the other women are gathering them into piles (see also 2:16).[222] The imperfect תְּלַקֵּט has a permissive sense: "she *may/has permission to* glean."[223]

וְלֹא תַכְלִימוּהָ:—The imperfect (Hiphil masculine plural of כָּלַם, "cause shame, disgrace, abuse," with third feminine singular suffix) with the absolute negative (לֹא) forms an emphatic imperative, common in OT legislation,[224] and thus fitting for an order to workers: "you shall in no way humiliate her!"

2:16 וְגַם שֹׁל־תָּשֹׁלּוּ לָהּ—After the emphatic negative imperative (imperfect with לֹא) at the end of 2:15, the imperfect תָּשֹׁלּוּ (Qal of שָׁלַל) has the force of a positive imperative (Williams, § 173),

---

[221] Williams, § 379; Hubbard, *Ruth*, 176.
[222] Gerleman, *Ruth, Das Hohelied*, 27; Matthews, *Judges and Ruth*, 230.
[223] See Williams, § 170; Joüon, § 113 l; Hubbard, *Ruth*, 171, n. 5.
[224] See Waltke-O'Connor, §§ 31.5d; 34.2.1b.

Ruth 2:1–17

literally, "And even you shall surely pull out for her." The emphatic וְגַם, "and even," is translated "yes." Heavy stress is further underscored for the positive command by the infinitive absolute שֹׁל (Qal of שָׁלַל) before the finite verb. שֹׁל is the expected form for the infinitive construct of שָׁלַל and is unusual as the form of the infinitive absolute.²²⁵ This שָׁלַל may mean "to draw/pull out"; if so, it occurs only here in the OT, though there are Arabic cognates.²²⁶ But the verb here may be the common שָׁלַל, whose Qal means "to plunder, capture, rob" (*HALOT*, s.v. שלל II). The workers were told to "plunder" some ears out of the piles to drop them on the ground for Ruth to glean. In either case, the verb presumes an internal object: "plunder/pull out for her [*some stalks*]." The LXX translated: καί γε παραβάλλοντες παραβαλεῖτε αὐτῇ, "And surely you shall throw aside [stalks] for her."²²⁷

מִן־הַצְּבָתִים— The noun צֶבֶת occurs only here in the OT. It may be related to Akkadian *sabatu* ("seize") and the Hebrew verb צָבַט, meaning either "to seize, grasp" or "to heap/pile up" (see the textual note on it in 2:14). The noun occurs in rabbinic Hebrew meaning a "pair, set" and can refer to sets of sheaves; it is related to the rabbinic Hebrew (צָבַת) and Aramaic (צְבַת) verbs meaning "to join" (see Jastrow). Thus הַצְּבָתִים probably refers to "the ears of the sheaf which are grasped in the left hand while being cut with the right" (*HALOT*, s.v. צְבָת). After the men cut handfuls of ears, they left them in piles for the women to gather up (see 2:15).²²⁸ תִּים מִן־הַצְּבָ is translated "from the piles."

---

²²⁵ GKC, § 67 o; Joüon, § 123 q; Hubbard, *Ruth*, 172, n. 7.
²²⁶ See BDB, s.v. שָׁלַל I; *HALOT* (s.v. שלל I), which gives "to slip out some stalks of wheat from the sheaves"; Campbell, *Ruth*, 103–4; Hubbard, *Ruth*, 177.
²²⁷ Preceding this, the LXX has an additional command: καὶ βαστάζοντες βαστάξατε αὐτῇ, "and you surely shall carry [stalks] for her." Cf. Bons, "Die Septuaginta-Version des Buches Rut," 215.
²²⁸ See Dalman, Arbeit und Sitte in Palästina, 3:42, 48–49; Rudolph, Das Buch Ruth, das Hohe Lied, die Klagelieder, 47; Campbell, Ruth, 104; Gerleman, Ruth, Das Hohelied, 27; Bush, Ruth, Esther, 126–27; Block, Judges, Ruth, 668.

וַעֲזַבְתֶּם וְלִקְּטָה—Both verbs are perfect with *waw* consecutive. The first has the force of an imperative because of the preceding imperfects with imperatival force (cf. Waltke-O'Connor, § 32.2.2b). Like וְתֹתַר at the end of 2:14 and שֹׁל in 2:16a, עָזֹב too implies an object: "you shall leave [*stalks*]." The second verb forms a purpose clause with an implied object: "*so she can glean* [them]."

וְלֹא תִגְעֲרוּ־בָהּ:—As at the end of 2:15, an imperfect (Qal of גָּעַר, "rebuke") with the absolute negative לֹא forms an emphatic prohibition: "And do not at all rebuke her!"

2:17 וַתְּלַקֵּט בַּשָּׂדֶה עַד־הָעָרֶב—The *waw* consecutive follows the permission of Boaz as the consequential action: "*so she gleaned ...*" (cf. 1:1b). "The evening" (הָעָרֶב) indicates that the sun was in the lower part of the sky, that is, the late afternoon. At the latitude of Israel, darkness follows quickly after sunset. Ruth still needed a couple of hours of light to thresh the straw from her gleaned ears. This may have been about the time of the evening sacrifice (Ex 29:38–41; Ps 141:2), which was prepared and offered before dark. According to rabbinic tradition, it was the priests' last offering of the day (Talmud, *Yoma,* 32b–33a).[229]

וַתַּחְבֹּט—The *waw* consecutive follows the previous clause in sequence: "*Then she beat out ...*" (cf. 1:4a). Ruth threshed what she had gleaned so she would not have to take the straw and husks home along with the ears. A small quantity of grain was "beaten out" with a flat, curved wooden stick, club, or hammer to remove the husks (as Gideon did in secret for even a large quantity [Judg 6:11]). The LXX translates this with ῥαβδίζω, "to beat with a stick."[230]

---

[229] See Kleinig, *Leviticus*, 156.
[230] See Dalman, *Arbeit und Sitte in Palästina*, 3:92; Gerleman, *Ruth, Das Hohelied*, 27; de Waard and Nida, *A Translator's Handbook on the Book of Ruth*, 39; Gray, *Joshua, Judges, Ruth*, 392; Hubbard, *Ruth*, 178.

Ruth 2:1–17

אֶת אֲשֶׁר־לִקֵּטָה—The relative pronoun אֲשֶׁר is treated as definite and so is preceded by אֶת (Joüon, § 125 g), marking this phrase as the direct object: she beat out "what she had gleaned." אֲשֶׁר followed by a verb (לִקֵּטָה) can form a substantival clause (Joüon, § 158 l).

וַיְהִי כְּאֵיפָה שְׂעֹרִים:—This is, literally, "And it was about an ephah of barley." In English, "it amounted to …" is more usual, also hinting at the large amount. Here the preposition כְּ indicates an approximation (as in 1:4b) not exactitude (the כְּ *veritatis*).[231] The quantity of the ephah is uncertain, but this measure of volume is estimated to have been somewhere between ten and forty liters, hence about a "bushel" (thirty-five liters) and probably between thirty and forty-five pounds of grain. It was astonishing that Ruth could glean so much in one day. Since one liter of barley was widely regarded in the ancient world as a daily ration of food, Ruth had gleaned enough for both herself and Naomi to last perhaps two weeks.[232]

---

[231] For these uses of כְּ, see Joüon, § 133 g.

[232] M. A. Powell, "Weights and Measures," *ABD* 6:903–4, estimates an ephah at between ten and twenty liters, whereas *HALOT* (s.v. אֵיפָה) follows those who advocate forty liters. Cf. Campbell, *Ruth*, 104; Hubbard, *Ruth*, 179; Block, *Judges, Ruth*, 670.

Additional Notes

Ruth 2:1–17

2:18 וַתִּשָּׂא֙ וַתָּב֣וֹא הָעִ֔יר וַתֵּ֥רֶא חֲמוֹתָ֖הּ אֵ֣ת אֲשֶׁר־לִקֵּ֑טָה
וַתּוֹצֵא֙ וַתִּתֶּן־לָ֔הּ אֵ֥ת אֲשֶׁר־הוֹתִ֖רָה מִשָּׂבְעָֽהּ׃
19 וַתֹּאמֶר֩ לָ֨הּ חֲמוֹתָ֜הּ אֵיפֹ֨ה לִקַּ֤טְתְּ הַיּוֹם֙ וְאָ֣נָה עָשִׂ֔ית
יְהִ֥י מַכִּירֵ֖ךְ בָּר֑וּךְ וַתַּגֵּ֣ד לַחֲמוֹתָ֗הּ אֵ֤ת אֲשֶׁר־עָשְׂתָה֙ עִמּ֔וֹ
וַתֹּ֗אמֶר שֵׁ֤ם הָאִישׁ֙ אֲשֶׁ֨ר עָשִׂ֧יתִי עִמּ֛וֹ הַיּ֖וֹם בֹּֽעַז׃
20 וַתֹּ֨אמֶר נָעֳמִ֜י לְכַלָּתָ֗הּ בָּר֥וּךְ הוּא֙ לַיהוָ֔ה
אֲשֶׁר֙ לֹא־עָזַ֣ב חַסְדּ֔וֹ אֶת־הַחַיִּ֖ים וְאֶת־הַמֵּתִ֑ים
וַתֹּ֧אמֶר לָ֣הּ נָעֳמִ֗י קָר֥וֹב לָ֨נוּ֙ הָאִ֔ישׁ מִֽגֹּאֲלֵ֖נוּ הֽוּא׃
21 וַתֹּ֖אמֶר ר֣וּת הַמּוֹאֲבִיָּ֑ה גַּ֣ם ׀ כִּי־אָמַ֣ר אֵלַ֗י
עִם־הַנְּעָרִ֤ים אֲשֶׁר־לִי֙ תִּדְבָּקִ֔ין
עַ֣ד אִם־כִּלּ֔וּ אֵ֥ת כָּל־הַקָּצִ֖יר אֲשֶׁר־לִֽי׃
22 וַתֹּ֥אמֶר נָעֳמִ֖י אֶל־ר֣וּת כַּלָּתָ֑הּ
ט֣וֹב בִּתִּ֗י כִּ֤י תֵֽצְאִי֙ עִם־נַ֣עֲרוֹתָ֔יו וְלֹ֥א יִפְגְּעוּ־בָ֖ךְ בְּשָׂדֶ֥ה אַחֵֽר׃
23 וַתִּדְבַּ֞ק בְּנַעֲר֥וֹת בֹּ֨עַז֙ לְלַקֵּ֔ט
עַד־כְּל֥וֹת קְצִֽיר־הַשְּׂעֹרִ֖ים וּקְצִ֣יר הַֽחִטִּ֑ים וַתֵּ֖שֶׁב אֶת־חֲמוֹתָֽהּ׃

2   ¹⁸Then she lifted [it] up and entered the town, and her mother-in-law saw what she had gleaned. | She also took out and gave to her what she had left over from her fullness.

¹⁹Then her mother-in-law said to her, "Where did you glean today, and where did you work? | May he who acknowledged you be blessed!" Then she told her mother-in-law him with whom she had worked: | "The name of the man with whom I worked today is Boaz."

²⁰Then Naomi said to her daughter-in-law, "May he be blessed by the LORD, | whose faithfulness has not forsaken the living and the dead!" | Then Naomi said to her, "This man is near to us; he is even one of our redeemers." |

²¹Then Ruth the Moabitess said, "Indeed, he also said to me, | 'Cling closely to the workers who are mine, | until they have finished all the harvest that is mine!' " |

²²Then Naomi said to Ruth her daughter-in-law: | "It is good, my daughter, that you go out with his young women, so men will not molest you in another field!" |

²³So, she clung closely to the young women of Boaz to glean | until the completion of the harvest of the barley and the harvest of the wheat. And she lived with her mother-in-law.

Ruth 2:1–17

2:18 וַתִּשָּׂא—With this and the following terse phraseology, the narrator rushes his audience from the previous main scene (2:1–17) into this transitional one (2:18–23).²³³ This Qal imperfect of נָשָׂא, with *waw* consecutive is sequential: "*Then* she lifted up …" (see also וַיִּשְׂאוּ, which begins 1:4). נָשָׂא can mean "lift up" and "carry" (BDB, Qal, 1 and 2, respectively), and here Ruth does both. As common when carrying heavy loads, especially among women, Ruth would have carried the grain on her head. Ruth would have placed the ephah of beaten-out grain (2:17) in a sack, but the narrator omits that detail. He also omits an object for this verb; the implied object is the sack of grain. The translation supplies "it."

וַתָּבוֹא הָעִיר—The verb בּוֹא often takes an accusative without a preposition, and in such cases it can mean "to enter," for example, a city (Joüon, § 125 n), as also in 1:19, 22; 3:15 (see the textual note on it in 1:19). הָעִיר is a definite object without the accusative marker אֵת, as also in 3:15. For its meaning as "town" in reference to Bethlehem, see the textual note on it in 1:19b.

וַתֵּרֶא חֲמוֹתָהּ—See the textual note on חָמוֹת in 1:14. The verb is the Qal third feminine singular imperfect of רָאָה with *waw* consecutive, "and her mother-in-law saw." The narrator describes Naomi's own perception of the situation. This "enables the reader to look through Naomi's eyes," and "her reaction to Ruth's gleaning success becomes the introduction to Naomi's change of mind with regard to Ruth and future life."²³⁴

The Syriac Peshitta and the Vulgate translate, "she *showed* to her mother-in-law" what she had gleaned. Those translations apparently vocalized the verb as וַתַּרְא, the Hiphil of רָאָה, and took חֲמוֹתָהּ as a first direct object, although they translated it as an indirect object (*socrui suae*, "*to* her mother-in-law"). In biblical Hebrew, the Hiphil of רָאָה often takes two direct objects, the first one a person and the second one a thing, in constructions meaning "to show someone something" (see *HALOT*, s.v. רָאָה, Hiphil, 1). A few

---

233 Hubbard, *Ruth*, 180.
234 Van Wolde, "Texts in Dialogue with Texts," 16–17.

86

Hebrew manuscripts support the Hiphil reading.[235] Some argue for the Hiphil not only because of the manuscript evidence, but also because Ruth would then be the subject of all the verbs in 2:18; that would be smoother than the MT, in which Naomi ("her mother-in-law") is the subject of only this one verb (וַתֵּרֶא, "and she saw"), while Ruth is the subject of all the other verbs in 2:18.[236] However, Campbell rightly affirms the Qal reading, which is supported by the LXX. Campbell dismisses the scant Hebrew manuscript evidence for the Hiphil and argues that the narrator would not omit the sign of the direct object (אֵת) where it would be needed to avoid confusion (the unpointed text would be ambiguous without אֵת to indicate that the verb is Hiphil rather than Qal). He also argues that elsewhere in Ruth the narrator moves the pace rapidly with a change of subject (2:14–15; 4:13), as happens here according to the MT with the Qal.[237]

אֵת אֲשֶׁר־לִקֵּטָה—This phrase is repeated from 2:17; see the textual note on it there.

וַתּוֹצֵא—From the context, Ruth must be the subject of this and the next two verbs. This is a Hiphil third feminine singular imperfect with *waw* consecutive of יָצָא. The *waw* conjunctive can have the adjunctive sense of "also" when introducing a further action,[238] hence "she *also* took out …" She would have taken the grain (from 2:17) out of the sack (not mentioned) in which she must have carried it (2:18a).

---

[235] Wright, *The Book of Ruth in Hebrew*, 34, states that four Hebrew manuscripts (two of which he had in his possession and two cited by another source) have אֵת, the sign of the direct object, before חֲמוֹתָהּ, which would fit if the verb were Hiphil. However, Wright says that in the two manuscripts with אֵת that he had, the verb is pointed וַתֵּרֶא (Qal). The *BHS* apparatus claims that a few Hebrew manuscripts have וַתַּרְא, but the apparatus does not cite the evidence for including אֵת.

[236] Wright, The Book of Ruth in Hebrew, 34.

[237] Campbell, *Ruth*, 104–5. Campbell seems to have misunderstood Wright, since Campbell (p. 104) wrongly states that Wright had two manuscripts that pointed the verb as Hiphil. In fact, Wright concedes that in the two manuscripts with אֵת that he had in his possession, the verb is pointed וַתֵּרֶא, that is, as a Qal (*The Book of Ruth in Hebrew*, 34).

[238] Williams, § 441, citing 1 Ki 2:22.

Ruth 2:1–17

וַתִּתֶּן־לָהּ—The verb is a Qal third feminine singular imperfect of נָתַן with *waw* consecutive, denoting sequential action: "and (then) she gave to her …"

אֵת אֲשֶׁר־הוֹתִרָה מִשָּׂבְעָהּ:—This clause ("what she had left over from her fullness") is the direct object of the two preceding verbs, וַתּוֹצֵא and וַתִּתֶּן. The relative pronoun אֲשֶׁר is treated as definite and so is preceded by אֵת (Joüon, § 125 g). אֲשֶׁר followed by a verb (הוֹתִרָה) forms a substantival clause (Joüon, § 158 l). This clause recalls 2:14, where Ruth "ate, was full, and had some left over" (וַתֹּאכַל וַתִּשְׂבַּע וַתֹּתַר). Now the audience learns what Ruth had done with her leftovers.[239] The Hiphil of יָתַר is repeated from 2:14, but here in the third feminine singular perfect, written defectively without the *yod* (הוֹתִרָה instead of הוֹתִירָה). מִשָּׂבְעָהּ is the noun שֹׂבַע, "satiety, abundance" (BDB) with the preposition מִן and the third feminine singular suffix. This noun is cognate to the verb שָׂבַע, "be full," in 2:14, and so it is translated "fullness." This is what was left over after Ruth had been fully satisfied.[240]

2:19 אֵיפֹה לִקַּטְתְּ הַיּוֹם וְאָנָה עָשִׂית—This is the only OT passage that has both of these two interrogative adverbs for "where?" (אֵיפֹה and אָנָה). They are parallel and both are used with verbs here. They are rarer than the common adverbs אֵי and אַיֵּה, both of which mean "where?" (and אַיֵּה is never used with a verb [BDB]). As Boaz's question in 2:8 amounts to an emphatic imperative (שָׁמַעַתְּ בִּתִּי הֲלוֹא, "Have you not heard, my daughter?" is translated "Pay attention, my daughter!"), so these two questions may be emphatic ejaculations.[241] אֵיפֹה (the combination of אֵי and פֹּה) has the same consonants as אֵיפָה (2:17), perhaps providing wordplay, as if Naomi

---

[239] Hubbard, *Ruth*, 181.
[240] Campbell, *Ruth*, 105; Hubbard, *Ruth*, 180, n. 4.
[241] Cf. Cassel, *Ruth*, 33, n. 2; Hyman, "Questions and the Book of Ruth," 17–18.

Ruth 2:18–23

asked, "Where [*'ephoh*] did you glean to get the bushel [*'ephah*]?" יוֹם with the article often means "today" (BDB, s.v. יוֹם, 7 a (1)), as also in 3:18; 4:9–10, 14. אָ֫נָה is אָן with locative *he* and often means "whither?" or "*to* where?" so here the clause may be pregnant for "To where did you go and then work?" since Naomi knew Ruth had traveled.[242] Alternatively, here it may simply ask, "Where did you work?"[243] עָשִׂ֫ית is Qal third feminine singular perfect of עָשָׂה, which has the nuance "to labor, work" here, as well as two more times in 2:19.[244]

יְהִי מַכִּירֵךְ בָּרוּךְ—This benediction is, literally, "May your acknowledger be blessed." יְהִי, the Qal third masculine singular jussive of הָיָה, is common in blessings with בָּרוּךְ, as here (also 1 Ki 10:9; Prov 5:18; 2 Chr 9:8; negated in Jer 20:14; cf. Deut 33:24), or with מְבֹרָךְ (Ps 113:2; Job 1:21). מַכִּירֵךְ, literally, "your acknowledger," is the Hiphil masculine singular participle of נָכַר with second feminine singular objective pronominal suffix. The verb has the same meaning as in 2:10 (לְהַכִּירֵ֫נִי), where Ruth noted that Boaz had "acknowledge[d]" or "recognize[d]" her by granting her exceptional privileges to glean. Naomi knew immediately that Ruth could not have gleaned so much without a generous benefactor. בָּרוּךְ is the Qal masculine singular passive participle of בָּרַךְ, "to bless." It recurs in Ruth 2:20; 4:14; and (feminine) 3:10. Such a benediction prays for the LORD to grant abundant blessings by his grace. It may be compared to the reapers' blessing in 2:4 and to Boaz's prayer in 2:12 that Ruth would receive a "reward" that was "full from the LORD."[245] A blessing relies on the LORD's delight in doing good for his covenant people (Deut 28:63a; 30:9) and his gracious promises to do so (compare Deut 28:1–12 to Mt 5:1–12) for the sake of Christ, the "Seed" of Abraham through whom all peoples would be blessed (Gen 22:17–18; 26:3–4; 28:14).

---

[242] Gerleman (*Ruth, Das Hohelied*, 24) understands this as abbreviated speech for "Where did you (go and) work?"
[243] So Waltke-O'Connor, § 18.4f, example 27, and Campbell, *Ruth*, 105, citing Gen 37:30; 2 Ki 6:6; Is 10:3.
[244] Campbell, *Ruth*, 105; Hubbard, *Ruth*, 181, n. 3.
[245] Cf. Campbell, *Ruth*, 105–6; Hubbard, *Ruth*, 183–84; Mitchell, *The Meaning of* BRK *"To Bless" in the Old Testament*, 114.

Ruth 2:1–17

וַתַּגֵּד לַחֲמוֹתָהּ אֵת אֲשֶׁר־עָשְׂתָה עִמּוֹ—The first verb is Hiphil third feminine singular imperfect of נָגַד with *waw* consecutive, indicating sequential action: "*Then* she told …" The clause that is the direct object is, literally, "whom she worked with him." The relative pronoun אֲשֶׁר is followed by a redundant pronominal suffix on the preposition, עִמּוֹ (see Waltke-O'Connor, § 19.3b). Similar was כְּנָפָיו ... אֲשֶׁר in 2:12b. After the verb עָשָׂה, meaning "to work, labor," the preposition עִם ("with") has the nuance "in whose company, in whose field" (BDB, s.v. עָשָׂה, Qal, I 1 b).

Ruth's following speech has the same kind of construction: literally, "the name of the man whom I worked with him" (עִמּוֹ שֵׁם הָאִישׁ אֲשֶׁר עָשִׂיתִי). That repetitious speech prolongs the suspense by slowing the pace and delaying the name. The audience suffers the suspense with Naomi, who had to wait until Ruth's very last word in the verse to learn her benefactor's name: "Boaz" (see the textual note on his name in 2:1). Ruth's answer focused on what is essential for the story: identifying the man upon whom Naomi's blessing ("May he who acknowledged you be blessed!" 2:19) should rest. Both women may well have actually said much more at this juncture, but the narrator includes only the most important topic. Ruth's answer also contains alliteration, using the sounds *a*, *i*, *o*, and *sh*: *shem ha-ʾish ʾasher ʿasiti ʿimmo hayyom Boʿaz*.[246]

2:20 בָּרוּךְ הוּא לַיהוָה—This is, literally, "Blessed [is/be] he by the LORD." Naomi here employs a common blessing formula, "Blessed [Qal passive participle of בָּרַךְ] is/be someone by [לְ] God/the LORD," that is different than the blessing formulas in 2:4, 19; 4:14. This formula is an optative prayer for God to bless, and the uttering of it performs the action of one person blessing another.[247] The preposition לְ ("by") introduces the agent of the passive verb

---

[246] Campbell, *Ruth*, 106; Hubbard, *Ruth*, 184–85; Block, *Judges, Ruth*, 671.
[247] Thus such a blessing is a performative utterance. See Mitchell, *The Meaning of* BRK *"To Bless" in the Old Testament*, 7, 111.

("blessed").²⁴⁸ One manuscript and the Syriac omit לְ and so read: "Blessed be he, the LORD," which would be unique in the OT; that thought normally would be expressed by בָּרוּךְ יְהוָה, "Blessed is/be the LORD," as in 4:14.

אֲשֶׁר לֹא־עָזַב חַסְדּוֹ אֶת־הַחַיִּים וְאֶת־הַמֵּתִים—The antecedent of אֲשֶׁר is the preceding "LORD" (לַיהוָה). If he is also the subject of the verb עָזַב then this clause would mean "who has not forsaken his faithfulness with the living and with the dead" (so the LXX; KJV; BDB, s.v. עָזַב, Qal, 1 g; cf. NIV). The very similar blessing of the LORD in Gen 24:27 uses עָזַב and the combination of prepositions מֵעִם ("from with") in that sense. However, Ruth 2:20 would be the only passage where עָזַב takes the preposition אֵת (though that preposition, in combination with מִן, is used with חַסְדּוֹ in Ps 66:20).

The other possibility is that חַסְדּוֹ is the subject of עָזַב and אֵת is the direct object marker. Then this clause is, literally, "[the LORD], who his faithfulness has not forsaken the living and the dead" (see RSV; ESV). חַסְדּוֹ ("his [the LORD'S] faithfulness") would be somewhat personified, as in, for example, Pss 42:9 (ET 42:8); 57:4 (ET 57:3); 103:11. Compare Prov 3:3: "Let not faithfulness [חֶסֶד] and truth forsake [עָזַב] you."

חֶסֶד (*ḥesed*) may express God's goodness or grace as well as his fidelity. Here the reference is most likely to his faithfulness in his covenant relationship with his people, and thus even with them individually.²⁴⁹ The LORD is the one who blesses his people (see 2:4; 3:10; 4:11–14) and who in faithfulness has not abandoned "the living and the dead" (2:20). He has used Boaz to bless Ruth and Naomi, and perhaps *'azab* was chosen because of its alliteration with *Bo'az,* but since הַחַיִּים ("the living") is masculine plural, Naomi spoke in general terms, not referring only to herself and/or Ruth as the living beneficiaries of the LORD's faithfulness. "His faithfulness" must be

---

²⁴⁸ GKC, § 121 f; Joüon, § 132 f; Williams, § 280; Gerleman, *Ruth, Das Hohelied*, 24; Hubbard, *Ruth*, 185, n. 25. An inferior view of the function of לְ is advocated by Waltke-O'Connor, § 11.2.10d, example 26.

²⁴⁹ See the two other Ruth verses with חֶסֶד (*ḥesed*), 1:8 and 3:10.

Ruth 2:1–17

the LORD's, not Boaz's, for Boaz has not yet become the agent through whom the LORD will demonstrate "his faithfulness" toward "the dead" (הַמֵּתִים, masculine plural, probably referring to Elimelech, Mahlon, and Chilion). The LORD will do that when Boaz marries Ruth, widow of (deceased) Mahlon (4:10), to raise up an heir for (deceased) Elimelech.[250] But since "the dead" could not be aided through generosity with grain (2:18–19), Naomi must have thought of the possibility of Boaz marrying Ruth as a way in which the LORD would demonstrate "his faithfulness" toward "the dead" by reviving their dying family. Already in 1:9 (and later in 3:1) Naomi had thought of remarriage for Ruth as the way for her daughter-in-law to find "security."

קָרוֹב לָנוּ הָאִישׁ—This is, literally, "near to us is the man." Boaz was a relative of Elimelech (2:1; cf. 3:2), Naomi's late husband. By using the plural pronoun ("us"), Naomi acknowledges that Ruth too is also related (by marriage) to Boaz and is a potential recipient of a redeemer's duty.[251] Since Boaz is the object of conversation, the article on הָאִישׁ implies *"this man."*

מִגֹּאֲלֵנוּ הוּא:—Literally, "from our redeemers is he," this sentence heightens the relationship of Boaz to Naomi and Ruth, and so the translation adds "even." The preposition מִן is partitive (as with מִן־הַלֶּחֶם, "some of the food," in 2:14), and since the clause refers to only one person, "he is *one of* our redeemers" is appropriate. The context requires understanding גֹּאֲלֵנוּ (participle of גָּאַל with first common plural suffix) as plural and written defectively for גֹּאֲלֵינוּ. Some Hebrew manuscripts have the plene spelling of the plural,

---

[250] Compare 2 Sam 2:5–6, where David prays that the men of Jabesh Gilead may be blessed because they showed חֶסֶד ("faithfulness") to dead Saul by burying him (cf. 1 Sam 31:11–13). See Campbell, *Ruth*, 106; Sakenfeld, *The Meaning of Hesed in the Hebrew Bible*, 104–7; Porten, "Structure, Style, and Theme of the Scroll of Ruth," 15–16; Gerleman, *Ruth, Das Hohelied*, 28; Rebera, "Yahweh or Boaz?"; Hubbard, *Ruth*, 185–86; Lacocque, *The Feminine Unconventional*, 87; Thompson, "New Life amid the Alien Corn," 205; Block, *Judges, Ruth*, 673; but compare Bush, *Ruth, Esther*, 134–36.

[251] Trible, "Two Women in a Man's World," 263; Hubbard, *Ruth*, 189.

מִגֹּאֲלֵינוּ, and the LXX and Syriac translate with a plural.[252] All close male relatives could serve as "redeemers," though the closest one (in Ruth, the "redeemer" who enters the story in 3:12–13; 4:1–8) must be the first either to redeem or to pass the right to redeem to another close relative. The closest *go'el* (see 3:12) was the male relative who had the right or obligation to pay the redemption price for a dispossessed relative or property (Lev 25:25, 47–49). He could also avenge a relative's murder (Num 35:19). Here, Naomi must have in mind the redemption of the inherited property of Elimelech's family. Whoever would redeem the property of the deceased (Elimelech) would also be obligated to care for his widow (Naomi).

This is the first occurrence in Ruth of גָּאַל, which will recur in 3:9, 12, 13; 4:1, 3, 4, 6, 8, 14.[253]

2:21 גַּם ׀ כִּי־אָמַר אֵלַי—This is an emphatic way to introduce a quotation. Elsewhere, the combination גַּם כִּי (cf. BDB, s.v. גַּם, 6) means "even though" (Hos 8:10; Ps 23:4) or "also when" (Prov 22:6; Lam 3:8). The adverb גַּם usually introduces an additional idea ("also"). Here the conjunction כִּי could simply introduce the following quotation (cf. BDB, s.v. כִּי, 1 b), but more likely it is asseverative, "indeed, surely."[254] English requires reversing their Hebrew word order: "*Indeed*, he *also* said ..."

עִם־הַנְּעָרִים אֲשֶׁר־לִי תִּדְבָּקִין—Ruth moves from Boaz's identity (2:19) to the exceptionally generous permission he granted her. The idiom דָּבַק עִם ("cling with/to") is the same as used in Boaz's words in 2:8 (see the textual note there). The placement of the prepositional phrase before the verb emphasizes it: literally, "To the workers who are mine cling closely." Although the audience might

---

[252] Keil, *Joshua, Judges, Ruth*, 480; Steenstra in Cassel, *Ruth*, 34, n. 3; Campbell, *Ruth*, 106–7; Hubbard, *Ruth*, 182, n. 5.
[253] Cf. also H. Ringgren, "גאל," *TDOT* 2:351–52; J. J. Stamm, "גאל," *TLOT* 1:289–91; Sasson, *Ruth*, 60–61; Hubbard, *Ruth*, 188–89; *HALOT*; *DCH*.
[254] Cf. BDB, s.v. כִּי, 1 d and e; Williams, § 449; Joüon, § 157 a, footnote 2. Campbell, *Ruth*, 107, paraphrases: "There's more!"

Ruth 2:1–17

hear הַנְּעָרִים as "the young men" (it referred to the male reapers in 2:9), here (as in 2:15) it refers Boaz's workers in general, regardless of gender (GKC, § 122 g). Boaz had actually told her to cling to "my young women" (נַעֲרֹתָי, 2:8), who followed the reaping men and gathered the cut ears into sheaves.

Ruth uses a periphrastic construction to express the relationship of the workers to Boaz: "the workers who belong to me," אֲשֶׁר with לְ denoting possession.²⁵⁵ This is more cumbersome than a pronominal suffix ("my/his young women," 2:8, 22; 3:2; "his workers," 2:15). There seems to be no particular reason for the periphrastic construction אֲשֶׁר־לִי (Joüon, § 130 e), which recurs at the end of the verse (see the next textual note). The construction represents the turgid speech (repetition without emphasis) of an older person (Boaz), reproduced even in Ruth's quotation of him.²⁵⁶ Another archaism is the form of תִדְבָּקִין, the Qal second feminine singular imperfect with paragogic *nun* (see the last textual note on 2:8).

עַד אִם־כִּלּוּ אֵת כָּל־הַקָּצִיר אֲשֶׁר־לִי—The combination אִם עַד serves as a conjunction meaning "until," as elsewhere only in Gen 24:19, 33; Is 30:17.²⁵⁷ Otherwise in Ruth, "until X happens" is usually expressed by עַד with the infinitive construct (1:19; 2:23; 3:3).²⁵⁸ The verb כִּלּוּ is the Piel perfect of כָּלָה, "to finish, complete." In this context, following עַד אִם, the perfect refers to an act to be completed in the future, and so it could be translated as a future perfect, "until they *will have* finished" (see Joüon, § 112 i). The construction כָּל־הַקָּצִיר אֲשֶׁר־לִי (literally, "all the harvest that belongs to me," with לְ of possession; see the previous textual note) is periphrastic compared to one with a pronominal suffix ("all my harvest").

In the agricultural year the barley ripened and was harvested first, then the wheat harvest followed. The ancient Gezer Calendar from the tenth century B.C. includes the "month of the harvest of barley" (ירח קצר שערם) followed on the next line by the "month

---

²⁵⁵ See BDB, s.v. לְ, 5 a; *HALOT*, s.v. לְ I, 10, 11. See also the לְ for possession in 1:11–13.
²⁵⁶ See Campbell, *Ruth*, 107; Hubbard, *Ruth*, 190.
²⁵⁷ See Williams, § 457; Campbell, *Ruth*, 107; Hubbard, *Ruth*, 190, n. 47.
²⁵⁸ Campbell, *Ruth*, 107.

of harvest" (ירח קצר), which must refer to that of wheat.²⁵⁹ Since Boaz did not limit "the harvest" only to that of barley, the implication of "all the harvest that is mine" is that Ruth may glean in Boaz's field throughout the barley harvest and then also throughout the following wheat harvest. That implication is confirmed by the narrator's statement in 2:23. Together the barley and wheat harvests constituted the bulk of the harvest season and lasted about seven weeks, roughly late April to early June. The barley harvest started about Passover, and the first bread of wheat was offered at Shavuoth, that is, Pentecost.²⁶⁰ In modern times, however, barley is harvested in late June and wheat in early July in the Bethlehem area.²⁶¹

2:22 טוֹב בִּתִּי כִּי תֵצְאִי עִם־נַעֲרוֹתָיו—Probably טוֹב is a predicate adjective (rather than the homographic verb or noun), and כִּי introduces the verbal clause that is the subject, as also with כִּי ... טוֹב in Job 10:3 and Lam 3:27. תֵצְאִי is Qal second feminine singular imperfect of יָצָא and here means "*go forth ... to work*" (see BDB, s.v. יָצָא, Qal, 2 a). A translation reflecting the Hebrew subject and predicate would be "That you go out with his young women [is] good, my daughter," but our translation follows the Hebrew word order. Naomi clarifies that Ruth should associate only with "his young women," the *female* workers, not with the "young men" (2:9) or "reapers" (2:3–7, 14), who could have been included in "the workers" (הַנְּעָרִים) to whom Ruth referred in 2:21. Yet, considering the following clause, the strongest emphasis is that Ruth stick with "*his* young women," for in light of Boaz's order in 2:9, it would be better

---

[259] Gezer Calendar, lines 4–5. For the Hebrew text and an analysis, see Gibson, *Textbook of Syrian Semitic Inscriptions*, 1:2–4. An older translation is in *ANET*, 320.
[260] See Ex 34:22; Lev 23:10–21; Deut 16:9–12; Dalman, *Arbeit und Sitte in Palästina*, 1^(II):414–17; Campbell, *Ruth*, 108; Hubbard, *Ruth*, 190, 192; Kleinig, *Leviticus*, 498–503.
[261] Campbell, *Ruth*, 108.

Ruth 2:1–17

for Ruth to work near Boaz's young men than for her to take her chances in someone else's field.[262]

וְלֹא יִפְגְּעוּ־בָךְ בְּשָׂדֶה אַחֵר:—The verb פָּגַע often takes the preposition בְּ and can have a wide range of meanings, including "to **fall upon** someone ... intending to kill them," to "assault," and "to molest a woman" (*HALOT*, Qal, 2 a, b, and c, respectively, citing only Ruth 2:22 for "molest"). In this context it is synonymous with נָגַע ("touch") in 2:9, but stronger. Since the plural verb (יִפְגְּעוּ) is impersonal, with no named subject, grammatically it could be translated passively, "so that you will not be molested."[263] However, the masculine form, as well as its meaning, make it preferable to translate it with "men" as the subject. Naomi is more concerned with male physical abuse than with verbal abuse, which Ruth could suffer from from both genders.[264]

On the basis of 2 Sam 18:3, perhaps the preceding clause could be taken as comparative in relation to this clause: "It is *better*, my daughter, that you go out with his young women *than* that men molest you in another field" (so the Vulgate; cf. Joüon, § 141 g). However, such a construal of this *waw* and imperfect (וְלֹא יִפְגְּעוּ) is unattested elsewhere. The contrast is between something good ("with his young women") and something potentially dangerous ("in another field"), not between something better versus something good. Therefore it is best to understand this as a purpose clause, "*so* men will not molest you" (cf. the LXX and Syriac).[265]

2:23 As in 1:22 at the end of chapter 1, the narrator supplies the last verse to close chapter 2. The verse also points toward the next chapter, moving the reader quickly from the beginning to the end of

---

[262] See Hubbard, *Ruth*, 191.
[263] GKC, § 144 f; Campbell, *Ruth*, 108; Hubbard, *Ruth*, 191–92; Block, *Judges, Ruth*, 677.
[264] On potential abuse from men and women, see the textual note on "my young women" in 2:8; the textual notes on "his workers" and "you shall in no way humiliate her" in 2:15.
[265] Campbell, *Ruth*, 107; Hubbard, *Ruth*, 182, n. 10; 191.

the harvest season.²⁶⁶ Naomi and Ruth returned to Bethlehem at the beginning of the barley harvest (1:22), and the action in 2:1–22 took place soon afterward. Then the story skips to action near the end of the harvest season (2:23; see the fourth textual note on 3:2).

וַתִּדְבַּ֞ק בְּנַעֲר֥וֹת בֹּ֖עַז לְלַקֵּ֑ט—The narrator uses דָּבַק, "cling," with the preposition בְּ as in 1:14. (In 2:21 דָּבַק takes עִם.) As did Naomi (see the first textual note on 2:22), so too the narrator here clarifies that Ruth worked beside the "young women." The Piel infinitive construct (לְלַקֵּט) with לְ could express purpose ("to glean") or be circumstantial ("while gleaning").

עַד־כְּל֥וֹת קְצִֽיר־הַשְּׂעֹרִ֖ים וּקְצִ֥יר הַחִטִּֽים—The temporal clause has the Qal infinitive construct of כָּלָה, "to be finished, completed," translated as a noun ("until *the completion*"). The LXX translated, "until he [Boaz] completed [συνετέλεσεν] the harvest," probably reading its unpointed Hebrew text as if the infinitive were the transitive Piel (כַּלּוֹת), "to finish, complete." The Piel infinitive (with suffix) is in a similar temporal clause in 3:3: עַד כַּלֹּתוֹ. Compare the Piel perfects כִּלּוּ in 2:21 and כִּלָּה in 3:18. For the durations of the two harvests, see the last textual note on 2:21.

וַתֵּ֖שֶׁב אֶת־חֲמוֹתָֽהּ:—The Qal third feminine singular imperfect of יָשַׁב with *waw* consecutive means "and she *dwelt/lived* with her mother-in-law." It is contemporaneous with the preceding part of the verse: throughout the harvest season Ruth returned to Naomi after each day's work in Boaz's field. A few Hebrew manuscripts read אֶל וַתָּשָׁב (Qal imperfect of שׁוּב), "and she returned to" her mother-in-law, which is supported by the Vulgate (in 3:1). The MT is structurally preferable, for chapters 1 and 3 each conclude with a summary statement that also points forward to the next chapter (1:22; 3:18), and "she lived with her mother-in-law" leads into the strategy Naomi devised and proposed to Ruth while they were living together (3:1–6).

---

²⁶⁶ Hubbard, *Ruth*, 192–93.

Ruth 2:1–17

This clause recalls the period when the whole family "lived" together in Moab (וַיֵּשְׁבוּ, 1:4), and Ruth's promise to Naomi, "Wherever you lodge, I shall lodge" (with לִין, 1:16). While the clause underscores that Ruth is fulfilling her promise to Naomi and the LORD (1:16–17), Naomi's hope for Ruth (1:9) remains unfulfilled for now.[267]

---

[267] Campbell, *Ruth*, 108; Hubbard, *Ruth*, 183, n. 12; 193.

Text, Translation, and Notes

Chapter 3

Ruth 3:1–6

3:1 וַתֹּאמֶר לָהּ נָעֳמִי חֲמוֹתָהּ
בִּתִּי הֲלֹא אֲבַקֶּשׁ־לָךְ מָנוֹחַ אֲשֶׁר יִיטַב־לָךְ׃
2 וְעַתָּה הֲלֹא בֹעַז מֹדַעְתָּנוּ אֲשֶׁר הָיִית אֶת־נַעֲרוֹתָיו
הִנֵּה־הוּא זֹרֶה אֶת־גֹּרֶן הַשְּׂעֹרִים הַלָּיְלָה׃
3 וְרָחַצְתְּ ׀ וָסַכְתְּ וְשַׂמְתְּ שִׂמְלֹתַיִךְ עָלַיִךְ
וְיָרַדְתִּי הַגֹּרֶן אַל־תִּוָּדְעִי לָאִישׁ עַד כַּלֹּתוֹ לֶאֱכֹל וְלִשְׁתּוֹת׃
4 וִיהִי בְשָׁכְבוֹ וְיָדַעַתְּ אֶת־הַמָּקוֹם אֲשֶׁר יִשְׁכַּב־שָׁם
וּבָאת וְגִלִּית מַרְגְּלֹתָיו וְשָׁכָבְתִּי וְהוּא יַגִּיד לָךְ אֵת אֲשֶׁר תַּעֲשִׂין׃
5 וַתֹּאמֶר אֵלֶיהָ כֹּל אֲשֶׁר־תֹּאמְרִי ֗ ֗ אֶעֱשֶׂה׃
6 וַתֵּרֶד הַגֹּרֶן וַתַּעַשׂ כְּכֹל אֲשֶׁר־צִוַּתָּה חֲמוֹתָהּ׃

3 ⁱNaomi, her mother-in-law, said to her, | "My daughter, should I not seek for you security, so that it will be good for you? |
²Now, is not Boaz our relative, with whose young women you have been? | Look, he is winnowing at the threshing floor of barley tonight. |
³So bathe, anoint yourself, and put your cloak on yourself, | and go down to the threshing floor. Do not make yourself known to the man until he has finished eating and drinking. |
⁴But when he lies down, note the place where he lies down. | Then approach, uncover the place of his feet, and lie down. He himself will tell you what you should do." |
⁵Then she [Ruth] said to her, "All that you say to me, I will do!" |
⁶So she went down to the threshing floor, and she did according to everything that her mother-in-law had commanded her.

Ruth 3:1–6

3:1 וַתֹּאמֶר לָהּ נָעֳמִי חֲמוֹתָהּ—The first word of chapter 3 begins with a simple *waw* consecutive verb, which is sequential. However, the end of the previous chapter (2:23) indicates that a time interval of perhaps seven weeks elapsed between 2:23 and 3:1.[268] Naomi was the last person to speak (2:22). After the short narrative conclusion in 2:23, נָעֳמִי חֲמוֹתָהּ, "Naomi, her mother-in-law," resumes speaking in 3:1–4. See the textual note on חֲמוֹתָהּ in 1:14. The third feminine singular suffixes, "to her" (לָהּ) and "her" (הָ-), refer to Ruth, even though she is not named in this chapter until 3:9.

בִּתִּי—That Naomi calls Ruth "my daughter" indicates Ruth's age inferiority and also a close relationship of familiarity between the two. Naomi calls Ruth "my daughter" also in 2:2, 22; 3:16, 18, and Boaz addresses Ruth in that way in 2:8; 3:10–11.

הֲלֹא אֲבַקֶּשׁ־לָךְ מָנוֹחַ—The Piel imperfect אֲבַקֶּשׁ has a modal nuance: "I *must/should* seek" (see Joüon, § 113 m). The negative rhetorical question, "Should I not seek for you … ?" does not expect an answer. Instead, by it Naomi declares her motivation for formulating the plan she will outline to Ruth (cf. Boaz's question with הֲלוֹא in 2:8 that was a declaration). In the OT the noun מָנוֹחַ, derived from the verb נוּחַ, usually refers to a physical "resting place" (e.g., Deut 28:65; Is 34:14; Lam 1:3) rather than abstract "rest" (Ruth 3:1 ESV). Naomi had used its cognate synonym מְנוּחָה to refer to "security" in the house of a husband in 1:9. The larger context here too suggests that מָנוֹחַ pertains both to marriage (hence "a home," Ruth 3:1 NIV) and to rest from the toil of the manual labor necessary for the widow to eke out a living.[269] "Security" (NASB) conveys both aspects.

אֲשֶׁר יִיטַב־לָךְ:—The same phrase (but with לְךָ instead of לָךְ) is in Deut 4:40; 6:3, to which Naomi may allude. As there, the relative pronoun אֲשֶׁר introduces a purpose or result clause, "so that" (BDB, s.v. אֲשֶׁר, 8 b). The Qal imperfect of יָטַב is impersonal, with no stated subject: "it will be good/go well for you" means "your

---

[268] See the last textual note on 2:21 and Hubbard, *Ruth*, 196, n. 1.
[269] See De Waard and Nida, A Translator's Handbook on the Book of Ruth, 47; Bush, Ruth, Esther, 147; Block, Judges, Ruth, 681.

Ruth 3:1–6

circumstances/life will be good." See the similar expressions in Gen 12:13; Deut 5:16; 2 Ki 25:24.

3:2 וְעַתָּ֗ה הֲלֹ֥א בֹ֙עַז֙ מֹֽדַעְתָּ֔נוּ—Literally, "and now," וְעַתָּ֗ה introduces a new phase in the conversation: Naomi's quest for security for Ruth leads her to focus on Boaz. As in 2:8 and 3:1, the negative rhetorical question with הֲלֹא is actually a strong assertion.[270] מֹֽדַעְתָּ֔נוּ is the feminine noun מֹדַעַת, "relative" (*HALOT*), with first common plural suffix (usually ־נוּ but here ־ָֽנוּ).[271] מֹדַעַת occurs only here in the OT,[272] but the corresponding masculine noun מוֹדַע, "relative," was the Qere in 2:1. The feminine form of the noun may have an abstract nuance; BDB (s.v. מֹדַעַת, under יָדַע) gives "kindred, kinship." Or it may have an intensive nuance, "close relative."[273] Since it is from יָדַע, "to know," it exemplifies the narrator's frequent use of words from this root (see the first textual note on 2:1).

אֲשֶׁ֥ר הָיִ֖ית אֶת־נַעֲרוֹתָֽיו—This is, literally, "Boaz ... *who you were with his young women*." In Hebrew אֲשֶׁר ("who") regularly takes a pronoun complement ("his" on נַעֲרוֹתָיו) that is redundant in English, as also in 2:2 (בְּעֵינָיו) and 2:12 (כְּנָפָיו). English requires rearranging the syntax and translating אֲשֶׁר by "whose," as in 2:20.

---

[270] De Waard and Nida, *A Translator's Handbook on the Book of Ruth*, 48; Hubbard, *Ruth*, 197, n. 4.
[271] On the form of the suffix, see GKC, § 91 f; Joüon, § 94 h.
[272] It occurs in rabbinic Hebrew with the weaker meaning "acquaintance" or "friend" (Jastrow).
[273] Joüon, § 89 b; Hubbard, *Ruth*, 199, including n. 16. To support this point Hubbard cites GKC, § 141 c, which states that the construction here, with a noun as the predicate of a nominal clause, is more emphatic than if the predicate were an adjective. However, Bush, *Ruth, Esther*, 148, rejects the view that the nuance here is intensive.

Ruth 3:1–6

הִנֵּה־הוּא זֹרֶה ... הַלָּיְלָה —The interjection הִנֵּה ("look!") serves to attract attention and introduce a statement (as in 1:15). זֹרֶה is the Qal participle of זָרָה, "to scatter; winnow," that is, to toss the threshed stalks into the air with a winnowing fork or shovel so that the wind would blow away the chaff and separate the lighter straw from the grain, which would fall at the feet of the winnower. This was often done in the evening, when the breeze was optimal. In this context the participle could be translated as a future ("will be winnowing") because the verse ends with הַלָּיְלָה ("the night," that is, "tonight," in pause with *qamets*, -לָ-), a temporal accusative that identifies the time of an action.[274]

אֶת־גֹּרֶן הַשְּׂעֹרִים —The most likely literal meaning of this phrase is that Boaz was winnowing "at the threshing floor of the barley," though it could be paraphrased as "he is winnowing barley at the threshing floor."[275] The noun גֹּרֶן, "threshing floor," will recur in 3:3, 6, 14. It refers to "a flat surface of rock or pounded earth located in an open place exposed to the wind."[276] The construct phrase גֹּרֶן הַשְּׂעֹרִים uses "barley" as an attributive genitive of species,[277] equivalent to "the threshing floor *for* barley" or "the barley threshing floor."

The syntax of the phrase within the verse is challenging. After the preceding participle זֹרֶה, "winnowing," one would expect אֵת to introduce the direct object (e.g., אֶת־הַשְּׂעֹרִים "winnowing the barley") since the Qal of זָרָה usually takes a direct object. But גֹּרֶן intervenes, and the "threshing floor" itself cannot be the object of "winnowing." With גֹּרֶן one might expect a preposition, for example, בַּגֹּרֶן, "winnowing *at* the threshing floor," which would be similar to "I winnowed ... *at* [בְּ] the gates" in Jer 15:7. Here אֵת could be the preposition, which normally means "with," though the Qal of זָרָה does not take the preposition אֵת elsewhere. However, the second

---

[274] Waltke-O'Connor, § 10.2.2c; Dalman, *Arbeit und Sitte in Palästina*, 3:126–31; Bush, *Ruth, Esther*, 150.
[275] So Bush, *Ruth, Esther*, 149–50; many English translations also have this reading or one similar.
[276] H. N. Richardson, "Threshing," *IDB* 4:636.
[277] For examples of genitives of species, see Waltke-O'Connor, § 9.5.3g.

occurrence of אֵת in 1 Sam 7:16 may be another instance where it means "at" (BDB, s.v. אֵת II, 2).

Commentators have also pointed out an apparent chronological difficulty. Ruth 2:23 seems to indicate that this scene of Boaz winnowing barley occurred after both the barley and wheat harvests were completed. Normally the barley was harvested before the wheat, and the two harvests together lasted about seven weeks.[278] It strikes some commentators as unlikely that Boaz did not winnow the barley until after he finished harvesting the wheat, several weeks after the barley harvest was completed. An alternative chronology of the story seems even more unlikely: that this scene is a "flashback" that occurred at the end of the barley harvest but before the wheat harvest. Since Boaz married Ruth (4:10) within a day or so of this scene (3:18), that alternative chronology would mean that Ruth continued to glean (and live with her mother-in-law) even after Boaz had married her, until the wheat harvest too was completed (2:23).

Campbell argues that הַשְּׂעֹרִים, "the barley," should be emended to הַשְּׁעָרִים, "the gates," in which case the construct phrase גֹּרֶן הַשְּׁעָרִים would be a genitive of location,[279] and the clause would mean "he is winnowing (the grain of) the threshing floor near the gate."[280] Campbell gives the following reasons for his emendation: (1) The consonants שׂ and שׁ were not distinguished in writing until the Masoretes added the pointing (ca. sixth–ninth centuries A.D.), and

---

[278] See the last textual note on 2:21.
[279] For examples of genitives of location, see Waltke-O'Connor, § 9.5.2f.
[280] Campbell, *Ruth*, 114, 117–19. His translation (p. 114) assumes that אֵת is the direct object marker. It also follows the proposal by Joüon (*Ruth*, 67) that "threshing floor" is metonymy for "(the grain of) the threshing floor" (Campbell's translation on page 114), even though Campbell seems skeptical of Joüon's proposal when he refers to it on page 117. To explain why he translates his emended plural הַשְּׁעָרִים as the singular "gate," Campbell argues that "gates" theoretically could refer to a single entryway consisting of an inner and an outer gate; in 2 Sam 18:24, "two gates" refers to the double-entry gate structure common in ancient cities. However, Bush (*Ruth, Esther*, 149) argues against the emendation of הַשְּׂעֹרִים, "the barley," to הַשְּׁעָרִים, "the gate(s)," and considers the suggestion that the plural הַשְּׁעָרִים (produced by the emendation) could refer to a single city gate "quite unexampled, both in Ruth (4:1, 10, 11) and in the rest of the OT."

Ruth 3:1–6

before that both were written as שׂ. Thus in Gen 26:12, the LXX and Syriac (ancient translations that predate the Masoretes) read "barley" where the MT has שְׂעָרִים.[281] (2) The narrator of Ruth may be creating wordplay between "barley" and "gate," as one finds in some other OT passages (2 Ki 7:1–20). "Barley" was important in Ruth 1:22; 2:17, 23, and the story will turn its focus to the action at Bethlehem's city "gate" in 3:11; 4:1, 10–11. (3) Threshing floors were often situated near the town gate (1 Ki 22:10; Jer 15:7).

However, evidence against Campbell's emendation includes the fact that the LXX, Syriac, and Vulgate all translate the phrase in 3:2 as "threshing floor of barley." Also, Boaz will fill Ruth's shawl with "barley" in 3:15, and "barley" remains in focus in the story through 3:17.

The conclusion must be that, although Boaz and his workers harvested the barley first, they did not winnow it until after the wheat had been harvested too. Thus the story is sequential, and 3:1–6 takes place after the months of harvesting briefly narrated in 2:23. Whether or not the harvested wheat was also on the threshing floor at this time, the point is that Ruth's work of gleaning during the harvests had ended (2:23), but Boaz had not yet completed his work of winnowing the barley.

3:3 וְרָחַצְתְּ—After Naomi's introductory statements in 3:1–2, this verb begins an extended set of directives to Ruth. It is the first in a series of eight verbs in 3:3–4:

וְרָחַצְתְּ ׀ וָסַכְתְּ
וְשַׂמְתְּ ... וְיָרַדְתְּ ... וְיָדַעַתְּ ... וּבָאת
וְגִלִּית ... וְשָׁכָבְתְּ

---

[281] In Gen 26:12 שְׂעָרִים probably is the plural of a homograph שַׁעַר that refers to some kind of "measure" (BDB, s.v. שַׁעַר II). Since it follows "one hundred," it is usually translated by the suffix on "hundred*fold*" (so KJV, RSV, NIV, ESV).

Ruth 3:1–6

Each of these verbs is a second feminine singular perfect with *waw* consecutive with an imperatival meaning ("bathe, anoint yourself, and put ... and go down ... note ... approach, uncover ... and lie down"). The verbs are sequential: Ruth is to perform the actions in that order, one after the other. All are Qal except וְנָגְלִית, which is Piel. The forms themselves could either have *waw* consecutive or conjunctive *waw*: with *waw* consecutive the accent on a perfect verb usually shifts to the final syllable if possible (Joüon, § 43; Waltke-O'Connor, § 32.1.1b–d), but that shift is not possible with most of these second feminine singular perfect forms because final תְּ- cannot be accented. Two of the forms already have the accent on the final syllable regardless of the *waw* (וּבָאת וְנָגְלִית). That all these forms have *waw* consecutive is an inference from the fact that often elsewhere Hebrew uses a perfect with *waw* consecutive to express an imperative (GKC, § 112 x, aa). Often a series begins with an imperative form, which is then followed by perfects with *waw* consecutive that have an imperatival meaning.[282]

וְסַכְתְּ—The Qal of סוּךְ can have a reflexive meaning, "anoint oneself," as here, or a transitive meaning, to "anoint" someone else (BDB, s.v. סוּךְ I, Qal, 1 and 2, respectively). The *waw* consecutive is pointed with *qamets* (-ָ) before the tone syllable, though rarely as here when not in pause (GKC, § 104 g). Elsewhere the verb is often used with שֶׁמֶן, "oil" (Deut 28:40; 2 Sam 14:2; Ezek 16:9; Micah 6:15). It refers to applying perfumed olive oil as a cosmetic, and thus it could be translated, "put on scented oil."[283] Ruth would not have adorned herself with oil while she was still mourning for her deceased husband. For her now to apply fragrant olive oil would signal that her mourning was over and that she was available for marriage.

וְשַׂמְתְּ שִׂמְלֹתַיִךְ עָלָיִךְ—This clause with the Qal second feminine singular perfect of שִׂים is, literally, "and put your clothing upon yourself." This means that Ruth should wear her normal clothing, not mourning attire. The definite direct object lacks the

---

[282] Joüon, §119 l; Waltke-O'Connor, § 32.2.2b. See also Campbell, *Ruth*, 119–20; Hubbard, *Ruth*, 197, n. 9; Bush, *Ruth, Esther*, 150.
[283] Cf. Hubbard, *Ruth*, 197, n. 6; Bush, *Ruth, Esther*, 150.

Ruth 3:1–6

object marker אֵת.²⁸⁴ The Qere is the plural noun with second feminine singular suffix, שִׂמְלֹתַיִךְ, "your clothes," which is the reading in a few manuscripts, but preferable is the Kethib, which is the singular שִׂמְלֹתֵךְ, "your clothing," the reading in many manuscripts. שִׂמְלָה refers to an "outer garment, cloak, mantle" (*HALOT*, 1) that can be worn for sleeping at night for warmth (as in Ex 22:26 [ET 22:27]).²⁸⁵ Hubbard proposes that "the context suggests the probable meaning 'to get dressed up, to dress one's best' " and cites the Vulgate and Targum for support.²⁸⁶ The Vulgate has *cultioribus vestimentis*, "finer clothes," and the Targum has תכשיטיך, "your adornments/jewelry." However, Bush correctly states that the Hebrew term refers to a large outer garment "covering the entire body and extending well down on the legs"; neither here nor in any other context does it refer to dressy clothes.²⁸⁷ A different term in 3:15 refers to a "shawl" she also wore.

וְיָרַדְתִּי הַגֹּרֶן—The Qere, וְיָרַדְתְּ, is the regular Qal second feminine singular perfect of יָרַד, while the Kethib, וְיָרַדְתִּי, has an archaic form of the second feminine singular perfect ending, as also does the Kethib וְשָׁכַבְתִּי in 3:4.²⁸⁸ Because these archaic forms occur in Ruth only in this speech by Naomi, they indicate the speech of an older person. After the verb of motion, the noun הַגֹּרֶן is an accusative of place indicating direction (see Williams, § 54; Waltke-O'Connor, § 10.2.2b): "and go down to the threshing floor."

אַל־תִּוָּדְעִי לָאִישׁ—The Niphal can have a causative-reflexive meaning, and the imperfect (Qal second feminine singular of יָדַע) with אַל forms a negative imperative: "*do* not *make yourself known* to the man" (Waltke-O'Connor, § 23.4h, example 21).

עַד כַּלֹּתוֹ לֶאֱכֹל וְלִשְׁתּוֹת:—The preposition עַד and Piel infinitive construct of כָּלָה with third masculine singular suffix forms

---

²⁸⁴ Another such case was in 2:14. See Waltke-O'Connor, § 10.3b.
²⁸⁵ Bush, *Ruth, Esther*, 150–51.
²⁸⁶ Hubbard, *Ruth*, 197, n. 7.
²⁸⁷ Bush, *Ruth, Esther*, 150–51.
²⁸⁸ See Joüon, § 42 f; GKC, § 44 h; Myers, *The Linguistic and Literary Form of the Book of Ruth*, 11; Hubbard, *Ruth*, 197, n. 8; Sasson, *Ruth*, 245. This archaic ending also appears in Jeremiah and Ezekiel.

a temporal clause: "until he has finished" (see Waltke-O'Connor, § 36.2.2b, including example 8). Following are two Qal infinitive constructs with לְ, לֶאֱכֹל (from אָכַל) and וְלִשְׁתּוֹת (from שָׁתָה), that serve as verbal complements (cf. Waltke-O'Connor, § 36.2.3b, including examples 5–11): "until he has finished *eating* and *drinking*."

3:4 וִיהִי בְשָׁכְבוֹ—The first verb is the Qal jussive of הָיָה with conjunctive *waw*. וִיהִי is much less common than וְהָיָה, which commonly introduces a command or wish (GKC, § 112 bb), but וִיהִי can have the same force (GKC, §§ 109 k; 112 z). Here (as also in 1 Sam 10:5; 2 Sam 5:24 ‖ 1 Chr 14:15; 1 Ki 14:5), וִיהִי is followed by an infinitive construct with preposition and suffix, forming a temporal clause. בְשָׁכְבוֹ is the Qal infinitive construct of שָׁכַב (Joüon, § 65 b) with the preposition בְּ and a third masculine singular suffix. The temporal clause introduces the following commands,[289] literally, "and may it be, when he lies down ..." However, a translation of the imperatival jussive ("and may it be") is not needed in English because the following verbs are translated as imperatives.

וְיָדַעַתְּ אֶת־הַמָּקוֹם אֲשֶׁר יִשְׁכַּב־שָׁם—The first verb is the next in the series of Qal second feminine singular perfects with *waw* consecutive that have an imperatival meaning (see the first textual note on 3:3). Here יָדַע means that Ruth is to "take note of" (see BDB, Qal, 1 b) the place, a different meaning than יָדַע had in 3:3b. Hebrew characteristically uses the pleonastic adverb שָׁם, literally, "the place where he lies *there*," which need not be translated.

וּבָאת—This is the Qal second feminine singular perfect of בוֹא with *waw* consecutive. From the perspective of Boaz, Ruth is to "come to" or "approach" him.

---

[289] Bush, *Ruth, Esther*, 152.

Ruth 3:1–6

וְגִלִּית מַרְגְּלֹתָיו—The verb is the Piel perfect second feminine singular of גָּלָה with *waw* consecutive. The Piel of גָּלָה, "to uncover, reveal," with the object עֶרְוָה, "nakedness," is often used in reference to forbidden sexual relations (e.g., Lev 18:6–19; 20:17–21; Ezek 22:10; 23:10, 18). But its object here is מַרְגְּלֹתָיו, literally, "his foot-places," meaning "the place of (or the area around) his feet." מַרְגְּלוֹת occurs also in Ruth 3:7, 8, 14 and elsewhere only in Dan 10:6. The noun is a feminine plural of extension, referring to a location (GKC, § 124 b; Waltke-O'Connor, § 7.4.1c; cf. § 7.1d). It corresponds to מְרַאֲשׁוֹת, the "place at the head" (BDB) of someone lying down (Gen 28:11, 18; 1 Sam 19:13, 16; 1 Ki 19:6). The clause "uncover the place of his feet" avoids the suggestion of sexuality that could have been present if the object were רַגְלָיו, "uncover his feet."[290] In the OT the verb גָּלָה is never used with רֶגֶל, but in other contexts רַגְלַיִם ("legs/feet") occasionally seems to be euphemistic, though never does it pertain to sexual intimacy.[291] But מַרְגְּלֹתָיו clearly has a literal meaning in 3:8, 14 (see the last textual note on 3:8), which makes it implausible that its meaning here is euphemistic.

Naomi's instruction to Ruth cannot mean "uncover yourself at his feet,"[292] for that would require a Niphal verb.

וְשָׁכָבְתִּי—The Qere is וְשָׁכַבְתְּ, the normal form, while the Kethib is וְשָׁכָבְתִּי, an archaic form of the Qal second feminine singular perfect of שָׁכַב with *waw* consecutive.[293] It continues the imperatival series: "and lie down." Like the preceding Piel of גָּלָה, this verb too can have sexual overtones in other contexts.

---

[290] Bush, *Ruth, Esther*, 153; cf. Campbell, *Ruth*, 121; Joüon, *Ruth*, 69; Sasson, *Ruth*, 69–70; Hubbard, *Ruth*, 203.

[291] According to some commentators and lexicons it may refer to the pubic region in Ex 4:25; Is 6:2; 7:20, though in none of those passages is the context one of sexual intimacy. It is used in idioms for relieving oneself in Judg 3:24; 1 Sam 24:4 (ET 24:3); and the Qere in 2 Ki 18:27 (|| Is 36:12).

[292] Van Wolde, "Texts in Dialogue with Texts," 19–20, argues for that understanding.

[293] Joüon, § 42 f; GKC, § 44 h; Myers, The Linguistic and Literary Form of the Book of Ruth, 11.

וְהוּא יַגִּיד־לָךְ אֵת אֲשֶׁר תַּעֲשִׂין:—The pronoun הוּא is grammatically unnecessary with the third masculine singular verb (יַגִּיד, Hiphil imperfect of נָגַד), so it emphasizes the shift from Ruth's activity to that of Boaz: "*He himself* will tell you what you should do." תַּעֲשִׂין, the Qal imperfect second feminine singular of עָשָׂה, has a final paragogic *nun* (see the last textual note on 2:8). The imperfect has the modal nuance of obligation, "*should* do" (see Joüon, § 113 m; Waltke-O'Connor, § 31.4g, including example 16).

3:5 וַתֹּאמֶר אֵלֶיהָ—Naomi spoke to Ruth in 3:1–4. The following context will clarify that this clause, literally, "And she said to her … ," means that Ruth is now speaking to Naomi.

כֹּל אֲשֶׁר־תֹּאמְרִי ... אֶעֱשֶׂה:—The first part of the clause ("all that you say …") is the direct object of the verb at the end of the verse, אֶעֱשֶׂה ("I will do"). Here and in 3:11 אֵת is not used in the כֹּל אֲשֶׁר־ phrase that precedes and is the direct object of a form of עָשָׂה. It is used in 3:16, where the phrase forming the direct object (אֵת כָּל־אֲשֶׁר…) follows the verb, there the Hiphil of נָגַד (Joüon, § 125 i).

Since Naomi has already spoken, it is unusual for Ruth to use the imperfect תֹּאמְרִי, "all that you say/will say," instead of a perfect. Yet Boaz will use the identical imperfect when he assures Ruth, "All that you say [תֹּאמְרִי], I will do for you!" (3:11), as he responds to Ruth's (completed) words and actions. See a similar promise with an imperfect (of צָוָה) in 2 Sam 9:11. The imperfect can be used for past actions whose effect continues (GKC, § 107 h).[294] Another explanation is that the imperfect is used formulaically here. In some passages, a person uses an imperfect in a formula of obedience that he speaks before he receives the commands he is to obey (e.g., "All that you will say to me, I shall do" [Num 22:17]; similar are Gen 41:55;

---

[294] See Rudolph, *Das Buch Ruth, das Hohe Lied, die Klagelieder*, 52–53; Hubbard, *Ruth*, 198, n. 12; Bush, *Ruth, Esther*, 154.

Deut 17:11; 2 Ki 10:5). The imperfect here may reflect such formulaic language even though Ruth has already received the commands from Naomi.

According to the Kethib the verse ends with תֹּאמְרִי אֶעֱשֶׂה. But the inserted vowels indicate that the Qere is תֹּאמְרִי אֵלַי אֶעֱשֶׂה ("that you say *to me* I will do"), and אֵלַי appears in many manuscripts, but is not represented in the LXX. Likewise in 3:17 אֵלַי is absent from the Kethib but indicated for the Qere. In both verses it makes for a smoother reading, but is not necessary.

3:6 וַתֵּרֶד הַגֹּרֶן—The verb is Qal third feminine singular imperfect of יָרַד with *waw* consecutive, with a consequential meaning: "*So* she went down to the threshing floor." After the verb of motion, the noun הַגֹּרֶן is an accusative of place. The verb יָרַד indicates that the threshing floor was located somewhat lower than the city. If it were as high on the hill as the city, the wind might be too strong for winnowing, perhaps blowing some kernels away with the chaff (cf. 1 Ki 22:10; Jer 15:7).[295]

וַתַּעַשׂ כְּכֹל אֲשֶׁר־צִוַּתָּה חֲמוֹתָהּ:—The Qal third feminine singular imperfect of עָשָׂה with *waw* consecutive has a sequential meaning: "And (then) she did ..." כְּכֹל is, literally, "according to all." A few manuscripts omit the preposition כְּ, and it is not reflected in the Syriac and Vulgate. However, the combination כְּכֹל is common in OT passages where someone does (עָשָׂה) what was commanded (the verb צִוָּה). Note also Gen 6:22; 7:5; Ex 29:35; 31:11; 39:32. צִוַּתָּה is the Piel third feminine singular perfect of צִוָּה with a third feminine singular suffix that lacks the usual *mappiq* (הּ). In this context the meaning of צִוַּתָּה is pluperfect: "she *had commanded* her."[296]

---

[295] Dalman, *Arbeit und Sitte in Palästina*, 3:71–72.
[296] On Hebrew pluperfects, see Waltke-O'Connor, § 30.5.2b; GKC, § 106 f. On the loss of *mappiq* in the suffix on צִוַּתָּה, see GKC, § 91 e (see also § 58 g); Myers, *The Linguistic and Literary Form of the Book of Ruth*, 18. On the penultimate accent of צִוַּתָּה, see GKC, § 59 g.

Additional Notes

Ruth 3:7–18

3:7 וַיֹּ֨אכַל בֹּ֤עַז וַיֵּשְׁתְּ֙ וַיִּיטַ֣ב לִבּ֔וֹ
וַיָּבֹ֕א לִשְׁכַּ֖ב בִּקְצֵ֣ה הָעֲרֵמָ֑ה וַתָּבֹ֣א בַלָּ֗ט וַתְּגַ֛ל מַרְגְּלֹתָ֖יו וַתִּשְׁכָּֽב׃
8 וַיְהִי֙ בַּחֲצִ֣י הַלַּ֔יְלָה וַיֶּחֱרַ֥ד הָאִ֖ישׁ וַיִּלָּפֵ֑ת
וְהִנֵּ֣ה אִשָּׁ֔ה שֹׁכֶ֖בֶת מַרְגְּלֹתָֽיו׃
9 וַיֹּ֖אמֶר מִי־אָ֑תּ וַתֹּ֗אמֶר אָנֹכִי֙ ר֣וּת אֲמָתֶ֔ךָ
וּפָרַשְׂתָּ֤ כְנָפֶ֙ךָ֙ עַל־אֲמָ֣תְךָ֔ כִּ֥י גֹאֵ֖ל אָֽתָּה׃
10 וַיֹּ֗אמֶר בְּרוּכָ֨ה אַ֤תְּ לַֽיהוָה֙ בִּתִּ֔י
הֵיטַ֛בְתְּ חַסְדֵּ֥ךְ הָאַחֲר֖וֹן מִן־הָרִאשׁ֑וֹן
לְבִלְתִּי־לֶ֗כֶת אַחֲרֵי֙ הַבַּ֣חוּרִ֔ים אִם־דַּ֖ל וְאִם־עָשִֽׁיר׃
11 וְעַתָּ֣ה בִּתִּי֮ אַל־תִּֽירְאִי֒ כֹּ֥ל אֲשֶׁר־תֹּאמְרִ֖י אֶֽעֱשֶׂה־לָּ֑ךְ
כִּ֤י יוֹדֵ֙עַ֙ כָּל־שַׁ֣עַר עַמִּ֔י כִּ֛י אֵ֥שֶׁת חַ֖יִל אָֽתְּ׃
12 וְעַתָּה֙ כִּ֣י אָמְנָ֔ם כִּ֥י אִם־גֹּאֵ֖ל אָנֹ֑כִי וְגַ֛ם יֵ֥שׁ גֹּאֵ֖ל קָר֥וֹב מִמֶּֽנִּי׃
13 לִ֣ינִי ׀ הַלַּ֗יְלָה וְהָיָ֤ה בַבֹּ֙קֶר֙ אִם־יִגְאָלֵ֥ךְ טוֹב֙ יִגְאָ֔ל
וְאִם־לֹ֨א יַחְפֹּ֧ץ לְגָֽאֳלֵ֛ךְ וּגְאַלְתִּ֥יךְ אָנֹ֖כִי חַי־יְהוָ֑ה שִׁכְבִ֖י עַד־הַבֹּֽקֶר׃
14 וַתִּשְׁכַּ֤ב מַרְגְּלוֹתָו֙ עַד־הַבֹּ֔קֶר וַתָּ֕קָם בְּטֶ֛רֶם יַכִּ֥יר אִ֖ישׁ אֶת־רֵעֵ֑הוּ
וַיֹּ֙אמֶר֙ אַל־יִוָּדַ֔ע כִּי־בָ֥אָה הָאִשָּׁ֖ה הַגֹּֽרֶן׃
15 וַיֹּ֗אמֶר הָ֠בִי הַמִּטְפַּ֧חַת אֲשֶׁר־עָלַ֛יִךְ וְאֶֽחֳזִי־בָ֖הּ וַתֹּ֣אחֶז בָּ֑הּ
וַיָּ֤מָד שֵׁשׁ־שְׂעֹרִים֙ וַיָּ֣שֶׁת עָלֶ֔יהָ וַיָּבֹ֖א הָעִֽיר׃
16 וַתָּבוֹא֙ אֶל־חֲמוֹתָ֔הּ וַתֹּ֖אמֶר מִי־אַ֣תְּ בִּתִּ֑י
וַתַּ֨גֶּד־לָ֔הּ אֵ֛ת כָּל־אֲשֶׁ֥ר עָֽשָׂה־לָ֖הּ הָאִֽישׁ׃
17 וַתֹּ֕אמֶר שֵׁשׁ־הַשְּׂעֹרִ֥ים הָאֵ֖לֶּה נָ֣תַן לִ֑י
כִּ֚י אָמַ֣ר ‎ ‎ אַל־תָּב֥וֹאִי רֵיקָ֖ם אֶל־חֲמוֹתֵֽךְ׃
18 וַתֹּ֙אמֶר֙ שְׁבִ֣י בִתִּ֔י עַ֚ד אֲשֶׁ֣ר תֵּֽדְעִ֔ין אֵ֖יךְ יִפֹּ֣ל דָּבָ֑ר
כִּ֣י לֹ֤א יִשְׁקֹט֙ הָאִ֔ישׁ כִּֽי־אִם־כִּלָּ֥ה הַדָּבָ֖ר הַיּֽוֹם׃

3 ⁷After Boaz ate and drank and his heart was in good spirits, | he went to lie down at the edge of the grain heap. Then she [Ruth] approached in secret, and she uncovered the place of his feet and lay down. |

⁸In the middle of the night, the man shivered and turned over. Behold, | a woman was lying at the place of his feet! |

⁹He said, "Who are you?" She said, "I am Ruth, your handmaid. | Spread out your 'wing' over your handmaid, for you are a redeemer!" |

¹⁰Then he said, "May you be blessed by the LORD, my daughter! | You have made your last faithfulness better than the first | by not going after the young men, whether a poor man or a rich man! |

¹¹So now, my daughter, do not be afraid! All that you say, I will do for you! | For the whole gate of my people [everyone in my town] knows that you are an honorable woman! |

¹²And now it is indeed true—certainly I am a redeemer—but also there is a redeemer nearer than I. |

¹³Spend the night [here] tonight. If in the morning he redeems you, good; let him redeem. | But if he does not desire to redeem you, then I will redeem you myself, as the LORD lives! Lie down until the morning." |

¹⁴So she lay down at the place of his feet until the morning. She arose before a man could recognize his neighbor. | But he thought, "Let it not be known that the woman came to the threshing floor!"

¹⁵So he said, "Give me the shawl that is on you, and take hold of it!" And she took hold of it. | He measured out six [measures] of barley and placed it upon her. Then he entered the town.

¹⁶When she came to her mother-in-law, she [Naomi] said, "How are you, my daughter?" | Then she [Ruth] told her all that the man had done for her. |

¹⁷She emphasized, "These six [measures] of barley he gave to me, | for he said, 'You shall not come empty-handed to your mother-in-law!'" |

¹⁸Then she [Naomi] said, "Sit still, my daughter, until you know how the matter will turn out. | For the man will not rest unless he has fulfilled his word today!"

Ruth 3:7–18

3:7 וַיֹּאכַל בֹּעַז וַיֵּשְׁתְּ וַיִּיטַב לִבּוֹ—These three clauses with three Qal imperfects with *waw* consecutive are, literally, "And Boaz ate, and he drank, and his heart was good." Different forms of the first two verbs were in Naomi's instruction in 3:3. Since those three clauses are preliminary to the following one ("he went to lie down"), they can be rendered as temporal clauses, either "When he had eaten ..." (cf. וַתֵּרֶא, "When she saw ... ," in 1:18), or more smoothly in English, "After Boaz ate ..."[297] The idiom with לֵב as the subject of יָטַב, "be glad, joyful" (BDB, Qal, 1), means "be in good spirits" and can result from a satisfying meal (Judg 19:6; 1 Ki 21:7).[298]

וַיָּבֹא לִשְׁכַּב בִּקְצֵה הָעֲרֵמָה—The Qal imperfect of בּוֹא literally states that Boaz "came" to the heap of grain, but for the audience's perspective, in some contexts בּוֹא is better translated "go" (BDB, Qal, 4) or "went." The *waw* is sequential and need not be translated after the preceding temporal clauses. The Qal infinitive construct of שָׁכַב with לְ forms a purpose clause: "to lie down," meaning in this context, "to go to bed for the night," thus implying sleep (Ruth 3:13; Prov 6:22; 1 Sam 3:5–6).[299] עֲרֵמָה can refer to a "heap" of grain (Jer 50:26; Hag 2:16; Song 7:3 [ET 7:2]; Neh 13:15) or of grain and fruit (2 Chr 31:5–9). Here it refers to the pile of barley grain on the threshing floor.[300]

וַתָּבֹא בַלָּט—This clause is, literally, "And she approached in the secrecy." The *waw* consecutive is sequential so it can be translated, "Then ..." as in 1:4. The action denoted by בּוֹא ("approach") corresponds to the same verb in Naomi's instruction (וּבָאת) in 3:4. It follows a time interval after Boaz had fallen asleep. The noun לָט or לָאט, "secrecy," always has the preposition בְּ of circumstance ("*in* secret"), and such phrases with בְּ may be translated adverbially (Waltke-O'Connor, § 11.2.5d). The generic article can be used with abstract terms denoting states (Waltke-O'Connor, § 13.5.1g). Compare הַמָּוֶת in 1:17.

---

[297] See Bush, *Ruth, Esther*, 158 and 159, n. 7a.
[298] Hubbard, *Ruth*, 206–7, n. 2.
[299] Hubbard, *Ruth*, 207, n. 3.
[300] Compare the references to barley in Ruth 2:23; 3:2, 15, 17, and see Dalman, *Arbeit und Sitte in Palästina*, 3:135–36.

Even though לָט is absent from the account of Lot, possibly there is a Hebrew pun between לָט (laṭ, "secrecy") in Ruth 3:7 and the name לוֹט, loṭ, "Lot," whose daughters plied him with wine so they could secretly have intercourse with him to have children, one of whom was Moab (Gen 19:30–38), the ethnic progenitor of Ruth the Moabitess.[301] The verb form here in Ruth 3:7 (וַתָּבֹא) is the same as in Gen 19:33 (וַתָּבֹא), where Lot's older daughter "approached" him for the purpose of intercourse, and different forms of the verb בּוֹא in that context have the same sexual meaning (לָבוֹא in Gen 19:31 and וּבֹאִי in Gen 19:34). The account of Lot also uses the verb שָׁכַב, "to lie (with someone)" (Gen 19:32–35, the first verses in the OT where that verb has the sexual meaning), and שָׁכַב is also in Ruth 3:4, 7, 8, 13, 14 (the only verses in Ruth where it occurs). Yet Lot's drunkenness and incest (Gen 19:32–35) contrast with Boaz's drinking in moderation (Ruth 3:3, 7) and chastity (3:13–14).

וַתְּגַל מַרְגְּלֹתָיו וַתִּשְׁכָּב:—These clauses repeat the vocabulary in Naomi's instructions in 3:4 (וְגִלִּית מַרְגְּלֹתָיו וְשָׁכָבְתְּ). The two verbs are the Piel of גָּלָה and Qal of שָׁכַב, here both third feminine singular imperfect with *waw* consecutive. The noun with suffix, מַרְגְּלֹתָיו, is the same as in 3:4. Ruth did exactly what Naomi counseled, laying back part of Boaz's outer garment to expose his feet, and then lying down. She most likely remained awake, anxiously awaiting Boaz's arousal from sleep, when she would offer her marriage proposal to him.

3:8 וַיְהִי בַּחֲצִי הַלַּיְלָה וַיֶּחֱרַד הָאִישׁ—This is, literally, "And it occurred in the half of the night, and the man shivered." וַיְהִי, which may be omitted in translation, introduces the temporal idiom for some time "in the middle of the night" as the ensuing action's circumstance. This indicates that a period of time elapsed after Ruth

---

[301] Linafelt, *Ruth*, 52.

"lay down" (3:7) and before Boaz awoke. וַיֶּחֱרַד is the third masculine singular Qal imperfect of חָרַד with *waw* consecutive. This verb usually means "tremble" or "shudder" in fear, or sometimes "be startled" (BDB, 2, which gives "*start up* (out of sleep)" for this verse). But in this context, the best view is that Boaz "shivered" from the cold because his feet were uncovered.[302]

וַיִּלָּפֵת—This is the Niphal third masculine singular imperfect with *waw* consecutive of לָפַת, which only occurs thrice in the OT. The Qal in Judg 16:29 means "**grasp**, perh[aps] with [a] twisting motion" (*DCH*). The Niphal in Job 6:18 refers to paths that "wind" or "twist," or perhaps to caravans that "turn aside" from their paths (*DCH*, Niphal, 2). The Arabic cognate *lafata* means "twist, bend." Thus here the verb may mean "**turn oneself over**, in bed" (*DCH*, Niphal, 1) or "bend over."[303] Others argue for the meaning "grope,"[304] which is supported by the Qal in Judg 16:29.

וְהִנֵּה אִשָּׁה שֹׁכֶבֶת מַרְגְּלֹתָיו—"Behold, a woman [was] lying at the place of his feet!" indicates surprise from Boaz's viewpoint (cf. וְהִנֵּה in 2:4). The Syriac translated with two verbs that are absent in the Hebrew: "and *he was startled* because *he saw* a woman." The Vulgate (*viditque mulierem*) and Targum (וחמא והא איתתא) also added the verb "and *he saw* a woman."[305] שֹׁכֶבֶת is the Qal feminine singular participle of שָׁכַב, modifying אִשָּׁה. Here and in 3:14 מַרְגְּלֹתָיו (which was translated in 3:4, 7 as "uncover *the place of his feet*") is used adverbially: Ruth was lying "at the place of his feet."[306] Since it obviously has that literal meaning in 3:8, 14, the sexually euphemistic meaning that some interpreters propose for it in 3:4, 7 is much less plausible. Instead of a euphemism, in 3:4, 7 Ruth was to (and did) uncover (i.e., pull back) the garment that covered Boaz's feet.

---

[302] See Block, *Judges, Ruth*, 689–90.
[303] Bush, *Ruth, Esther*, 163.
[304] Campbell, *Ruth*, 122, and Block, *Judges, Ruth*, 690, including n. 35.
[305] Cf. Berlin, Poetics and Interpretation of Biblical Narrative, 91–92; Hubbard, Ruth, 207, n. 7.
[306] BDB, s.v. מַרְגְּלוֹת. See also Waltke-O'Connor, § 10.2.2b, example 5; Joüon, § 126 h.

3:9 מִי־אָ֑תְּ—This is a question of identification: "*Who* are you?" (Waltke-O'Connor, § 18.2b, example 1). The second person feminine singular pronoun is usually pointed אַתְּ (GKC, §§ 10 k, 32 h). Here Leningradensis has אָ֑תְּ, but most other manuscripts have אַתְּ.

אָנֹכִי֙ ר֣וּת אֲמָתֶ֔ךָ—Twice in 3:9, first here, Ruth uses אָמָה: "I am Ruth, your *handmaid*." The penultimate accent and *seghol* (-תֶ֔-) in אֲמָתֶ֔ךָ are because it is in pause. In the next clause, אֲמָתְךָ֙ is not in pause (hence -תְ-) even though it too has the disjunctive *zaqeph* accent (-֔). When an accent is repeated on nearby words, the first has the greater force (Joüon, § 15 k), hence the first occurrence of the identical terms (אֲמָתֶ֔ךָ) is in pause and the second (אֲמָתְךָ֙) is not.

"Handmaid" (אָמָה) may be a socially higher designation for Ruth than the term she used for herself earlier, שִׁפְחָה, "maidservant" (twice in 2:13). Often in the OT the two terms are used as synonyms, but some authorities maintain that originally these two terms designated two classes of people that were clearly differentiated from one another: שִׁפְחָה, "maidservant" (2:13), referred to a servile girl or woman who was still unmarried and whose primary duty was to serve the woman of the house, while אָמָה, "handmaid," referred to a servile woman who could be a man's secondary wife or the wife of a slave.[307]

וּפָרַשְׂתָּ֤ כְנָפֶ֙ךָ֙ עַל־אֲמָ֣תְךָ֔—Ruth's response includes this explicit petition and a second, implied petition (see the next textual note). The translation "Spread out your 'wing' over your handmaid" preserves the connection between "wing" here and the LORD's "wings" in 2:12. The quotation marks around "wing" indicate that Ruth uses it with a metaphorical meaning: she is requesting that Boaz marry her.

The verb is the second masculine singular Qal perfect with *waw* consecutive of פָּרַשׂ, which can refer to a person "spreading out" a garment (e.g., Deut 22:17; Judg 8:25) or a covering (2 Ki 8:15; Ezek 16:8). It can also refer to a bird "spreading" its "wings" (Deut 32:11; Jer 48:40; 49:22; Job 39:26). The most common usage of פָּרַשׂ

---

[307] See *HALOT*, s.v. שִׁפְחָה, 1 a, and C. Westermann, "עֶבֶד," *TLOT* 2:823, both of which rely on A. Jepsen, "AMA and SCHIPHCHA," *Vetus Testamentum* 8 (1958): 293–97.

Ruth 3:7–18

with כָּנָף is for the cherubim on the ark of the covenant and against the back wall of the Holy of Holies in the temple, who "spread" their "wings" over the ark. Note Ex 25:20; 37:9; 1 Ki 6:27; 8:7; 2 Chr 3:13; 5:8. In two verses פָּרַשׂ with כָּנָף refers metaphorically to a groom "spreading" his "wing" or "hem" of his robe over a bride as symbolic of marrying her (Ezek 16:8; Ruth 3:9). The perfect verb with consequential *waw* consecutive can serve as an imperative (GKC, § 112 x, aa; cf. Joüon, § 119 w), as also in 3:3–4 (see the first textual note on 3:3), hence "*Spread out* your 'wing' over your handmaid."

The noun כָּנָף usually refers to a "wing," whether of a bird, cherub, seraph, or the LORD himself. (Note Pss 17:8; 36:8 [ET 36:7]; 57:2 [ET 57:1]; 61:5 [ET 61:4]; 63:8 [ET 63:7]; 91:4; Ruth 2:12). It can also refer to the skirt or "hem" of a garment (*HALOT*, 3). The marginal Masorah explains that according to the western Masoretes (of Israel and Syria) כְנָפֶךָ is defectively written for כְנָפֶיךָ, "your wings," the plural or dual form that many Hebrew manuscripts have. However, according to the eastern Masoretes (of Babylonia) the text is כְנָפֶךָ, "your wing," and the LXX and Syriac translate it as singular.[308] Some commentators prefer כְנָפֶיךָ (plural or dual) and take it, meaning "wings," as a metaphor for protection, which Ruth requests from Boaz, rather than a metaphor specifically for marriage.[309] The plural/dual would recall the plural/dual כְּנָפָיו in Boaz's prayer for Ruth in 2:12 ("the LORD ... to whom you have come to seek refuge under *his wings*").

However, in the context of 3:9, the singular is preferable because כָּנָף in the singular is used in idioms that pertain to marriage in Deut 23:1 (ET 22:30); 27:20; Ezek 16:8.[310] In Ezek 16:8 the LORD uses the same idiom (פָּרַשׂ כָּנָף) as Ruth in 3:9 to say that he "spread" his "wing/hem" over Jerusalem (personified) when he took her to be his wife. The idiom "uncover the wing/hem of his father" (גִּלָּה כְּנַף־אָבִיו) is used in the divine prohibition (Deut 23:1 [ET

---

[308] For explanations of the terms in the marginal Masorah that refer to western and eastern Masoretes, see Yeivin, *Introduction to the Tiberian Masorah*, pp. 99, 104.
[309] Wright, *The Book of Ruth in Hebrew*, 46; Steenstra in Cassel, *Ruth*, 40, n. 2; Morris, *Ruth*, 289–90.
[310] Campbell, *Ruth*, 123; cf. Linafelt, *Ruth*, 55.

22:30]) and curse (Deut 27:20) against a man having sexual relations with his father's wife; such sin violates the father's sacrosanct marital union (cf. Heb 13:4).

כִּי גֹאֵל אָתָּה:—This clause with causal כִּי, "for you are a redeemer," contains an implicit request. Ruth phrases it as an explanation for the first part of her proposal, "Spread out your 'wing' over your handmaid," which was her request that Boaz marry her. This second part of the proposal appeals to Boaz to act not simply for Ruth's sake, but also for the sake of Naomi, Ruth's mother-in-law. Since Boaz is a close relative of Naomi's deceased husband (2:1), he is a potential "redeemer" for Naomi. On גֹאֵל, "redeemer," see the last textual note on 2:20.

3:10 בְּרוּכָה אַתְּ לַיהוָה—Literally, "blessed be you by the LORD," this is the same blessing formula that Naomi used for Boaz in 2:20 (see the textual note there), but with the second person feminine singular pronoun אַתְּ, so the Qal passive participle בְּרוּכָה is feminine too. Compare the different blessing formulas in 2:4, 19; 4:14.

בִּתִּי—Boaz first called Ruth "my daughter" in 2:8; see the textual note there. He repeats this term for her in 3:10–11.

הֵיטַבְתְּ חַסְדֵּךְ הָאַחֲרוֹן מִן־הָרִאשֹׁון—The verb is the Hiphil second feminine singular perfect of יָטַב. The Hiphil can mean "to do something well" (*HALOT*, 3), or, as here, it can have a causative meaning, to "make a thing good, right" (BDB, 4). (The Qal of יָטַב, "be good," was in 3:1, 7.) Here the verb with the preposition מִן ("than") expresses the comparative degree: "You have made your last faithfulness *better than* the first [faithfulness]." This definite direct object lacks the object marker אֵת, omitted also in 2:14 (see Waltke-O'Connor, § 10.3b).

This is the only OT verse in which חֶסֶד is the object of יָטַב (though חֶסֶד follows the Qal of יָטַב in Gen 40:14 and Esth 2:9). It is also the only verse where חֶסֶד is modified by the adjective אַחֲרוֹן, "latter, last." The only other verse where חֶסֶד is modified by רִאשׁוֹן,

Ruth 3:7–18

"former, first," is Ps 89:50 (ET 89:49), where the psalmist Ethan asks about the LORD's "former lovingkindesses" (KJV) which he had promised to David.

לְבִלְתִּי־לֶכֶת אַחֲרֵי הַבַּחוּרִים—The verb לֶכֶת is the Qal infinitive construct of הָלַךְ. The particle בִּלְתִּי (here with preposition לְ) is used to negate an infinitive construct (Joüon, § 124 e; as also in 1:13), hence literally, "not to go." Here as often the infinitive has the meaning of a gerund (Joüon, § 124 o), "by not going." To "go after" could refer to seeking sexual relations (הָלַךְ אַחֲרֵי in Prov 7:22; Hos 2:7 [ET 2:5]),[311] but here it refers to seeking a husband. בָּחוּר denotes a "**young** (fully-grown, vigorous, unmarried) man" (*HALOT*) which fits this context particularly well, for it carries the nuance of choice, eligible bachelors in their prime. It contrasts with נַעַר, "servant; worker; young man" in 2:5–6, 9, 15, 21, which referred to Boaz's subordinate workers.[312]

אִם־דַּל וְאִם־עָשִׁיר:—The construction with repeated אִם is alternative: "either (whether) … or" (Williams, § 455). The antonyms דַּל, "a poor man," and עָשִׁיר, "a rich man," form a merism: Ruth did not pursue any of "the young men" regardless of their wealth.

3:11 וְעַתָּה בִּתִּי—"So now, my daughter" indicates that Boaz is drawing a conclusion on the basis of previous statements. When followed by an imperative, עַתָּה signals special urgency.[313] Compare וְעַתָּה in 3:2 followed by the imperatival verbs in 3:3–4.

אַל־תִּירְאִי—The imperfect (Qal second feminine singular of יָרֵא) with אַל forms a negative imperative: "Do not be afraid!"

כֹּל אֲשֶׁר־תֹּאמְרִי אֶעֱשֶׂה־לָּךְ—With this clause, "*All* that you say, I will do for you," Boaz pledges to fulfill both parts of Ruth's

---

[311] Block, *Judges, Ruth*, 693.
[312] Sasson, *Ruth*, 85; Block, *Judges, Ruth*, 693.
[313] BDB, s.v. עַתָּה (under the root ענה I), 1 e; 2 b; Sasson, "The Issue of Geʾullāh in *Ruth*," 56; Waltke-O'Connor, § 39.3.1h.

Ruth 3:7–18

request in 3:9: he will marry Ruth and also act as redeemer for Naomi (unless the closer redeemer does so; see 3:12). Boaz repeats to Ruth the same words she spoke in her promise to Naomi in 3:5, with the addition of לָךְ, "for you." A few manuscripts include אֵלַי ("say *to me*"), which is supported by most of the ancient versions (the Greek recension of Origen, Peshitta, Vulgate, and Targum) and harmonizes these words to the Qere in 3:5. The textual note on 3:5 discussed possible reasons for the use of the imperfect תֹּאמְרִי referring to words already spoken (here by Ruth; in 3:5 by Naomi).

כָּל־שַׁעַר עַמִּי—Literally, "the whole gate of my people," this means "everyone in my town," that is, everyone who passes in and out of the walled town through the gate. This exact expression occurs only here, but שַׁעַר עַמִּי is in Obad 13 and Micah 1:9, and another expression with שַׁעַר in Ruth 4:10 refers to the townspeople.[314]

אֵשֶׁת חַיִל—"An honorable woman" corresponds to the description of Boaz as "an honorable gentleman" (אִישׁ גִּבּוֹר חַיִל) in 2:1. Here, it could be rendered "virtuous"[315] in reference to her strength of faith and fidelity. A former pagan, she had confessed her belief in the LORD and her unswerving commitment to Naomi (1:16–17), as Boaz (2:11–12) and presumably the rest of the town had heard. Ruth's labor in Boaz's field (chapter 2) was a public demonstration that she was faithfully fulfilling her commitment to Naomi. In effect, Boaz declared, "Everyone in town respects you highly!"

3:12 וְעַתָּה—As in 3:2, 11, "now ..." introduces an urgent consideration and is followed by an imperative (לִינִי in 3:13). In 3:11 Boaz had agreed in principle both to marry Ruth and to act as

---

[314] De Waard and Nida, *A Translator's Handbook on the Book of Ruth*, 56; Bush, *Ruth, Esther*, 173.
[315] Steenstra in Cassel, *Ruth*, 40, n. 4; Campbell, *Ruth*, 125; Bush, *Ruth, Esther*, 173–74.

Ruth 3:7–18

redeemer for Naomi. No obstacle would prevent him from marrying Ruth. However, in 3:12–13 Boaz addresses a major obstacle that could prevent him from acting as redeemer for Naomi: there is a closer redeemer who has priority over him. But before stating that in the last clause of 3:12, he first will affirm the last part of Ruth's petition, where she, speaking on behalf of Naomi, said to him, "You are a redeemer!" (3:9).[316]

כִּי אָמְנָם כִּי אִם גֹּאֵל אָנֹכִי—Boaz affirms, "Certainly I am a redeemer." The asseverative conjunction כִּי and the adverb אָמְנָם here mean "indeed (it is) true"[317] or "truly." Compare the expression of Jesus, ἀμὴν ἀμήν, "amen, amen," or "truly, truly" (e.g., Jn 1:51). The second כִּי too is asseverative. The lack of pointing on אִם indicates that אִם is part of the Kethib (one written textual tradition) but absent in the Qere (the preferred textual variant that was to be read aloud). If included, it goes with the second כִּי as after an oath. כִּי אִם would thus introduce "an emphatic assurance"[318] and is thus rendered "certainly." For גֹּאֵל, "redeemer," see the last textual note on 2:20.

וְגַם יֵשׁ גֹּאֵל קָרוֹב מִמֶּנִּי׃—Introducing a contrast, וְ here is adversative ("but," as in 2:8b), and גַּם is additive ("also").[319] יֵשׁ is a particle denoting existence: "*There is* a kinsman-redeemer nearer than I" (Waltke-O'Connor, § 4.5b, example 4). Naomi had used the adjective קָרוֹב in 2:20 to describe Boaz as a "near" relative. Here the adjective with the preposition מִן (with first common singular suffix: מִמֶּנִּי) forms a comparative: "nearer than I." A comparative מִן occurs also in 1:13 (מִכֶּם, "than for you"); 3:10; 4:15. The other relative, who will be called "the redeemer" in 4:1–8, is more closely related to Naomi than is Boaz. Yet even that closer relative apparently was not a

---

[316] Cf. Sasson, "The Issue of Geʾullāh in *Ruth*," 56–57.
[317] Williams, § 449; see also Sasson, "The Issue of *Geʾullāh* in *Ruth*," 57–58.
[318] GKC, § 163 d, citing Ruth 3:12; 2 Ki 5:20; and other passages. See also Keil, *Joshua, Judges, Ruth*, 485; Steenstra in Cassel, *Ruth*, 40, n. 5; cf. Sasson, *Ruth*, 88–89.
[319] Williams, §§ 378, 432; Hubbard, *Ruth*, 208, n. 14.

Ruth 3:7–18

brother-in-law of Naomi, but more distantly related, so neither he nor Boaz was obligated to enter into a levirate marriage with Naomi.[320]

3:13 לִינִי ׀ הַלַּיְלָה—The verb is the Qal feminine singular imperative of לִין. As in 1:16, the verb by itself (without לַיְלָה) can mean "lodge" or "spend the night." The adverb "here" is implied by the verb in its context ("Spend the night [here] tonight"), as also in Gen 24:54; Judg 19:6.[321] This imperative ("spend the night") at the beginning of 3:13 and the imperative שִׁכְבִי ("lie down") toward the end of the verse form an inclusio of commands around Boaz's sketch of the next morning's action in the middle of the verse.[322] In this context, neither imperative carries sexual connotations. The verb לִין "is really more concerned with denoting the passage of time than in determining the manner in which this time is spent."[323] Some commentators assert that לִין never has sexual connotations.[324] However, לִין is part of double entendres in Song 1:13; 7:12 (ET 7:11).[325] Nevertheless, לִין rarely has such sexual implications, while שָׁכַב, "lie down," which has no overt sexual connotations in Ruth 3:4, 7, 8, 13, 14, often does in other contexts.

וְהָיָה בַבֹּקֶר—This is, literally, "and it will be in the morning." The perfect of הָיָה with *waw* consecutive introduces the temporal description that indicates the future time of an occurrence. Compare וְהָיָה introducing a prayer in 4:15, and וַיְהִי introducing past temporal descriptions in 1:1; 3:8.

---

[320] On levirate marriage, see Deut 25:5–10.
[321] Hubbard, *Ruth*, 208, n. 16; Block, *Judges, Ruth*, 695.
[322] Trible, "A Human Comedy," 179–80.
[323] Sasson, *Ruth*, 90.
[324] Sasson, *Ruth*, 90; Campbell, *Ruth*, 138; Hubbard, *Ruth*, 218.
[325] For a philological and theological analysis, see Mitchell, *The Song of Songs*, 290, 294, 633–34, 651–53, 1116, 1135–36.

Ruth 3:7–18

אִם־יִגְאָלֵךְ טוֹב יִגְאָל—A Hebrew imperfect can have the modal and volitional nuance "to *want* to do" something.³²⁶ יִגְאָלֵךְ (Qal of גָּאַל with second feminine singular suffix) may mean "if he wants to redeem you," especially because it stands in contrast to the following clause with יַחְפֹּץ, "but if he does not *desire* to redeem you." All four occurrences in this verse of גָּאַל may be rendered "act as (your) redeemer," especially the second one (יִגְאָל), where the verb lacks an object.³²⁷ For גֹּאֵל, "redeemer," see the last textual note on 2:20. The adjective טוֹב, "good," is shorthand for "that would be good," as also in English idiom. יִגְאָל could be either imperfect or jussive in form, but in either case its meaning in this context must be jussive: "let him redeem."

וְאִם־לֹא יַחְפֹּץ לְגָאֳלֵךְ—The *waw* is adversative, "but" (as also in וְגַם in 3:12). When חָפֵץ is followed by an infinitive (here לְגָאֳלֵךְ, Qal infinitive construct of גָּאַל), it means to desire to do something (BDB, s.v. חָפֵץ, Qal, 2 b; cf. *HALOT*, Qal, 3 a–b).

וּגְאַלְתִּיךְ אָנֹכִי—The *waw* consecutive with perfect verb is sequential: "*then* I will redeem you." The pronoun is redundant for emphasis: "I ... *myself*."

חַי־יְהוָה—The verb חַי is an irregular third masculine singular perfect form of חָיָה, "to live," so this is, literally, "the LORD is alive." This clause is a common oath formula of invocation, usually translated "as the LORD lives!" Compare the oath formula in 1:17.

שִׁכְבִי עַד־הַבֹּקֶר—This is, literally, "Lie down until the morning." The Qal feminine singular imperative of שָׁכַב, "lie down," may imply "to sleep," as it does in reference to Boaz in 3:7a. Even though שָׁכַב in 3:7b refers to Ruth lying down, she may have remained awake until Boaz awoke (3:8), anxiously waiting to see how Boaz would respond to her proposal (3:9). Here Boaz may have intended that after Ruth had lain down again, she would sleep for the

---

³²⁶ Joüon, § 113 n; GKC, § 107 n; Waltke-O'Connor, § 31.4h; Beattie, "Ruth III," 45; Hubbard, *Ruth*, 208, n. 17.

³²⁷ Most of the occurrences of גָּאַל in 4:4, 6 also lack a grammatical object, though in the context Boaz refers to the property that was the object (what would be redeemed).

Ruth 3:7–18

duration of the night, but 3:14 does not clearly indicate whether she was able to sleep after the momentous conversation. Her eager anticipation that the matter would be resolved after daybreak ("If in the morning he redeems you ...," 3:13) and her desire to arise early so as not to be noticed by others may have kept her awake.

3:14 וַתִּשְׁכַּב מַרְגְּלֹתָו עַד־הַבֹּקֶר—The vocabulary repeated from the preceding clause (עַד־הַבֹּקֶר ... שָׁכַב) shows that Ruth obeyed Boaz's instruction exactly. The *waw* consecutive (וַתִּשְׁכַּב) is consequential: "*So* she lay down ..." This does not mean that she lay down after having stood up, but that she remained lying at his feet. The Qere, which is the sole reading in many manuscripts, is מַרְגְּלוֹתָיו, which has the same form of the third masculine singular pronominal suffix for the plural noun as on מַרְגְּלֹתָיו in 3:4, 7, 8. The Kethib probably should be vocalized מַרְגְּלֹתָו so that the feminine noun is plural and the third masculine singular suffix is written defectively (וֹ-) instead the normal plene form (יו-). The alternative vocalization of the Kethib would be מַרְגְּלָתוֹ; the noun would be singular with the appropriate form of the third masculine singular suffix. Both the Qere and the Kethib (with either vocalization) have the same adverbial meaning, "at the place of his feet," as did מַרְגְּלֹתָיו in 3:4, 7, 8.

וַתָּקָם—Literally, "and she got up," this is the Qal third feminine singular imperfect of קוּם with *waw* consecutive.

בְּטֶרוֹם יַכִּיר אִישׁ אֶת־רֵעֵהוּ—The adverb טֶרֶם by itself or (as here) with the preposition בְּ means "before" (BDB, s.v. טֶרֶם, 2). The Qere is בְּטֶרֶם, which is the sole reading in many manuscripts. The Kethib, בְּטֶרוֹם, is inexplicably written with "a superfluous *waw*" according to the marginal Masoretic note (יתיר ו).[328] יַכִּיר is the Hiphil third masculine singular imperfect of נָכַר, meaning "to

---

[328] Cf. Campbell, *Ruth*, 115, n. *o*; Gerleman, *Ruth, Das Hohelied*, 30.

Ruth 3:7–18

recognize," with the modal nuance of capability (Waltke-O'Connor, § 31.4c; cf. GKC, § 107 c): "before a man could recognize his neighbor." The idiom רֵעֵהוּ ... אִישׁ could also be rendered more generally, "one person ... another." נָכַר was also in 2:10, 19, where it meant "acknowledge," and נכר is the root of נָכְרִיָּה, "foreigner," in 2:10.

וַיֹּאמֶר—The Qal of אָמַר can mean "to think" (as in 4:4), possibly by way of "to say to oneself" or "say in the heart" (see *HALOT*, 4; BDB, 2).[329] The following probably is an unspoken thought, and is the motivation for Boaz's action in 3:15. The *waw* consecutive may be rendered "but ..." to bring out a contrast (cf. BDB, 2 (b)): it was still too dark for Ruth to be recognized, but Boaz still was concerned that someone might misconstrue what took place, and so he took a precaution.

אַל־יִוָּדַע—The Niphal imperfect or jussive of יָדַע with the negative means "let it not be known." Naomi used the negated Niphal imperfect of יָדַע with a similar meaning in 3:3. The Qal is in 2:11; 3:4, 11, 18; 4:4, and a Pual participle ("acquaintance") is the Kethib in 2:1.

כִּי־בָאָה הָאִשָּׁה הַגֹּרֶן׃—"The woman" is a typical way to refer to a woman who is known to the speaker (or as here, to the one thinking about her).[330] It may be used here instead of her name "to heighten the sense of privacy" and "mystery."[331] Unlike the corresponding English, the Hebrew does not connote disrespect. Compare the discussion of הָאִישׁ ("the man") in the last textual note on 3:16. Compare also Jesus' use of γύναι, "woman" (vocative), in Mt 15:28; Jn 2:4; 4:21; 20:15, which surely was not meant dishonorably.

הַגֹּרֶן is an accusative of place, "*to* the threshing floor," as also in 3:3, 6.

---

[329] Bush, *Ruth, Esther*, 177.
[330] Cf. Hubbard, *Ruth*, 220, n. 5.
[331] Campbell, *Ruth*, 130.

3:15 וַיֹּ֕אמֶר—After 3:14b, the *waw* consecutive is consequential: "*So* he said …"

הָ֠בִי הַמִּטְפַּ֧חַת אֲשֶׁר־עָלַ֛יִךְ—The verb is a Qal feminine singular imperative, evidently of יָהַב, with the general meaning "*give* (me)" (BDB, s.v. יָהַב, Qal, 1; cf. *HALOT*, s.v. יהב), hence, literally, "give the shawl that is on you," that is, the shawl Ruth was wearing.[332] Boaz did not mean that Ruth should give the shawl to him, but that she should hold it out so he could fill it with grain. The verb's accent and vocalization are unusual; the expected form would be הָבִ֫י (GKC, § 69 o). The definite direct object lacks the marker אֵת, as also in 2:14 and 3:10. מִטְפַּ֫חַת, "shawl" (*HALOT*), occurs elsewhere in the OT only in Is 3:22, in a list of women's elegant clothing. It must refer to a large outer garment of strong material.[333] It is a different Hebrew term than that for the "cloak" Naomi instructed Ruth to wear in 3:3.

וְאֶֽחֳזִי־בָ֖הּ—The verb is the Qal feminine singular imperative of אָחַז, which idiomatically takes the preposition בְּ, meaning "take hold" of something. The *chateph qamets* (-ֳ-) is reduced from the original *holem* (GKC, § 64 c; Joüon, § 69 b). The suffix on בָּהּ is feminine to match its antecedent, הַמִּטְפַּ֫חַת. The implication is that she was to hold the four corners of her shawl, two in each hand, and extend it so Boaz could pour grain into it as a makeshift container. She would have had to hold the shawl tightly because of the large amount of grain he was about to pour into it.

וַתֹּ֣אחֶז בָּ֑הּ—The repetition of the verb אָחַז (here third feminine singular imperfect with *waw* consecutive) and the prepositional phrase בָּהּ shows that Ruth followed Boaz's instruction exactly, holding out the shawl for him to fill.

וַיָּ֤מָד שֵׁשׁ־שְׂעֹרִים—The verb is the Qal third masculine singular imperfect of מָדַד, "to measure," with *waw* consecutive. Hebrew commonly omits units of measure after numerals,[334] and here

---

[332] See Brockelmann, § 6a; Gerleman, *Ruth, Das Hohelied*, 30; Bush, *Ruth, Esther*, 178; Block, *Judges, Ruth*, 697.
[333] See Gerleman, *Ruth, Das Hohelied*, 33.
[334] See GKC, § 134 n; Joüon, § 142 n; Hubbard, *Ruth*, 222. Ancient sources also often omitted the measure of payment (Wiseman, *The Alalakh Tablets*, 13).

Ruth 3:7–18

the phrase must mean that he measured "six *measures* of barley," as also in 3:17. For the measure, and the reason for using it so that the appropriate numeral would be "six."

וַיָּ֫שֶׁת עָלֶ֫יהָ—A direct object must be supplied in translation: "And he put [it] upon her," referring to the shawl now filled with grain. He would have lifted it and placed it onto her head. The verb is the Qal third masculine singular imperfect of שִׁית with *waw* consecutive.

וַיָּבֹא הָעִיר:—The Qal third masculine singular imperfect of בּוֹא with *waw* consecutive is sequential: "*Then* he entered the town." בּוֹא can mean "to enter" when it is followed by an accusative of place (here הָעִיר, "the town"); see Joüon, § 125 n, and the second textual note on 1:19. Many Hebrew manuscripts and the Syriac and Vulgate read, "and she entered," imagining that the subject is Ruth, but it is logical for the narrator to conclude Boaz's involvement in this episode before concentrating on Ruth in 3:16–18.[335]

3:16 וַתָּבוֹא אֶל־חֲמוֹתָהּ—This is translated as a temporal clause ("*When* she [Ruth] came to her mother-in-law …") subordinate to the following main clause. On חֲמוֹתָהּ, see the textual note on it in 1:14.

The speakers in 3:16–18 are not identified by name in the Hebrew text. Boaz was the subject at the end of 3:15, but the feminine verb beginning 3:16 (וַתָּבוֹא, third feminine singular imperfect of בּוֹא with *waw* consecutive) indicates that the subject is now Ruth. In 3:16 the implied subject changes rapidly from Ruth, to Naomi, and then back to Ruth. Their names are added in brackets in the translation. It must be Ruth who "came to her mother-in-law." Naomi then must have addressed Ruth as "my daughter." Ruth must have related to Naomi "all that the man had done for her."

וַתֹּ֫אמֶר מִי־אַ֫תְּ בִּתִּי—The context indicates that now Naomi (the referent of חֲמוֹתָהּ, "her mother-in-law," in the preceding clause)

---

[335] Sasson, *Ruth*, 98–99; Bush, *Ruth, Esther*, 179.

is the subject of this feminine verb, and she is speaking to Ruth, whom she repeatedly calls בִּתִּי, "my daughter" elsewhere (also in 2:2, 22; 3:1, 18; cf. 1:11–13). In 3:9 Boaz used מִי־אָתְּ to ask Ruth, "Who are you?" Here Naomi poses the same Hebrew question, but מִי־אַתְּ is best taken as an interrogative of condition: "*How* are you?"[336]

וַתַּגֶּד־לָהּ—The verb (Hiphil third feminine singular imperfect of נגד) with *waw* consecutive is sequential: "*Then* she told her." The subject of the feminine verb must be Ruth, speaking to Naomi.

הָאִישׁ:—Ruth, speaking to Naomi, calls Boaz "the man," which is a customary way to refer to a known person who is not present.[337] It might be used for someone who is a social superior to prevent "the impression of presumptive familiarity."[338] Like "the woman" (see the last textual note on 3:14), it could be used instead of a personal name "to heighten the sense of privacy" and "mystery."[339] The Hebrew usage does not have the connotation of disrespect that "the man" may have in English. Naomi will call Boaz "the man" in 3:18; see "the man" in speech also in 2:19–20; 3:3.

3:17 וַתֹּאמֶר—Since 3:16 already stated that Ruth "told" Naomi "all that the man had done for her," this (literally, "and she said") may be rendered, "She emphasized …" The following words were particularly important and so have been included in the narrative.

שֵׁשׁ־הַשְּׂעֹרִים הָאֵלֶּה נָתַן לִי—Ruth's Hebrew word order emphasizes the large amount of grain by placing it first in her statement: "Six [measures] of barley, these, he gave to me."

כִּי אָמַר—After "for he said," the Qere (as in 3:5), indicated by the pointing (ֵ), is אֵלַי, "to me," which is absent from the

---

[336] See מִי also in Amos 7:2 and *HALOT*, s.v. מִי, 7 a; Waltke-O'Connor, 18.2d, example 20; Gerleman; *Ruth, Das Hohelied*, 33; Block, *Judges, Ruth*, 699.
[337] See Hubbard, *Ruth*, 224.
[338] Block, *Judges, Ruth*, 699.
[339] Campbell, *Ruth,* 130.

Ruth 3:7–18

Kethib, hence the marginal Masoretic note, קְרֵ ולא כתֿ, an abbreviation for קרי ולא כתיב, "Qere but not Kethib." See Joüon, § 16 e.

אַל־תָּבֽוֹאִי רֵיקָם אֶל־חֲמוֹתֵֽךְ׃—The negated imperfect verb (second feminine singular of בּוֹא) is a negative imperative, literally, "you shall/should not come emptily to your mother-in-law." From Naomi's perspective, Ruth came to her; from Boaz's perspective, Ruth went to her. Compare וַיָּבֹא, "and he went," in 3:7. The adverb רֵיקָם, literally, "emptily," is repeated from 1:21, but here is rendered "empty-handed." Its repetition here is a reminder that Naomi had returned from Moab "empty" (1:21), that is, without a husband or sons and hungry for food, but Boaz is the human agent through whom God filled her with food (through allowing Ruth to glean in his part of the field [chapter 2]), as he does again now (the six measures of barley). Moreover, Boaz will fill her family emptiness through his marriage to Ruth and fathering of an heir, who will continue the family line (chapter 4).

3:18 שְׁבִ֣י בִתִּ֔י—The Qal feminine singular imperative of יָשַׁב in this context means "sit still," that is, to wait for Boaz to resolve the matter. Compare יָשַׁב in Ex 24:14: "to wait for" (*HALOT*, s.v. יָשַׁב, Qal, 4).

עַד אֲשֶׁ֣ר תֵּדְעִ֔ין.—As a temporal conjunction, עַד is often followed by the relative pronoun אֲשֶׁר and an imperfect verb referring to future time (BDB, s.v. עַד III, II 1 a (*b*)), hence "until you know." The verb is the Qal second feminine singular imperfect of יָדַע with paragogic *nun* (Waltke-O'Connor, §§ 20.2f; 31.7.1a; Joüon, § 44 f), other examples of which (on other words) were in 2:8, 9, 21; 3:4. Here יָדַע may have the nuance "learn, find out." Its meaning here

Ruth 3:7–18

fills out a full range of nuances for the verb in Ruth; see it also in 2:11; 3:3–4, 11, 14; 4:4; and as Kethib in 2:1.[340]

אֵיךְ יִפֹּל דָּבָר—This idiom, literally, "how a word will fall," occurs in this sense only here, where it must mean "how the matter will turn out." The verb is the Qal third masculine singular imperfect of נָפַל, which here must mean "turn out, result" (BDB, Qal, 5). דָּבָר can refer to a "matter" or "affair" (BDB, IV 3), and it lacks the definite article here.

כִּי לֹא יִשְׁקֹט הָאִישׁ—The verb שָׁקַט, only here in Ruth, means "be at peace, at rest, quiet." For הָאִישׁ, see the last textual note on 3:16.

כִּי־אִם־כִּלָּה הַדָּבָר הַיּוֹם:—The combination of conjunctions כִּי־אִם, "unless,"[341] introduces an exception clause, stating a condition that must be fulfilled for the preceding to come to pass ("the man will ... rest"). The verb is the Piel perfect of כָּלָה, here meaning to "accomplish, fulfil, bring to pass" (BDB, 1 e) his promise that either he or the nearer relative would act as redeemer (3:12–13). דָּבָר can refer to a human "promise" (BDB, I 1 f; or a divine promise [BDB, I 2 b]). It has the definite article, which sometimes is equivalent to a possessive pronoun (Joüon § 137 f (2)), hence הַדָּבָר, "the word," can be rendered "his word" or "his promise." The article on הַיּוֹם serves as a demonstrative (GKC, § 126 b), "this day, today."

---

[340] Campbell, *Ruth*, 131.
[341] GKC, § 163 c; Joüon, § 173 b; Campbell, *Ruth*, 129.

Additional Notes

Text, Translation, and Notes

Chapter 4

Ruth 4:1–12

4:1 וּבֹ֨עַז עָלָ֣ה הַשַּׁ֘עַר֮ וַיֵּ֣שֶׁב שָׁם֒ וְהִנֵּ֨ה הַגֹּאֵ֤ל עֹבֵר֙ אֲשֶׁ֣ר דִּבֶּר־בֹּ֔עַז וַיֹּ֛אמֶר ס֥וּרָה שְׁבָה־פֹּ֖ה פְּלֹנִ֣י אַלְמֹנִ֑י וַיָּ֖סַר וַיֵּשֵֽׁב:
2 וַיִּקַּ֞ח עֲשָׂרָ֧ה אֲנָשִׁ֛ים מִזִּקְנֵ֥י הָעִ֖יר וַיֹּ֣אמֶר שְׁבוּ־פֹ֑ה וַיֵּשֵֽׁבוּ:
3 וַיֹּ֙אמֶר֙ לַגֹּאֵ֔ל חֶלְקַת֙ הַשָּׂדֶ֔ה אֲשֶׁ֥ר לְאָחִ֖ינוּ לֶאֱלִימֶ֑לֶךְ מָכְרָ֣ה נָעֳמִ֔י הַשָּׁ֖בָה מִשְּׂדֵ֥ה מוֹאָֽב:
4 וַאֲנִ֨י אָמַ֜רְתִּי אֶגְלֶ֧ה אָזְנְךָ֣ לֵאמֹ֗ר קְ֠נֵה נֶ֥גֶד הַֽיֹּשְׁבִים֮ וְנֶ֣גֶד זִקְנֵ֣י עַמִּי֒ אִם־תִּגְאַל֙ גְּאָ֔ל וְאִם־לֹ֨א יִגְאַ֜ל הַגִּ֣ידָה לִּ֗י וְאֵֽדְעָה֙ כִּ֣י אֵ֤ין זוּלָֽתְךָ֙ לִגְא֔וֹל וְאָנֹכִ֖י אַחֲרֶ֑יךָ וַיֹּ֖אמֶר אָנֹכִ֥י אֶגְאָֽל:
5 וַיֹּ֣אמֶר בֹּ֔עַז בְּיוֹם־קְנוֹתְךָ֥ הַשָּׂדֶ֖ה מִיַּ֣ד נָעֳמִ֑י וּ֠מֵאֵת ר֣וּת הַמּוֹאֲבִיָּ֤ה אֵֽשֶׁת־הַמֵּת֙ קָנִ֔יתִי לְהָקִ֥ים שֵׁם־הַמֵּ֖ת עַל־נַחֲלָתֽוֹ:
6 וַיֹּ֣אמֶר הַגֹּאֵ֗ל לֹ֤א אוּכַל֙ לִגְאָל־לִ֔י פֶּן־אַשְׁחִ֖ית אֶת־נַחֲלָתִ֑י גְּאַל־לְךָ֤ אַתָּה֙ אֶת־גְּאֻלָּתִ֔י כִּ֥י לֹא־אוּכַ֖ל לִגְאֹֽל:
7 וְזֹאת֩ לְפָנִ֨ים בְּיִשְׂרָאֵ֜ל עַל־הַגְּאוּלָּ֤ה וְעַל־הַתְּמוּרָה֙ לְקַיֵּ֣ם כָּל־דָּבָ֔ר שָׁלַ֥ף אִ֛ישׁ נַעֲל֖וֹ וְנָתַ֣ן לְרֵעֵ֑הוּ וְזֹ֥את הַתְּעוּדָ֖ה בְּיִשְׂרָאֵֽל:
8 וַיֹּ֧אמֶר הַגֹּאֵ֛ל לְבֹ֖עַז קְנֵה־לָ֑ךְ וַיִּשְׁלֹ֖ף נַעֲלֽוֹ:
9 וַיֹּאמֶר֩ בֹּ֨עַז לַזְּקֵנִ֜ים וְכָל־הָעָ֗ם עֵדִ֤ים אַתֶּם֙ הַיּ֔וֹם כִּ֤י קָנִ֙יתִי֙ אֶת־כָּל־אֲשֶׁ֣ר לֶֽאֱלִימֶ֔לֶךְ וְאֵ֛ת כָּל־אֲשֶׁ֥ר לְכִלְי֖וֹן וּמַחְל֑וֹן מִיַּ֖ד נָעֳמִֽי:
10 וְגַ֣ם אֶת־ר֣וּת הַמֹּאֲבִיָּה֩ אֵ֨שֶׁת מַחְל֜וֹן קָנִ֧יתִי לִ֣י לְאִשָּׁ֗ה לְהָקִ֤ים שֵׁם־הַמֵּת֙ עַל־נַ֣חֲלָת֔וֹ וְלֹא־יִכָּרֵ֧ת שֵׁם־הַמֵּ֛ת מֵעִ֥ם אֶחָ֖יו וּמִשַּׁ֣עַר מְקוֹמ֑וֹ עֵדִ֥ים אַתֶּ֖ם הַיּֽוֹם:

Ruth 4:1–12

Note: The translation of 4:3 employs the sign ‖ before and after a relative clause that stands at the end of the second line of the Hebrew verse, but which must be translated earlier for the sake of English.

4 ¹Boaz went up to the gate, and he sat down there. And behold, the redeemer about whom Boaz had spoken was indeed passing by. | He [Boaz] said, "Turn aside! Sit down here, So-and-so!" So he turned aside and sat down. |
²Then he [Boaz] took ten men from the elders of the town, and he said, "Sit down here!" And they too sat down. |
³Then he said to the redeemer, "Naomi, ‖ who returned from the region of Moab, ‖ is putting up for transfer the portion of the field that belongs to our brother Elimelech. |
⁴On my part, I thought I should get your attention in order to say, 'Acquire [it] in the presence of these residents and in the presence of the elders of my people.' | If you will redeem, redeem! But if you will not redeem, declare [that] to me. | I know that there is no one before you to redeem, and I am after you." And he said, "I will indeed redeem!" |
⁵Then Boaz said, "On the day you acquire the field from the hand of Naomi, | then from Ruth the Moabitess, the wife of the deceased, I will acquire | [the means] to perpetuate the name of the deceased on his inheritance!" |
⁶Then the redeemer said, "I am not able to redeem for myself, lest I ruin my inheritance. | You redeem for yourself my redemption, because I am not able to redeem!" |
⁷This formerly in Israel [was the custom] regarding the transfer of the right of redemption, |to confirm every matter: a man took off his sandal and gave [it] to his counterpart. | Such was the attestation in Israel. |
⁸So the redeemer said to Boaz, "Acquire it for yourself!" and he took off his sandal. |
⁹Then Boaz said to the elders and all the people, "You are witnesses today that I have acquired | all that belonged to Elimelech and all that belonged to Chilion and Mahlon from the hand of Naomi! |
¹⁰Furthermore, Ruth the Moabitess, the wife of Mahlon, have I acquired for myself for a wife | to perpetuate the name of the deceased on his inheritance, | so that the name of the deceased shall not be cut off from his brethren and from the gate of his place. You are witnesses today!"

11 וַיֹּאמְר֨וּ כָל־הָעָ֧ם אֲשֶׁר־בַּשַּׁ֛עַר וְהַזְּקֵנִ֖ים עֵדִ֑ים
יִתֵּן֩ יְהוָ֨ה אֶֽת־הָאִשָּׁ֜ה הַבָּאָ֣ה אֶל־בֵּיתֶ֗ךָ
כְּרָחֵ֤ל ׀ וּכְלֵאָה֙ אֲשֶׁ֨ר בָּנ֤וּ שְׁתֵּיהֶם֙ אֶת־בֵּ֣ית יִשְׂרָאֵ֔ל
וַעֲשֵׂה־חַ֣יִל בְּאֶפְרָ֔תָה וּקְרָא־שֵׁ֖ם בְּבֵ֥ית לָֽחֶם:
12 וִיהִ֤י בֵֽיתְךָ֙ כְּבֵ֣ית פֶּ֔רֶץ אֲשֶׁר־יָלְדָ֥ה תָמָ֖ר לִֽיהוּדָ֑ה
מִן־הַזֶּ֗רַע אֲשֶׁ֨ר יִתֵּ֤ן יְהוָה֙ לְךָ֔ מִן־הַֽנַּעֲרָ֖ה הַזֹּֽאת:

¹¹Then all the people and the elders who were in the gate said,
"Witnesses! |
The LORD make the woman who is coming into your household
be like Rachel and like Leah, the two who built the house of Israel, |
so that you prosper in Ephrathah
and become famous in Bethlehem! |
¹²May your house become like the house of Perez,
whom Tamar bore to Judah, |
from the seed whom the LORD will give to you
from this young woman!"

Ruth 4:1–12

4:1 וּבֹ֤עַז עָלָ֣ה הַשַּׁ֔עַר—This clause is circumstantial, introducing a new scene and directing the attention to Boaz: "(As for) Boaz, he went up ..."[342] Since it begins with a name (cf. 1:2; 2:1) instead of a *waw* consecutive verb, it does not indicate a temporal sequence after the preceding verse (3:18), but distinguishes the new scene without expressly indicating whether the time was earlier, simultaneous, or later.[343] However, Naomi had said (3:18) that Boaz would attend to the matter on the very day after Ruth's nocturnal proposal to him (3:9–13), so 4:1–12 must have taken place no more than a few hours after Ruth arrived home toward sunrise (3:16–18). Boaz had "entered the town" after bestowing his gift of grain upon Ruth for her and Naomi (3:15).

The idiom עָלָה הַשַּׁעַר, "go up to the gate," probably has the legal meaning "go to court," as in Deut 25:7 (cf. Deut 17:8).[344] Cities usually were situated on hills, so the city gate would be at a higher elevation than the threshing floor outside the city, hence עָלָה, "go *up*." As often in Ruth (e.g., הַגֹּרֶן in 3:3, 6, 14), the destination (here: הַשַּׁעַר) is an accusative of place[345] without a Hebrew preposition or directional *he* ending (ה ָ-), but English translation requires "*to* the gate."

וַיֵּ֣שֶׁב שָׁ֑ם—The verb is the third masculine singular Qal imperfect of יָשַׁב with *waw* consecutive. It means "to sit down," as also in 2:14 (cf. 2:7); twice more in 4:1; and in 4:2, 4.

וְהִנֵּ֨ה הַגֹּאֵ֤ל עֹבֵר֙—Literally, "and behold, the redeemer was passing by," this introduces a new actor in the drama, denoted by the Qal participle of גָּאַל, "to redeem" (see the last textual note on 2:20). Naomi's closest male relative is referred to as "the redeemer" (4:1, 3, 6, 8). Here that participle is modified by the Qal participle of עָבַר, "pass by," which pictures his action in progress. The providential element of surprise indicated by הִנֵּה is not that the nearer relative

---

[342] See Morris, *Ruth*, 296–97; Berlin, *Poetics and Interpretation of Biblical Narrative*, 104; Hubbard, *Ruth*, 232, n. 4; Bush, *Ruth, Esther*, 196; Block, *Judges, Ruth*, 704.

[343] Gerleman, *Ruth, Das Hohelied*, 35; de Waard and Nida, *A Translator's Handbook on the Book of Ruth*, 63, contra Sasson, *Ruth*, 104, who believes it indicates simultaneity with 3:16–18.

[344] Keil, *Joshua, Judges, Ruth*, 487; Hubbard, *Ruth*, 231, n. 1.

[345] See Waltke-O'Connor, § 10.2.2b; Joüon, § 126 h.

passed by just as Boaz sat down, but, from his point of view, that the man he sought indeed came by.³⁴⁶ As also in 2:4, הִנֵּה is followed by a participle, indicating providential surprise.

אֲשֶׁר דִּבֶּר־בֹּעַז—This relative clause is, literally, "whom Boaz spoke." In such phrases with verbs of speaking, Hebrew often omits a preposition meaning "about, concerning," which must be supplied in English translation, hence "*about* whom Boaz had spoken" (see Joüon, § 158 i (1)). That speaking took place in 3:12–13, where Boaz told Ruth that he would redeem her if the closer relative did not.

סוּרָה שְׁבָה־פֹּה—The two Qal masculine singular imperatives, of סוּר and יָשַׁב, have the emphatic ending (ה-ָ), which sometimes has an honorific connotation (Joüon, § 48 d). The syntax is asyndetic ("Turn aside! Sit down ... !"), as is common with adjacent Hebrew imperatives (Joüon, § 177 e). (In contrast, the verbs describing the fulfillment are joined with *waw*: וַיָּסַר וַיֵּשֵׁב, "he turned aside *and* sat down.") The adverb פֹּה immediately follows an imperative of יָשַׁב also in 4:2 ("sit down *here*").

פְּלֹנִי אַלְמֹנִי—This phrase occurs thrice in the OT (1 Sam 21:3 [ET 21:2]; 2 Ki 6:8; Ruth 4:1). A conflation of the two words, פַּלְמוֹנִי, is used in Dan 8:13. In each case, the speaker must have used a proper name, but the biblical author substituted this expression for the name. Perhaps the name was not known by the author, but more likely he decided that the name should not be recorded.³⁴⁷ It can be translated "so-and-so" here, where it refers to a person's name (as the conflation does in Dan 8:13), or "such-and-such" in 1 Sam 21:3 (ET 21:2); 2 Ki 6:8, where it refers to a place name (cf. Joüon, § 147 f). The etymologies are uncertain, but פְּלֹנִי may be derived from פָּלָה and mean "a certain, distinct one," and אַלְמֹנִי may come from אָלַם, "be silent, speechless," so the combination would mean "a certain unnamed one."³⁴⁸ The form

---

³⁴⁶ Berlin, *Poetics and Interpretation of Biblical Narrative*, 92–93.
³⁴⁷ Another example where a biblical author altered a name to which he objected is the substitution of Mephibosheth (2 Sam 4:4; *bosheth* means "shame") in place of Merib-baal (1 Chr 8:34; 9:40), which could be understood to mean "one who contends for Baal" even if the meaning intended by the Israelites was "one who contends for the Lord."
³⁴⁸ See BDB, s.v. פְּלֹנִי, under the root פלה; *HALOT*, s.v. פְּלֹנִי; Gerleman, *Ruth, Das Hohelied*, 35; Cassel, *Ruth*, 46.

Ruth 4:1–12

suggests a farrago, an alliterative wordplay intelligible in context, for example, "hodgepodge."[349] The LXX renders it here as κρύφιε, "O hidden one." Some LXX manuscripts render it ὁ δεῖνα, "such a one," and one Old Latin manuscript reads *quicumque es*, "whoever you are."[350]

Since Boaz would never have addressed the redeemer in this way, but only by his proper name, the narrator must have decided to omit the redeemer's name and substitute this phrase. The only other time the narrator intrudes into the story of Ruth in such an obvious way is the whole of 4:7, which the narrator supplied for historical background.

וַיָּסַר וַיֵּשֵׁב:—The verbs with *waw* consecutive (Qal third masculine singular imperfects of סוּר and יָשַׁב) are logically consequential: "*So he turned aside and sat down.*" They express the fulfillment of Boaz's request, which used Qal imperatives of the same two verbs (סוּרָה שְׁבָה). Only the meaning required by the context indicates that וַיָּסַר must be Qal ("he turned aside") rather than Hiphil ("he removed [something]"; see GKC, § 72 t). וַיֵּשֵׁב is the pausal form of וַיֵּשֶׁב earlier in the verse (GKC, § 69 p).

4:2 וַיִּקַּח—The Qal imperfect of לָקַח with *waw* consecutive is sequential: "*Then he took …*"

הָעִיר—For the meaning of this phrase as "the town," see the textual note on it in 1:19.

שְׁבוּ־פֹה וַיֵּשֵׁבוּ:—The Qal masculine plural imperative and imperfect are of יָשַׁב, meaning "to sit down," as in 2:14; 4:1. When given at the gate, the command "sit down here" (4:1–2) may be a formula for invitation to participate in a legal proceeding.[351] The *waw* consecutive is adjunctive: "they *too* sat down" (see also וַתּוֹצֵא in 2:18).

---

[349] Berlin, *Poetics and Interpretation of Biblical Narrative*, 99–101; Hubbard, *Ruth*, 234; Lawrenz, *Judges, Ruth*, 250; Block, *Judges, Ruth*, 705–6.
[350] Bush, *Ruth, Esther*, 196.
[351] Hubbard, *Ruth*, 236.

4:3 The Hebrew word order first has the object phrase ("the portion of the field that belongs to our brother Elimelech"), then the verb ("is putting up for transfer"), and lastly the subject phrase ("Naomi, who returned from the region of Moab"). English requires the order subject, verb, object.

הַשָּׂדֶ֗ה—חֶלְקַת֙ הַשָּׂדֶ֔ה אֲשֶׁ֥ר לְאָחִ֖ינוּ לֶאֱלִימֶ֑לֶךְ—Here too חֶלְקַת֙ is followed by לְ indicating possession or ownership ("that belongs to our brother") instead of having a three-word construct chain (see Waltke-O'Connor, § 9.7b, including example 10; GKC, § 129 d). אָח ("brother") may refer to any male blood relative, for example, a cousin (*HALOT*, s.v. אָח II, 3).

מָכְרָ֤ה—With Naomi as subject, the verb is third feminine singular Qal perfect. In this context, the perfect is appropriate for a legal declaration of imminent or present action indicating resolve,[352] hence "Naomi … is [now] putting up for transfer" (NIV and ESV have "is selling"). Since מָכַר often entails no payment, it may refer to "transfer of ownership."[353] "The verb does not apply specifically to the semantic field 'buy/sell,' but designates a delivery of goods, generally in return for valuables, with or without the intention of passing ownership," and it can refer to a transferal of rights and claims for a limited time.[354]

An alternative interpretation is that the perfect here has a pluperfect sense: "Naomi had sold" the field, referring to the sale of the property's usufruct by Elimelech before he left for Moab (1:1). This interpretation considers Naomi, the family's last survivor, to be named here in place of the actual seller, Elimelech, her husband. Such substitutions sometimes occur in OT narrative, for example, as Saul is substituted for Jonathan in 1 Sam 13:3–4.[355] This interpretation would not alter the implication of Boaz's statement, that the question of

---

[352] Waltke-O'Connor, § 30.5.1d, including example 30. See also the textual notes on the perfect קָנִ֫יתִי in 4:5 and 4:9.

[353] Morris, *Ruth*, 299; Campbell, *Ruth*, 143–44; Gerleman, *Ruth, Das Hohelied*, 35; Gordis, "Love, Marriage and Business in the Book of Ruth," 254–56; Sasson, *Ruth*, 109–10, 136; Hubbard, *Ruth*, 239; Gow, *The Book of Ruth*, 148, n. 1; Bush, *Ruth, Esther*, 200–2, 215; Block, *Judges, Ruth*, 709–10.

[354] E. Lipiński, "מכר," *TDOT* 8:291–93.

[355] Westbrook, Property and the Family in Biblical Law, 65–66.

Ruth 4:1–12

redeeming the property must be settled. However, because a wife could not sell property in her husband's name, it is doubtful that she would have been indicated here as the seller, even in the form of a substitution.

נָעֳמִ֛י הַשָּׁ֥בָה מִשְּׂדֵ֖ה מוֹאָֽב׃—The verb (הַשָּׁ֥בָה) is the Qal third feminine singular perfect of שׁוּב with definite article, as also in 1:22 (see the textual note there) and 2:6. It is the equivalent of a relative clause, "who returned." On the meaning "from the *region* of Moab" for מִשְּׂדֵ֖ה מוֹאָֽב, see the textual note on בִּשְׂדֵ֣י מוֹאָ֑ב in 1:1b.

4:4 וַאֲנִ֣י אָמַ֗רְתִּי—This is, literally, "and I, I said/thought." The disjunctive *waw* signals a change of focus from Naomi's intention to Boaz's present action (see Waltke-O'Connor, § 39.2.3c). Boaz's statement begins with emphasis upon himself, which is conveyed in translation with the English idiom "on my part." אָמַר may mean "to say to oneself, to think," as in 3:14 (see the textual note there; see also Gen 20:11; 26:9; 2 Sam 12:22; 2 Ki 5:11).[356]

אֶגְלֶ֣ה אָזְנְךָ֗—Literally, this is "let me uncover your ear." The verb is the Qal first common singular imperfect or cohortative of גָּלָה. The idiom גָּלָה אֹזֶן could be a polite idiom for imparting information to someone (see it in 1 Sam 20:2, 12, 13; 22:8, 17); it can also be used for divine revelation (e.g., 1 Sam 9:15; 2 Sam 7:27; 1 Chr 17:25). However, what Boaz imparted in 4:3 would have been expected by the closer redeemer, and what Boaz goes on to say in 4:4 is not new information but a firm request for the redeemer to take action. Thus, the force of the idiom here is rather to "get someone's attention" (as also in Job 33:16; 36:10, 15).[357]

לֵאמֹ֔ר—This Qal infinitive construct of אָמַר does not merely introduce a direct quotation here, as commonly elsewhere, but since a command follows, it also indicates purpose: "in order to say."[358]

---

[356] Bush, *Ruth, Esther*, 205; Block, *Judges, Ruth*, 711.
[357] Block, *Judges, Ruth*, 711; cf. *HALOT*, s.v. גלה, Qal, 1; Campbell, *Ruth*, 144; Hubbard, *Ruth*, 239–40; Bush, *Ruth, Esther*, 205–6.
[358] See Waltke-O'Connor, 36.2.3d; Block, *Judges, Ruth*, 711.

קְנֵה—This is the masculine singular Qal imperative of קָנָה, "acquire!" Although often a commercial term for buying, this verb is more general than "buy" (NASB, NIV, ESV). Often in Hebrew and other Semitic languages it means "acquire" or "obtain."[359] It can refer to God as the one who "created" the universe (e.g., Gen 14:19, 22); to God the Father, who from eternity "begot" God the Son, who is wisdom incarnate (Prov 8:22); or to a mother who gives birth (Gen 4:1), and in all those cases no money was involved. In Ruth it occurs only in 4:4–10, and it is best rendered "acquire" throughout this context, both in reference to marriage (4:5, 10; see the third textual note on 4:5) and in reference to acquiring property (4:4, 8, 9). Its imperative (4:4, 8) is technically a legal petition for the addressee to acquire.[360] The verb קָנָה lacks a direct object here (also in 4:5b, 8). In 4:4, 8, the implied object is "the portion of the field ..." in 4:3, so the translation supplies "it": "acquire it!" For other examples of Hebrew verbs with direct objects that are only implied, see 2:14b and גָּאַל in 4:4, 6.[361]

In this entire context (4:3–10) "acquire" and "redeem" do not mean that the closer redeemer or Boaz would take absolute and permanent possession of the land inheritance of Elimelech's family, but only that one of them would obtain the *legal right* to redeem that property.

נֶגֶד הַיֹּשְׁבִים וְנֶגֶד זִקְנֵי עַמִּי—This terminology indicates a legal situation: the transaction will take place "in the presence of the residents and in the presence of the elders of my people," who are the valid "witnesses" (עֵדִים, 4:9, 10, 11). The Qal masculine plural participle הַיֹּשְׁבִים (of יָשַׁב) probably indicates "residents" or "inhabitants," that is, adult citizens of Bethlehem besides the ten chosen elders. The term could mean "the sitting/seated ones," but then it would refer only to the elders because they alone, besides the two proponents (Boaz and the primary redeemer), are mentioned as having seated themselves at Boaz's invitation (4:2). The comparatively limited space in the gate of a small town did not permit

---

[359] See *HALOT*, s.v. קנה, and Qal, 2; BDB, s.v. קָנָה I, and Qal 1.
[360] Gow, *The Book of Ruth*, 169; *HALOT*, s.v. קנה, Qal, 1 d.
[361] Williams, § 588; Bush, *Ruth, Esther*, 207.

Ruth 4:1–12

seating for a large number.³⁶² Since both 4:9 and 4:11 clearly refer to "all the people" (כָּל־הָעָם) at the gate as a second group of witnesses distinct from "the elders," most likely הַיֹּשְׁבִים here refers to that same second group of townspeople, here translated "residents."³⁶³ הַיֹּשְׁבִים refers only to "the residents" assembled at the gate (not to all "the residents" of the town), so with the article it is translated "*these* residents." The repetition of נֶגֶד, "in the presence of," at the start of each prepositional phrase supports the view that the two phrases refer to two distinct groups.³⁶⁴ The article may have demonstrative force, referring to "*these* residents" who were present. While grammatically only זִקְנֵי is in construct with עַמִּי, "my people" may modify both nouns ("residents" and "elders"), indicating that the local adult "residents" are also Israelites and thus are legally eligible for participation as witnesses (cf. עַמִּי also in 3:11). As an example of how bystanders could function at least implicitly as witnesses at a trial, note "all the people" who witnessed Jeremiah's trial (Jer 26:7–9, 11).³⁶⁵

אִם־תִּגְאַל גְּאָל—Following the hypothetical particle אִם are the Qal second masculine singular imperfect and masculine singular imperative (in pause) of גָּאַל: "If you will redeem, redeem!" The imperfect can have a modal and volitional meaning, "to want, desire, or be willing to do something," and גָּאַל had that same meaning in Ruth 3:13.³⁶⁶ In this context, גָּאַל means to "pay [the] redemption price" (*DCH*, 1a), that is, to exercise the right of repurchase. See the last textual note on 2:20. All five occurrences of גָּאַל in this verse (and three in 4:6) lack a direct object, but Boaz in 4:3 mentioned "the portion of the field" that belonged to Elimelech, which was the implied direct object of קָנָה ("acquire!") earlier in 4:4 (and in 4:8), and that probably is the implied direct object of גָּאַל too.

---

³⁶² See the description of town gates in Campbell, *Ruth*, 154–55, and illustrations 5–9 (following p. 100).
³⁶³ See Hubbard, *Ruth*, 240–41.
³⁶⁴ Waltke-O'Connor, §§ 11.4.2a; Hubbard, *Ruth*, 240–41; Campbell, *Ruth*, 145.
³⁶⁵ Matthews, *Judges and Ruth*, 240.
³⁶⁶ See the third textual note on 3:13 and Joüon, § 113 n; GKC, § 107 n; Waltke-O'Connor, § 31.4h.

Alternatively, גָּאַל could have an intransitive meaning in 4:4, 6, "to act/serve as redeemer."³⁶⁷ The imperative גְּאָל may be a legal petition, as was קְנֵה ("Acquire!") earlier in 4:4.

וְאִם־לֹא יִגְאַל—The Qal imperfect of גָּאַל in Leningradensis is *third* masculine singular, "if *he* will not redeem," which certainly is the harder reading. Sasson retains it and explains that Boaz at this point is addressing the elders, and so he refers to the redeemer in the third person.³⁶⁸ Many manuscripts have תִגְאַל, which is supported by the ancient versions and is consistent with the other second person verbs in the context.³⁶⁹ This reader follows תִגְאַל ("if you will not redeem") because the text gives no other hint that Boaz in this one short clause should address the elders, and all his other statements are addressed to the closer redeemer in the second person.

הַגִּידָה לִּי—The verb is the Hiphil emphatic masculine singular imperative of נָגַד, "declare." The implied direct object is the closer redeemer's decision not to redeem, hence the translation, "Declare [that] to me."

וְאֵדְעָ כִּי אֵין זוּלָתְךָ לִגְאוֹל וְאָנֹכִי אַחֲרֶיךָ—The first word is difficult. The Qere is וְאֵדְעָה, the Qal first common singular cohortative (with final *he*) of יָדַע. The Kethib is וְאֵדַע, the first common singular imperfect of יָדַע. The Masoretic accents indicate that the previous clause ended with לִּי (with the strong disjunctive *rebia'* accent, -ֿלִ) and that this clause begins with the verb (Qere or Kethib). Usually in the OT, "I know" in the present tense is expressed by יָדַעְתִּי, the perfect of יָדַע. However, sometimes it is expressed by the imperfect אֵדַע (1 Ki 3:7; Pss 51:5 [ET 51:3]; 73:22; Job 42:3), and that could be the case here. כִּי can introduce indirect discourse. Therefore, the most expedient way to understand the text is to follow the Kethib and translate this clause as a new sentence: "I know that there is no one before you to redeem, and I am after you."³⁷⁰

---

³⁶⁷ Hubbard, *Ruth*, 237, n. 5, citing Joüon, *Ruth*, 82.
³⁶⁸ Sasson, *Ruth*, 118.
³⁶⁹ Hubbard, *Ruth*, 237, n. 6.
³⁷⁰ Hubbard, *Ruth*, 237, n. 7, reflects this view.

Ruth 4:1–12

If we follow the Qere, which is the sole reading in many manuscripts, most likely we should disregard the accents and take the cohortative as a purpose clause concluding the previous clause: "… declare to me *so I will know*." Most commentators and English translations reflect this view. The sequence "declare … so we/they will know …" is expressed by a Hiphil of נָגַד followed by an imperfect of יָדַע in Is 19:12 and followed by a cohortative of יָדַע in Is 41:22, 23, 26. Then כִּי would begin a new clause and have a causal sense: "For there is no one …"

In either case, the כִּי clause explains the reason why Boaz has petitioned the unnamed primary redeemer to act first. Here אֵין has the absolute meaning "there is no one, none exists" (cf. GKC, § 152 o). In this context, "besides you" (זוּלָתְךָ, the preposition זוּלָה with second masculine singular suffix) in effect means "*before* you," since Boaz goes on to say to the closer relative, "I [וְאָנֹכִי] am after you [אַחֲרֶיךָ]." The Qal infinitive construct גְּאוֹל with לְ has the modal nuance: "none has *the right to redeem* (it) except you" (Waltke-O'Connor, 36.2.3f, including example 43).

אָנֹכִי אֶגְאָל:—The closer redeemer uses the redundant pronoun for emphasis: "I myself [אָנֹכִי] will redeem [אֶגְאָל]!" The imperfect אֶגְאָל (Qal first common singular of גָּאַל, "redeem") voices his intention to fulfill Boaz's request (the imperative גְּאַל earlier in 4:4). However, if he had wanted to declare decisively that he was exercising his prerogative to act as redeemer, he probably would have used the perfect, גָּאַלְתִּי, "I hereby redeem" (see Joüon, § 112 f). His imperfect leaves the way open for further negotiations.[371]

4:5 Boaz's declaration is couched in a chiasm:
    A   "On the day you acquire …
    B   from the hand of Naomi,
    B'   then from Ruth the Moabitess, …
    A'   I will acquire …"[372]

---

[371] Bush, *Ruth, Esther*, 210.
[372] Linafelt, *Ruth*, 69.

Ruth 4:1–12

בְּיוֹם־קְנוֹתְךָ הַשָּׂדֶה מִיַּד נָעֳמִי—Literally, "On the day of your acquiring the field from the hand of Naomi," this is equivalent to "When you acquire …" The verb is the Qal infinitive construct of קָנָה with second masculine singular suffix; see the textual note on the imperative קְנֵה in 4:4. This is a temporal conditional clause indicating that the action of the closer redeemer acquiring the field will be simultaneous with Boaz's action of acquiring from Ruth (described next).[373] "From the hand of Naomi" (מִיַּד נָעֳמִי) indicates the transferal of possession (as in Gen 33:19; 39:1; Lev 25:14),[374] akin to the English expression that property has "changed hands."

וּמֵאֵת רוּת הַמּוֹאֲבִיָּה אֵשֶׁת־הַמֵּת—This is, literally, "then *from with* Ruth the Moabitess, the wife of the deceased." After the major disjunctive accent *athnach* (-ָ֑- on נָעֳמִ֑י) at the end of the preceding phrase, this clause begins with a disjunctive *waw* (on וּמֵאֵת) that contrasts Boaz's action to that of his counterpart (see Waltke-O'Connor, § 39.2.3b). This could be rendered, "On the day *you* acquire … then/nevertheless … *I* will acquire …" מֵאֵת is the preposition מִן compounded with the preposition אֵת, "with," indicating that what Boaz intends to acquire "from" Ruth is now "with" Ruth. In English the combination can simply be rendered "from."

In the MT (reflected in the LXX), "Ruth" is part of a prepositional phrase with מִן (מֵאֵת), "then *from* Ruth …"[375] However, the Syriac, Old Latin, and Vulgate translated "Ruth" as a direct object of the following finite verb (a form of "acquire"), which suggests that instead of וּמֵאֵת רוּת they read וְגַם אֶת רוּת (the same consonants but with addition of ג).[376] Those translations apparently harmonized this

---

[373] Campbell, *Ruth*, 146; Sasson, *Ruth*, 119; Hubbard, *Ruth*, 243, n. 38; Waltke-O'Connor, § 11.2.5c.
[374] Bush, *Ruth, Esther*, 210–11.
[375] Waltke-O'Connor, § 39.2a, footnote 2, includes the proposal that the מ in וּמֵאֵת in Ruth 4:5 and Neh 5:11 is the enclitic *mem*, which the Masoretes misunderstood as the preposition מִן. If that were the case, Ruth would be the direct object, and the Syriac, Old Latin, and Vulgate translations would be accurate.
[376] See Würthwein, "Ruth," 19–20; Beattie, "The Book of Ruth as Evidence for Israelite Legal Practice," 263; Campbell, *Ruth*, 146; Gray,

Ruth 4:1–12

text to agree with 4:10, which begins with וְגַם אֶת־רוּת as the direct object of קָנִיתִי ("Furthermore, Ruth ... have I acquired," that is, "I have acquired Ruth"). There is no reason to emend 4:5 to be identical with 4:10.[377] The MT's prepositional phrase and following verb ("I will acquire") should be understood to be a pregnant construction: the reader needs to supply in thought the verb's direct object. Boaz will acquire from Ruth "[*the means*] to perpetuate ..." Ruth herself is actually the means, the one through/by whom Boaz will perpetuate the family line of the deceased (Mahlon, son of Elimelech).

"The wife of the deceased" (אֵשֶׁת־הַמֵּת) may be a technical legal term,[378] since it occurs also in Deut 25:5, which prescribes levirate marriage; compare also "the name of his brother, the deceased" (שֵׁם אָחִיו הַמֵּת) in Deut 25:6 and "the name of the deceased" (שֵׁם־הַמֵּת) later in Ruth 4:5. In such legal contexts, it is fitting to translate מֵת, the Qal masculine singular participle of מוּת, as "deceased" rather than "dead."

קָנִיתִי—This is a Qal perfect form of קָנָה, "to acquire"; see the textual note on קָנֵה in 4:4. The Kethib is קָנִיתִי, first common singular ("I acquire"), which is preferable for the context here. The perfect has the force of a legal declaration (as did מָכְרָה in 4:3), and since the legal transaction will take place in the future ("On the day you acquire ..."), it must be rendered in English as a future, "I will acquire." The Kethib fits as a contrast to the second person in the preceding dependent clause ("On the day you acquire ... I will acquire"). Boaz repeats the first person verb קָנִיתִי in 4:9, 10, and its context in 4:10 is quite similar to that here in 4:5. Thus the Kethib is consistent with the immediate and larger context.

The Qere is קָנִיתָה, second masculine singular ("you acquire") with final ה- as a vowel letter. (The Qere וְאֵדְעָה in 4:4 also has that final vowel letter.) The Qere is the sole reading in some Hebrew manuscripts and is supported by the LXX, Syriac, Vulgate, and Targum. Almost all English translations follow the Qere. However,

---

Joshua, Judges, Ruth, 380; Sasson, *Ruth*, 121–22; Hubbard, *Ruth*, 237, n. 8; Bush, *Ruth, Esther*, 216–17, 238.

[377] See major objections to emendation by Gow, *The Book of Ruth*, 153–67.
[378] Hubbard, *Ruth*, 243.

the Qere can be explained as secondary: the first person (קָנִיתִי) was changed to second person (קָנִיתָה) based on two erroneous assumptions. The first assumption was that this form of קָנָה should agree with the second masculine singular subjective suffix on the infinitive קְנוֹתְךָ earlier in the verse, so that the closer redeemer would be the subject of both forms of קָנָה in 4:5. The second assumption was that there was a connection in OT Law, or at least in Israelite custom, between the redemption of property (4:5a) and levirate marriage (4:5b); the Qere implies that the same man who redeems the property must also enter into a levirate marriage with the widow (Ruth) of the deceased property owner (Mahlon). However, no other OT passage supports that second assumption. Thus one can explain why the Kethib would have been changed to produce the Qere, but there is no good explanation why the Qere would have been changed to produce the first-person Kethib.[379] Thus the Kethib is the harder reading and is more likely to be the original.

Most commentators rightly agree that here in 4:5b the verb קָנָה means "acquire," regardless of which reading we follow, קָנִיתִי, "I will acquire," or קָנִיתָה, "you will acquire," and whether Ruth is the means ("from Ruth ... I/you will acquire") or the direct object ("I/you will acquire Ruth").[380] In this clause קָנָה does not mean "buy, purchase," as if a commercial transaction were involved. Though a so-called "bride-price" could be given to the bride's father by the groom or his father (e.g., 1 Sam 18:25), this is not to be compared to a price for property, for it was evidence of the groom's esteem for the bride. The OT thus avoids commercial terminology to refer to marriage.[381] Boaz twice had just used קָנָה to refer to the acquisition of the property ("acquire [it]," 4:4; "on the day you acquire the field," 4:5a), as he will again when the transaction is completed ("I have acquired all that belonged ... ," 4:9). Therefore, stylistically he uses

---

[379] Beattie, "The Book of Ruth as Evidence for Israelite Legal Practice," 263–64.
[380] See the second textual note on 4:5.
[381] Mace, Hebrew Marriage, 169–72; Boecker, Law and the Administration of Justice in the Old Testament and Ancient East, 101; W. H. Schmidt, "קנה," TLOT 3:1149; Westbrook, Old Babylonian Marriage Laws, 53–58; Bush, Ruth, Esther, 217–18.

Ruth 4:1–12

the same verb to refer to the acquisition of Ruth as a wife ("I/you will acquire," 4:5b), as he will again upon completion ("Ruth the Moabitess, the wife of Mahlon, have I acquired," 4:10).[382] Ruth 4:5 and 4:10 are the only OT verses where קָנָה pertains to marriage, but in rabbinic Hebrew, it can refer to acquiring a wife.[383]

However, Boaz uses "acquire" in respect to Ruth not just in harmony with the term for the property, but more specifically because Ruth became attached to Naomi through Ruth's conversion to faith in the LORD (see 1:16–17) and her return with Naomi to Bethlehem (1:19, 22). Ruth the Moabitess now was a true believer, and indeed all believers in Jesus Christ comprise the true Israel (Rom 9:6–8; 11:5–6, 25–26; Gal 6:16). Although Boaz in effect acknowledged Ruth as a true believer in Israel's God and as a relative (2:11–16, 20; 3:9–11), she would not formally be incorporated into Israelite society until she married an Israelite in Israel (4:10–12). After Boaz would marry Ruth, he could perpetuate the name of her deceased Israelite husband and his family through offspring from her (see the next textual note).

לְהָקִים שֵׁם־הַמֵּת עַל־נַחֲלָתוֹ—The first three words display alliteration with the repeated *mem*: *lehaqim shem-hammet*. The Hiphil infinitive construct of קוּם with לְ expresses purpose:[384] "in order to raise up/perpetuate the name of the deceased on his inheritance." More literally, it could be rendered, "to cause the dead man's name to stand upon his inheritance" (BDB, s.v. קוּם, Hiphil, 6 g). The first son born to the widow would perpetuate the deceased man's name, and since the son would inherit his property, the name would continue to be "on" (עַל) or attached to the inheritance. If the child were a girl, the inheritance could pass to her husband, according to Num 27:1–11 and 36:1–12. Boaz will repeat this Hebrew idiom verbatim in 4:10. It is drawn from Deut 25:6–7, where the LORD had commanded levirate marriage. The firstborn son of the widow, fathered by the brother of the deceased, would "arise on the name of his [the dead man's] brother, the deceased" (יָקוּם עַל־שֵׁם אָחִיו הַמֵּת, Deut 25:6).

---

[382] Steenstra in Cassel, *Ruth*, 45, n. 7; Weiss, "The Use of קנה in Connection with Marriage"; Morris, *Ruth*, 303–4; Campbell, *Ruth*, 145–47; Bush, *Ruth, Esther*, 218.

[383] See Jastrow, s.v. קני, קָנָה, Niphal and Hiphil.

[384] Williams, § 197; Waltke-O'Connor, § 36.2.3d.

Ruth 4:1–12

However, if the brother refused to unite with his deceased brother's widow, he thereby failed "to raise up/perpetuate for his brother a name in Israel" (לְהָקִים לְאָחִיו שֵׁם בְּיִשְׂרָאֵל, Deut 25:7).

4:6 וַיֹּאמֶר הַגֹּאֵל—On "the redeemer," see the third textual note on 4:1.

לֹא אוּכַל לִגְאָול־לִי—The first verb is the Qal first singular imperfect of יָכֹל, "to be able." Its imperfect often has a present meaning, hence here "I am not able." The second verb is the Qal infinitive construct of גָּאַל, "redeem," with the preposition לְ. Its Kethib is לִגְאוֹל־ with *holem* (וֹ, long "o" vowel), while its Qere is לִגְאָל־ with *qamets chatuph* (-אָ-, short "o" vowel). The Qere is the expected form because the infinitive is in construct with the following prepositional phrase, so the long vowel would be reduced to a short vowel. לִי, "for myself," the reflexive use of the preposition,[385] adds emphasis. A pronominal object of the verb is implied: "redeem *it* [the field]." See also "acquire [it]" in 4:4. The closer redeemer will repeat most of this clause at the end of 4:6.

פֶּן־אַשְׁחִית אֶת־נַחֲלָתִי—The adverb פֶּן introduces a negative purpose clause (Waltke-O'Connor, § 39.3.3a), expressed with the Hiphil first singular imperfect of שָׁחַת, "lest I ruin my inheritance/so that I do not ruin my inheritance." If he would redeem the property, he would damage his inheritance.

גְּאַל־לְךָ אַתָּה אֶת־גְּאֻלָּתִי—The closer redeemer relinquishes his own right and petitions Boaz to exercise the right to redeem Elimelech's estate. For emphasis, he uses both the reflexive prepositional phrase (לְךָ)[386] and the redundant pronoun (אַתָּה), literally, "redeem for yourself—you—my redemption." The noun גְּאֻלָּה is taken from the covenant laws regarding redemption. Here

---

[385] BDB, s.v. לְ, 5 h (a); GKC, § 119 s; Joüon, § 133 d; Campbell, *Ruth*, 147; Bush, *Ruth, Esther*, 229.
[386] BDB s.v. לְ 5 h (a); GKC, § 119 s; Joüon, § 133 d. Other examples are in Ruth 4:6a, 8, 10.

Ruth 4:1–12

and in 4:7, as in most of those laws, it denotes the "right of redemption" (BDB, 3), the right and obligation to repurchase property that formerly belonged to one's clan, so that the property is reincorporated into the clan before the next Jubilee, when it should automatically revert to the clan.[387]

לֹא־אוּכַל לִגְאָל׃—These were the first three words of the closer redeemer's reply in 4:6a. He emphatically repeats "I am not able to redeem," thus giving his statement a chiastic inclusio. The Syriac adds "through lack of faith," which may be a Christian gloss.[388]

4:7 וְזֹאת לְפָנִים בְּיִשְׂרָאֵל—This is, literally, "and this formerly in Israel." The feminine demonstrative pronoun זֹאת in a general, neutral sense[389] with disjunctive וְ beginning a nominal (verbless) clause signals that this is a parenthetical explanation by the narrator that supplies information relevant for the story (see Waltke-O'Connor, § 39.2.3c, including example 10; a similar construction began Ruth 1:2). The prepositional phrase לְפָנִים serves as a temporal adverb, "formerly," that may refer to a previous time in fairly close proximity or to one in antiquity, here at least before the adult lifetime of the readers.[390] The Hebrew lacks an explicit predicate, but the translation supplies one ("This formerly in Israel [*was the custom*]"), as did the ancient versions (LXX: τὸ δικαίωμα, "[was] the legal custom"; Vulgate: *erat mos*, "was the custom, action"; Peshitta: "[was] the custom of redemption").[391] The last clause of this verse is similar to this one but includes the predicate noun (with article) הַתְּעוּדָה, "This/such [was] *the attestation* in Israel."

עַל־הַגְּאוּלָה וְעַל־הַתְּמוּרָה—The preposition עַל twice here means "regarding, concerning" (see BDB, II 1 f *(h)*; *HALOT*, s.v. עַל

---

[387] See Kleinig, *Leviticus*, 540, 549–51.
[388] Campbell, *Ruth*, 149; Gray, *Joshua, Judges, Ruth*, 398–99; Hubbard, *Ruth*, 238, n. 14.
[389] Waltke-O'Connor, § 17.4.3b; Sasson, *Ruth*, 141.
[390] Campbell, *Ruth*, 147–48; Bush, *Ruth, Esther*, 233.
[391] Cf. Hubbard, *Ruth*, 247, n. 1; Bush, *Ruth, Esther*, 233.

II, 3). See the textual note on גְּאֻלָּה in 4:6; here it is written *plene*. Normally only a short vowel precedes a consonant with *daghesh* (e.g., -אַל-), so the *plene* form with a long vowel before a doubled consonant (-וּלּ-) is exceptional. The noun תְּמוּרָה, "exchange, transfer," occurs elsewhere only in Lev 27:10, 33; Job 15:31; 20:18; 28:17. Here it refers to the transaction to confirm the transfer of the right of redemption from the closer redeemer to Boaz. The two prepositional phrases, literally, "regarding the right of redemption and regarding the transfer," build a hendiadys: "regarding the transfer of the right of redemption."[392]

לְקַיֵּם כָּל־דָּבָר—The uncommon Piel[393] of קוּם (infinitive construct with לְ) in this context means to "confirm, ratify" (BDB, 2 a). דָּבָר refers to a legal "matter." In this context כָּל־דָּבָר does not mean "every (legal) matter," that is, every commercial transaction, but specifically every transfer of the right of redemption (see the preceding textual note). By handing over his sandal, the nearer redeemer transferred his right to Boaz.[394]

שָׁלַף אִישׁ נַעֲלוֹ וְנָתַן לְרֵעֵהוּ—The two perfect verbs have a frequentative or habitual nuance, referring to customary actions that were repeated at various times in the past: "a man would draw off [שָׁלַף] his sandal and would give [וְנָתַן] [it] to his counterpart."[395] נַעַל

---

[392] Brichto, "Kin, Cult, Land and Afterlife," 18, followed by Bush, *Ruth, Esther*, 233–34. With respect to sacrificial animals, תְּמוּרָה in Lev 27:10, 33, means "substitute" or "replacement." It is derived from מוּר, whose Hiphil in those verses means "to substitute" (Kleinig, *Leviticus*, 582–84, 591–92).

[393] The usual geminate conjugation of verbs with ו or י as their middle radical is the Polel (Joüon, § 80 h). For קוּם, the OT attests both the Piel (eleven occurrences) and the Polel (four occurrences).

[394] Rowley, "The Marriage of Ruth," 182; de Waard and Nida, *A Translator's Handbook on the Book of Ruth*, 70; Bush, *Ruth, Esther*, 234.

[395] GKC, § 106 k, cites other perfects that, like שָׁלַף, lack *waw* and refer to recurring actions, and compares them to the Greek gnomic aorist. GKC, § 112 h, cites other examples of a "frequentative perfect consecutive" (GKC, § 112 g) that, like וְנָתַן, have *waw* and follow a perfect. Waltke-O'Connor, § 30.4b, calls a perfect with "present/habitual significance" a "gnomic perfective."

can refer to a "sandal" or any kind of footwear,[396] and it is implied as the object in the second clause ("give [it]"; cf. "acquire [it]" in 4:4). The idiom אִישׁ ... לְרֵעֵהוּ, literally, "a man ... to his neighbor [רֵעַ]," refers in this context of Law or custom to the closest redeemer ("a man") and his legal counterpart ("his neighbor"), namely, the next-closest redeemer who agreed to carry out the redemption.[397] This ceremony before witnesses, in which the primary redeemer handed over his sandal to the man receiving the redemption right, apparently was no longer practiced or understood at the time Ruth was written, most likely predating the later practice of written documentation that came into vogue during the monarchy (see Jer 32:6–12).[398]

וְזֹאת הַתְּעוּדָה בְּיִשְׂרָאֵל:—This final clause of the verse is similar to the opening clause (וְזֹאת לְפָנִים בְּיִשְׂרָאֵל), so the narrator has framed his historical explanation with an approximate chiastic inclusio.[399] The speeches of the closer redeemer in 4:6 and of Boaz in 4:9–10 each also have a chiastic inclusio. Literally, "This [was] the attestation in Israel," this clause refers to the process for making the transfer legally binding.[400] The noun תְּעוּדָה (from the verb עוּד, "testify, witness") occurs elsewhere only in Is 8:16, 20.

4:8 וַיֹּאמֶר הַגֹּאֵל—On "the redeemer," see the third textual note on 4:1.

קְנֵה־לָךְ—The redeemer uses the same Qal masculine singular imperative of קָנָה, "acquire," that Boaz had directed to him in 4:4, and as there, the translation supplies an implied object ("it"), referring to "the portion of the field ..." (4:3). The reflexive use of the

---

[396] Bush, *Ruth, Esther*, 234, understands the singular as a collective for both sandals.
[397] Campbell, *Ruth*, 148; cf. *HALOT*, s.v. רֵעַ II, 5 a.
[398] Hubbard, *Ruth*, 33, including n. 62; 250; Block, *Judges, Ruth*, 717–18.
[399] Campbell, *Ruth*, 149.
[400] See Bush, *Ruth, Esther*, 236–37; Block, *Judges, Ruth*, 718; Sasson, *Ruth*, 146–47.

preposition (לָ֔ךְ, "for yourself")⁴⁰¹ appears to have the second feminine singular suffix, but it is the pausal form of לְךָ (with second masculine singular suffix).

וַיִּשְׁלֹ֥ף נַעֲלֽוֹ׃— This repeats the idiom in 4:7. To "and he drew off his sandal," the LXX adds "and he gave to him," an example of addition for clarification.

4:9 לַזְּקֵנִ֜ים וְכָל־הָעָ֗ם—"The elders" and "all the people" refer to the two groups present; see the fifth textual note on 4:4 (see also 4:11). The preposition לְ does double duty:⁴⁰² "to the elders and [*to*] all the people." The only other example in Ruth of a double-duty preposition is לְ in לְכִלְי֣וֹן וּמַחְל֔וֹן later in the verse.

עֵדִ֤ים אַתֶּם֙ הַיּ֔וֹם—This is a nominal (verbless) clause, literally, "witnesses [are] you today," with the predicate (עֵדִים) first for emphasis. By saying this, Boaz in effect puts those present under oath, so that in the future they will be obligated to testify, if needed, that the transfer of redemption was in fact completed in a legal and binding manner. Boaz will repeat this clause at the end of 4:10 for an inclusio around his speech in 4:9–10.

קָנִ֙יתִי֙ אֶת־כָּל־אֲשֶׁ֣ר לֶֽאֱלִימֶ֔לֶךְ—The verb form (Qal first common singular perfect of קָנָה) is identical to the Kethib in 4:5b and it is repeated in 4:10. It has a legal nuance, as did the perfects מָכְרָ֣ה in 4:3 and קָנִ֖יתִי (Kethib) in 4:5. Since it concludes the act of transferal, it is translated as an English perfect, "I have acquired," or perhaps it could be translated, "*I acquire* (here and now ... by my own words)."⁴⁰³

---

⁴⁰¹ BDB, s.v. לְ, 5 h (a); GKC, § 119 s; Joüon, § 133 d.
⁴⁰² Campbell, *Ruth*, 150–51; cf. Waltke-O'Connor, § 11.4.2a.
⁴⁰³ Joüon, § 112 f. Waltke-O'Connor, § 30.5.1d, example 27, translates, "I *acquire* (here and now)" and considers it to be an "*instantaneous perfective*" that represents the action as taking place at the same time the expression is spoken.

Ruth 4:1–12

לֶאֱלִימֶלֶךְ ... לְכִלְיוֹן וּמַחְלוֹן—The preposition לְ denotes possession:[404] "all that *belonged to* ..." The second לְ does double duty for both sons. Their order here ("Chilion ... Mahlon") is the reverse of that in 1:2, 5. The לְ is translated with a past tense, "belonged," because Boaz's declaration of assuming the right of redemption meant that he had also legally assumed the ownership of the property inheritance in question, so that it no longer belonged to its former owners.

4:10 וְגַם אֶת־רוּת הַמֹּאֲבִיָּה אֵשֶׁת מַחְלוֹן—As in 4:5b, Boaz places the phrase describing Ruth first for emphasis. Even though it is the direct object, in both verses it precedes the verb קָנִיתִי. Here it also begins with וְגַם ("and also/furthermore") for further emphasis. As necessary in a legal settlement, Boaz states Ruth's full legal name: "Ruth the Moabitess, the wife of Mahlon." For a resident alien like Ruth, a gentilic adjective (הַמֹּאֲבִיָּה, "the Moabitess") is the proper term; see also, for example, "Uriah the Hittite" (2 Sam 23:39). In contrast, the proper terminology for a native Israelite would be patronymic and/or loconymic, for example, "Elhanan the son of Dodo of Bethlehem" (2 Sam 23:24) or "Abiezer of Anathoth" (2 Sam 23:27).[405]

Only here does it become clear that Mahlon had been the husband of Ruth, and thus Chilion must have been Orpah's husband (see 1:2, 4).

קָנִיתִי לִי לְאִשָּׁה—"I have acquired for myself for a wife" is legal terminology. Boaz's act mirrors his intention, which he expressed in 4:5b with the same verb, though there קָנִיתִי looked to the immediate future ("I will acquire"). Here, as in 4:9, קָנִיתִי has a perfect meaning, "I have acquired." The reflexive use of לְ (לִי), "for

---

[404] BDB, s.v. לְ, 5 a; *HALOT*, s.v. לְ I, 10, 11.
[405] Bush, *Ruth, Esther*, 138, 238.

Ruth 4:1–12

myself")[406] lends emphasis. The preposition לְ on לְאִשָּׁה indicates a transition into a new status or relationship, so "for a wife" means "to become my wife."[407]

לְהָקִים שֵׁם־הַמֵּת עַל־נַחֲלָתוֹ—See the last textual note on 4:5, where Boaz first used this phrase.

וְלֹא־יִכָּרֵת שֵׁם־הַמֵּת מֵעִם אֶחָיו וּמִשַּׁעַר מְקוֹמוֹ—In this context, the negated Niphal imperfect of כָּרַת expresses purpose:[408] literally, "so that the name of the deceased shall not be cut off from [being] with his brethren and from the gate of his place." A man's name was associated with his progeny and with the property he owned and passed on to his descendants. To be "cut off" (Niphal of כָּרַת) meant to be terminated; if the family died out, the man's name would no longer be remembered as part of the genealogy of living Israelites. The provision of an heir would ensure that his name was perpetuated and remembered among "his brethren" (אֶחָיו). The redemption of his property ensured that his inheritance would remain within his family. "The gate of his place" probably refers to "the assembly [that meets at the gate] of his town" (cf. "the whole gate of my people" in 3:11) since מָקוֹם can refer to a town or to a man's dwelling place (e.g., מָקוֹם in Gen 18:24, 26; 20:11; 30:25; 32:1 [ET 31:55]).[409] The man's heir would take his place in the assembly at the town gate.[410]

עֵדִים אַתֶּם הַיּוֹם:—"Witnesses are you today" was declared by Boaz at the beginning (4:9) and now at the end of his statement for legal solemnity and emphasis as a chiastic inclusio (see other inclusios in 4:6, 7).[411]

---

[406] BDB, s.v. לְ, 5 h (a); GKC, § 119 s; Joüon, § 133 d. See also לִי in 4:6a; לָךְ in 4:6b; and לְךָ in 4:8.
[407] See BDB, s.v. לְ, 4; Williams, § 278; Waltke-O'Connor, § 11.2.10d.
[408] Cf. Waltke-O'Connor, § 39.2.2a.
[409] Campbell, *Ruth*, 151 (cf. p. 124); see also Bush, *Ruth, Esther*, 239; Block, *Judges, Ruth*, 720–21.
[410] Hubbard, *Ruth*, 253, n. 7; Bush, *Ruth, Esther*, 246.
[411] Bush, *Ruth, Esther*, 195, 239.

Ruth 4:1–12

4:11a כָּל־הָעָ֧ם אֲשֶׁר־בַּשַּׁ֛עַר וְהַזְּקֵנִ֖ים—This is, literally, "All the people who were in the gate and the elders," but it is translated "all the people and the elders who were in the gate" because it refers to the two groups who had congregated at the gate to witness the proceedings. "The elders" refers only to the ten elders assembled there, not all the town elders. See the fifth textual note on 4:4, and see also 4:9.

עֵדִים—The elders and other townspeople utter a terse affirmation in legal style, "Witnesses!" This is a verbless clause that implies a full declaration: "We are witnesses!" They thereby testify that the transaction has been duly completed. This is a powerful ellipsis that repeats only the first, key word of Boaz's repeated statement that had put them under oath, עֵדִים אַתֶּם הַיּוֹם, "Witnesses are you today" (4:9, 10). Similar is Josh 24:22, where Joshua elevated the Israelites' promise not to break the divine covenant to the status of a legally binding oath under God by saying to them, "Witnesses are you against yourselves" (עֵדִים אַתֶּם בָּכֶם), and the people respond affirmatively with the single word "Witnesses!" (עֵדִים).[412] Instead of using a word for "yes," the biblical Hebrew convention for answering a question affirmatively was to repeat a key word or phrase from the question.[413]

4:11b The rest of 4:11 and also 4:12 is poetic.

יִתֵּן֩ יְהוָ֨ה—The Qal of נָתַן with an accusative (אֶת־הָאִשָּׁ֜ה) and the prepositional phrases with כְּ (כְּרָחֵ֤ל ׀ וּכְלֵאָה֙) mean "to make someone/something be like someone/something else" (see BDB, s.v. נָתַן, 3 c). Here the jussive יִתֵּן֩ with יְהוָ֨ה as subject has the optative meaning appropriate for a benediction: "The LORD make …" This is stronger than a prayer ("*May* the LORD …") or a mere wish.[414]

---

[412] See Harstad, *Joshua*, 793.
[413] GKC, § 150 n; Campbell, *Ruth*, 152; Sasson, *Ruth*, 153; Hubbard, *Ruth*, 257; Bush, *Ruth, Esther*, 239; Block, *Judges, Ruth*, 721.
[414] Cf. Hubbard, *Ruth*, 254, n. 14.

אֶת־הָאִשָּׁה הַבָּאָה אֶל־בֵּיתֶךָ—"The *woman* who is coming into your house" is appropriate rather than "wife," for she had not yet entered Boaz's house; the marriage had been announced but not yet consummated.[415] The accent on the final syllable indicates that הַבָּאָה is the Qal feminine singular participle of בּוֹא, with the article serving as a relative pronoun[416] ("who is …"), depicting action in progress ("coming"). Contrast הַשָּׁבָה in 1:22; 2:6; 4:3, whose penultimate accent indicates that it is third feminine singular perfect (see the third textual note on 1:22). The preposition אֶל in this context denotes motion "into" (BDB, 2). בַּיִת has the literal meaning of "house," in which the marriage would be consummated. At the same time, it can have the common metaphorical meaning because Ruth, through marriage, will become part of Boaz's "household."

כְּרָחֵל ׀ וּכְלֵאָה—The preposition כְּ here indicates qualitative resemblance (BDB, 1 b): "like Rachel and like Leah." The townspeople place the more important wife, the mother of Judah, second.[417] Similarly, the narrator names "Orpah," then "Ruth" as the more important one in 1:4, 14. Jacob loved Rachel more than Leah (Gen 29:30), but Leah bore him six of his twelve sons: Reuben, the firstborn; Simeon; Levi, from whom the priests and Levites were descended; Judah, from whose line came the Davidic kings and the Messiah, Jesus Christ; Issachar; and Zebulun (Gen 29:31–35; 30:17–20; 35:23). Rachel bore Joseph and died giving birth to Benjamin (Gen 30:22–24; 35:16–20, 24).

אֲשֶׁר בָּנוּ שְׁתֵּיהֶם אֶת־בֵּית יִשְׂרָאֵל—This relative clause is, literally, "[Rachel and Leah,] who the two of them built the house of Israel." The two wives are credited not only with their own sons, but also with the sons born to their handmaidens, Bilhah and Zilpah (Gen 30:1–13; 35:25–26). בָּנוּ is the Qal third common plural perfect of בָּנָה, which can literally mean "to build" a house, town, or so forth. The idiom בָּנָה בַּיִת, "build a house," can have a metaphorical meaning, to "perpetuate and establish a family" (BDB, s.v. בָּנָה, Qal,

---

[415] Cf. Bush, *Ruth, Esther*, 239–40.
[416] See Williams, § 90; GKC, § 138 k; Joüon, § 145 e; Waltke-O'Connor, § 19.7d.
[417] Sasson, *Ruth*, 154, followed by Bush, *Ruth, Esther*, 240.

Ruth 4:1–12

2 a) or "to provide someone with offspring" (*HALOT*, s.v. בנה, Qal, 6). The idiom is used in Deut 25:9, which reviles a man who refuses to "build the house of his brother" by levirate marriage to the widow in order to father an heir for his deceased brother. The LORD used the same idiom in his promise that he would "build" David's "house" (2 Sam 7:27; 1 Ki 11:38; 1 Chr 17:10, 25; cf. Amos 9:11) by granting him a line of sons who would reign on his throne, culminating in the Son of David, Jesus Christ, who will reign on David's throne forever (1 Ki 8:20, 25; Is 9:5–6 [ET 9:6–7]; Ps 132:10–12; Lk 1:31–32). See also the Niphal of בָּנָה, "to be built," referring to children born by concubines in Gen 16:2; 30:3, and בַּיִת, "house," referring to family (Ex 1:21) and a dynasty (2 Sam 7:11).

שְׁתֵּיהֶם is the numeral שְׁתַּיִם, the feminine form of שְׁנַיִם, "two," with third masculine plural suffix. Hebrew often uses masculine forms even when they refer to feminine persons; see the last textual note on 1:8.

וַעֲשֵׂה־חַיִל בְּאֶפְרָתָה וּקְרָא־שֵׁם בְּבֵית לָחֶם—Following the jussive יִתֵּן earlier in the verse, the two Qal masculine singular imperatives with conjunctive *waw* (וַעֲשֵׂה ... וּקְרָא) form subordinate purpose clauses: literally, "The LORD make ... so that you *do* strength in Ephrathah and *call* a name in Bethlehem!" See GKC, §§ 110 i; 165 a; Williams, § 519; and the first textual note on 1:9, where too יִתֵּן is followed by an imperative (וּמְצֶאןָ). The idiom עָשָׂה חַיִל occurs in other OT passages, where it could be rendered "achieve might = do valiantly" (BDB, s.v. חַיִל, 1 b), though in this context it may mean "prosper!"[418] The only other instances of חַיִל in Ruth are in the idioms describing Boaz (אִישׁ גִּבּוֹר חַיִל, "an honorable gentleman," 2:1) and Ruth (אֵשֶׁת חַיִל, "an honorable woman," 3:11).

The idiom קָרָא שֵׁם ("call a name") commonly is followed by a proper name when a person or place is given a name, as in 4:17 (cf. 4:14).[419] Only here does the idiom have the meaning "proclaim [your

---

[418] Gray, *Joshua, Judges, Ruth*, 400; Hubbard, *Ruth*, 253–54; Bush, *Ruth, Esther*, 240–42; Block, *Judges, Ruth*, 723.
[419] The imperative occurs in the clause קְרָא שְׁמוֹ/שְׁמָהּ, "call his/her name ... ," in Is 8:3; Hos 1:4, 6, 9.

own] name," that is, "become famous!"[420] Similar are idioms with שֵׁם עָשָׂה, "make a name," for example, "Let us make for ourselves a name" (Gen 11:4); "I will make for you a great name" (2 Sam 7:9 ‖ 1 Chr 17:8); and in 2 Sam 8:13; Is 63:12, 14; Dan 9:15.

4:12 וִיהִ֤י בֵיתְךָ֙ כְּבֵ֣ית פֶּ֔רֶץ—The Qal of הָיָה with the preposition כְּ can mean "become like" (BDB, s.v. הָיָה, II 2 c). The jussive יְהִי (with conjunction וְ) continues the benediction in the form of a prayer: "May your house become like the house of Perez." Here בַּיִת in the context of the ancestor Perez refers to the "family of descendants" (BDB, 5 b). As in 4:11, the preposition כְּ indicates qualitative resemblance (BDB, 1 b). In 4:11 it was "the LORD" who would enable Ruth to be like Rachel and Leah, who built the "house" of Israel. Here the LORD is the implied agent who will enable Boaz's "house" to become like that of Perez through the seed the LORD will give Boaz through Ruth.

מִן־הַזֶּ֗רַע אֲשֶׁ֨ר יִתֵּ֧ן יְהוָ֛ה לְךָ֖—While יִתֵּן is identical in form to the jussive יִתֵּן in 4:11, the context here indicates that it is the imperfect, expressing the confident faith that the LORD "will give" seed.

מִן־הַֽנַּעֲרָ֖ה הַזֹּֽאת:—After Boaz has declared that Ruth is to be his wife (4:10) and she has received the blessing prayer of the witnesses (4:11), נַעֲרָה ("young woman") reminds the audience of her youthfulness compared to Boaz. The term first appeared in the book when both Boaz and his foreman used it for Ruth as Boaz first set eyes on her (נַעֲרָה in 2:5–6), and it refers to Ruth again only here. Its repetition here forms a thematic inclusio around the events between their introduction and their marriage.[421]

---

[420] De Waard and Nida, *A Translator's Handbook on the Book of Ruth*, 74; Hubbard, *Ruth*, 260; Bush, *Ruth, Esther*, 242–43.
[421] Campbell, *Ruth*, 154; Hubbard, *Ruth*, 262.

4:13 וַיִּקַּ֨ח בֹּ֤עַז אֶת־רוּת֙ וַתְּהִי־ל֣וֹ לְאִשָּׁ֔ה וַיָּבֹ֖א אֵלֶ֑יהָ
וַיִּתֵּ֨ן יְהוָ֥ה לָ֛הּ הֵרָי֖וֹן וַתֵּ֥לֶד בֵּֽן׃

14 וַתֹּאמַ֤רְנָה הַנָּשִׁים֙ אֶֽל־נָעֳמִ֔י
בָּר֣וּךְ יְהוָ֔ה אֲשֶׁ֣ר לֹ֥א הִשְׁבִּ֛ית לָ֥ךְ גֹּאֵ֖ל הַיּ֑וֹם
וְיִקָּרֵ֥א שְׁמ֖וֹ בְּיִשְׂרָאֵֽל׃

15 וְהָ֤יָה לָךְ֙ לְמֵשִׁ֣יב נֶ֔פֶשׁ וּלְכַלְכֵּ֖ל אֶת־שֵׂיבָתֵ֑ךְ
כִּ֣י כַלָּתֵ֤ךְ אֲשֶׁר־אֲהֵבַ֙תֶךְ֙ יְלָדַ֔תּוּ
אֲשֶׁר־הִיא֙ ט֣וֹבָה לָ֔ךְ מִשִּׁבְעָ֖ה בָּנִֽים׃

16 וַתִּקַּ֨ח נָעֳמִ֤י אֶת־הַיֶּ֙לֶד֙ וַתְּשִׁתֵ֣הוּ בְחֵיקָ֔הּ וַתְּהִי־ל֖וֹ לְאֹמֶֽנֶת׃

17 וַתִּקְרֶאנָה֩ ל֨וֹ הַשְּׁכֵנ֥וֹת שֵׁם֙ לֵאמֹ֔ר יֻלַּד־בֵּ֖ן לְנָעֳמִ֑י
וַתִּקְרֶ֤אנָֽה שְׁמוֹ֙ עוֹבֵ֔ד ה֥וּא אֲבִי־יִשַׁ֖י אֲבִ֥י דָוִֽד׃ פ

18 וְאֵ֙לֶּה֙ תּוֹלְד֣וֹת פָּ֔רֶץ פֶּ֖רֶץ הוֹלִ֥יד אֶת־חֶצְרֽוֹן׃

19 וְחֶצְרוֹן֙ הוֹלִ֣יד אֶת־רָ֔ם וְרָ֖ם הוֹלִ֥יד אֶת־עַמִּֽינָדָֽב׃

20 וְעַמִּֽינָדָב֙ הוֹלִ֣יד אֶת־נַחְשׁ֔וֹן וְנַחְשׁ֖וֹן הוֹלִ֥יד אֶת־שַׂלְמָֽה׃

21 וְשַׂלְמוֹן֙ הוֹלִ֣יד אֶת־בֹּ֔עַז וּבֹ֖עַז הוֹלִ֥יד אֶת־עוֹבֵֽד׃

22 וְעֹבֵד֙ הוֹלִ֣יד אֶת־יִשָׁ֔י וְיִשַׁ֖י הוֹלִ֥יד אֶת־דָּוִֽד׃

4 ¹³Then Boaz took Ruth, and she became his wife, and he went to her. | The LORD gave to her conception, and so she bore a son. | ¹⁴Then the women said to Naomi, |
> "Blessed is the LORD,
>> who has not deprived you of a redeemer today! |
> May his name be proclaimed in Israel! |
>> ¹⁵May he restore your soul
>> and care for your old age! |
> For your daughter-in-law who loves you has borne him, |
>> she who is better for you than seven sons!" |

¹⁶Then Naomi took the boy and put him on her lap; so she became his guardian. |

¹⁷The neighboring women named him, saying, "A son is born to Naomi!" | and they called his name Obed. He was the father of Jesse, the father of David. |

¹⁸Now these are the generations of Perez: Perez fathered Hezron; |

¹⁹Hezron fathered Ram; Ram fathered Amminadab; |

²⁰Amminadab fathered Nahshon; Nahshon fathered Salmah; |

²¹Salmon fathered Boaz; Boaz fathered Obed; |

²²Obed fathered Jesse; and Jesse fathered David.

Ruth 4:13–22

4:13 וַיִּקַּ֥ח בֹּ֛עַז אֶת־ר֖וּת—The Qal imperfect of לָקַח with *waw* consecutive is sequential: "*Then* Boaz took Ruth." The verb with a man as subject and a woman as object commonly means to "*take* in marriage" (BDB, Qal, 4 e; cf. *HALOT*, לקח I, Qal, 7). It might relate to the husband taking the woman to his home (cf. 1:4).[422]

וַתְּהִי־ל֣וֹ לְאִשָּׁ֗ה—This is, literally, "and she was to him for a wife." The *waw* consecutive here indicates "simple chronological succession."[423] וַתְּהִי is the Qal third feminine singular imperfect of הָיָה, which refers to a change in Ruth's circumstances and so here means "become" (BDB, Qal, II 2), and with לְאִשָּׁה specifically "become [a] wife" (BDB, II 2 d). The use of לְ on לְאִשָּׁה to indicate a person's change in status or relationship could be called purpose (Waltke-O'Connor, § 11.2.10d, including examples 43–45). לוֹ indicates possession (BDB, s.v. לְ, 5 a; *HALOT*, s.v. לְ I, 10, 11), hence "*his* wife."

וַיָּבֹ֥א אֵלֶ֖יהָ—This is "and he went (in)to her." The verb בּוֹא with preposition אֶל commonly means to "come in(to)" or "enter" (see BDB, s.v. בּוֹא, Qal, 1 and 2). Boaz would have entered Ruth's private chamber in their home to consummate the marriage (cf. Gen 39:14; Judg 15:1; 2 Sam 12:24). With a man and woman, this common Hebrew idiom (בּוֹא with אֶל) means "consummate a marriage" or "have intercourse."[424]

וַיִּתֵּ֨ן יְהוָ֥ה לָ֛הּ הֵרָי֖וֹן—This is a striking way to highlight that God truly is the one who gives each human life: "The LORD gave to her conception." This corresponds to the prayer of the witnesses in 4:12, which had the same subject, verb, and preposition: "the seed whom *the LORD will give to you*" (יִתֵּ֧ן יְהוָ֛ה לְךָ֖). The noun הֵרָיוֹן derives from the common verb הָרָה, "to conceive." The noun occurs elsewhere only in Hos 9:11. It is related to הֵרוֹן, "pregnancy," which

---

[422] De Waard and Nida, *A Translator's Handbook on the Book of Ruth*, 76; Hubbard, *Ruth*, 267, n. 1; Bush, *Ruth, Esther*, 253.
[423] Waltke-O'Connor, § 33.2.1a, quoting S. R. Driver, *A Treatise on the Use of the Tenses in Hebrew* (3d ed.; Oxford, Clarendon, 1892), 80.
[424] E.g., Gen 16:2; 30:3; Deut 22:13. Campbell, *Ruth*, 163; *HALOT*, s.v. בּוֹא, Qal, 1; Bush, *Ruth, Esther*, 253; Block, *Judges, Ruth*, 725.

occurs only in Gen 3:16. הֵרָיוֹן itself could refer to the "conception" of either a son or daughter; the next clause will reveal that Ruth had conceived a son.

וַתֵּלֶד בֵּן:—After the previous clause with "conception," the Qal third feminine singular imperfect of יָלַד, "to bear, give birth," with *waw* consecutive is sequential ("and *then* ..."), but is best rendered as consequential, " and *so* she bore a son." Qal forms of יָלַד commonly are feminine and refer to a woman who "bears, gives birth," as also in Ruth 1:12; 4:15. However, in some OT passages, the father is said to "beget" the child (see *HALOT*, s.v. ילד, Qal, 2). Hiphil forms of יָלַד commonly are masculine and refer to a man who causes the child to be born by impregnating the mother; hence he "fathers" a child, as in 4:18–22, where הוֹלִיד occurs nine times (see the last textual note on 4:18). The Qal passive of יָלַד ("to be born") occurs in 4:17. The cognate masculine noun יֶלֶד, "boy," occurs in 1:5; 4:16. The cognate feminine plural noun תּוֹלְדוֹת, "generations," in 4:18 begins the genealogy.

4:14 וַתֹּאמַרְנָה הַנָּשִׁים אֶל־נָעֳמִי—The *waw* consecutive (Qal third feminine plural imperfect of אָמַר) is sequential: "*Then* the women said to Naomi ..." "The women" are the same townswomen of Bethlehem who greeted Naomi in 1:19. They will be called הַשְּׁכֵנוֹת ("the neighboring women") in 4:17.

בָּרוּךְ יְהוָה אֲשֶׁר לֹא הִשְׁבִּית לָךְ גֹּאֵל הַיּוֹם—This is, literally, "Blessed is the LORD, who did not cause to be missing for you a redeemer today." The blessing formula with בָּרוּךְ (Qal passive participle of בָּרַךְ) and יְהוָה, " Blessed is/be the LORD ... ," is followed by a relative clause (אֲשֶׁר, "who ...") that gives the reason for this praise, as also in, for example, Gen 14:20; 24:27; Ex 18:10; 1 Sam 25:32, 39; 1 Ki 8:56. The similar formula in Ruth 2:20 blessed Boaz, but whereas here (and in the other verses cited above) אֲשֶׁר refers back to the LORD, in 2:20 the LORD's fidelity is the subject of the אֲשֶׁר clause ("whose faithfulness has not forsaken ..."). See also the textual notes on the blessings in 2:4, 19; 3:10.

In the Qal, שָׁבַת means "to cease, end." The Hiphil (הִשְׁבִּית is third masculine singular perfect) has causative meanings: "cause to cease, make something be absent, exterminate, destroy." The syntax here is unique, but the closest parallel is when the Hiphil refers to omitting salt from the grain offering: "You shall not cause salt ... to be absent from your offering" (וְלֹא תַשְׁבִּית מֶלַח ... מֵעַל מִנְחָתֶךָ, Lev 2:13; see BDB, Hiphil, 5; *HALOT*, Hiphil, 3 a). The direct object is גֹּאֵל (see the last textual note on 2:20), which elsewhere in the book refers either to Boaz or the nearer relative, but here גֹּאֵל must refer to the newborn son as a "redeemer." The prepositional phrase (לָךְ with second feminine singular suffix) probably serves as a dative of advantage (*dativus commodi,* Joüon, § 133 d; "a redeemer [to act] for you, for your benefit"), as also in 4:15a, or else possession ("a redeemer of yours"). With the verb it is best rendered in this joyous acclamation, "has not deprived you of a redeemer."[425]

וְיִקָּרֵא שְׁמוֹ בְּיִשְׂרָאֵל׃—The verb form (Niphal third masculine singular of קָרָא with conjunctive *waw*) could be imperfect, but the context indicates that it is jussive, expressing a prayer for the child. The Niphal of קָרָא can mean "be proclaimed" (BDB, s.v. קָרָא I, Niphal, 2 a), so this is, literally, "and may his name be proclaimed in Israel." Since the similar clause with the Qal imperative in 4:11 (וּקְרָא־שֵׁם, literally, "call a name") meant "become famous," this clause implies that the proclamation of the infant redeemer's name would make him "be famous" (BDB, s.v. קָרָא I, Niphal, 2 a).

In this context, the logical antecedent of the pronoun (שְׁמוֹ, "*his* name") is the newborn "son" (בֵּן, 4:13), who is also a "redeemer" (גֹּאֵל, 4:14) and to whom 4:15a refers. Nevertheless, there may be some intentional ambiguity about the antecedent.[426] Following "Blessed is the LORD," grammatically and theologically this clause could mean "May his [the LORD's] name be invoked/celebrated in Israel." The ambiguity reinforces that the LORD is to be praised for

---

[425] See Bush, *Ruth, Esther,* 253.
[426] See Morris, *Ruth,* 313; de Waard and Nida, *A Translator's Handbook on the Book of Ruth,* 78; Campbell, *Ruth,* 163–64; Bush, *Ruth, Esther,* 256–57.

Ruth 4:13–22

the conception and birth of the son, and that the son will be the LORD's human agent, the one through whom the LORD will accomplish redemption for Naomi. Thus the newborn son anticipates the future Son of David, Jesus Christ, who will be the LORD's human agent (true God and true man) to accomplish redemption for the whole world.

4:15 וְהָ֤יָה לָךְ֙ לְמֵשִׁ֣יב נֶ֔פֶשׁ—This is, literally, "may he become for you a restorer of life/soul." The perfect verb with conjunctive *waw* (וְהָיָה) continues the prayer. The combination of הָיָה and לְ (here on לְמֵשִׁיב) often means "to become" (see BDB, s.v. הָיָה, II 2 d). The implied subject is the newborn "son" (בֵּן, 4:13) and "redeemer" (גֹּאֵל, 4:14). לָךְ (לְ with second feminine singular suffix) serves as a dative of advantage (Joüon, § 133 d), "for you," but it is better rendered in English as a possessive, "restores *your* soul." מֵשִׁיב is the Hiphil participle of שׁוּב. The Hiphil of שׁוּב means "cause to return, bring back, restore" and takes נֶפֶשׁ as its object also in other verses, where it pertains to salvation from death (starvation, Lam 1:11, 19; physical and spiritual death, Ps 35:17; Job 33:30); consolation from grief (Lam 1:16); or restoration to life in all its fullness by God's Word (Ps 19:8 [ET 19:7]). See also the Polel of שׁוּב with נֶפֶשׁ in Ps 23:3: "He [the LORD] restores my soul." Here the clause means that the son would save Naomi's family from extinction, and would restore her spirit or vitality to fullness of joyful life according to the LORD's salvific purpose.[427]

וּלְכַלְכֵּ֖ל אֶת־שֵׂיבָתֵ֑ךְ—The Pilpel of כּוּל (this is the infinitive construct with לְ) means "sustain, support, nourish" (BDB, 1). It is unusual to have an infinitive construct parallel to a participle (מֵשִׁיב in the preceding clause), but see also Jer 44:19. After וְהָיָה beginning the verse, the infinitive construct continues the prayer, hence "and

---

[427] Cf. Rudolph, *Das Buch Ruth, das Hohe Lied, die Klagelieder*, 69; Campbell, *Ruth*, 164; Hubbard, *Ruth*, 269, n. 3; Bush, *Ruth, Esther*, 257.

Ruth 4:13–22

may he support/care for."[428] The direct object שֵׂיבָתֵךְ (שֵׂיבָה with second feminine singular suffix), "your old age," has this sense in English: "care for *you in your old age*."

כַּלָּתֵךְ אֲשֶׁר־אֲהֵבַתֶךְ—This is the seventh and last occurrence in Ruth of כַּלָּה, "daughter-in-law" (1:6–8, 22; 2:20, 22), here with second feminine singular suffix. The verb אֲהֵבַתֶךְ is Qal perfect third feminine singular of אָהֵב with second feminine singular object suffix: "your daughter-in-law, who *loves you*." In many manuscripts, the *bet* has *qamets* (-בָ-), which is the expected vocalization (see GKC, § 59 g, which explains the penultimate accent). With verbs for feeling, the perfect is used with present meaning (cf. Williams, § 163). אָהֵב can be used for "love" between various family members, but only here in the OT for a daughter-in-law's love for her mother-in-law (cf. BDB, Qal, 1; *DCH*, Qal, 1 a; 4 <SUBJ>כַּלָּה).

יְלָדַתּוּ—This is the Qal third feminine singular perfect of יָלַד with third masculine singular suffix: "she has borne him."

אֲשֶׁר־הִיא טוֹבָה לָךְ מִשִּׁבְעָה בָּנִים—Literally, "who she is better for you than seven sons," this is translated, "she who is better for you than seven sons!" The subject pronoun הִיא ("she") is retrospective (Joüon, § 158 g) since it refers back to כַּלָּתֵךְ, "your daughter-in-law," in the previous clause. This nominal clause with an adjective (טוֹבָה, "good") followed by the preposition מִן (on מִשִּׁבְעָה) expresses the comparative degree ("better … than").

4:16 וַתִּקַּח נָעֳמִי אֶת־הַיֶּלֶד—The *waw* consecutive is sequential: "*Then* Naomi took the boy." The only other instance of יֶלֶד, "boy," in Ruth was in 1:5. The two instances form an inclusio bracketing the entire book; see the second textual note on 1:5.

וַתְּשִׁתֵהוּ בְחֵיקָהּ—The verb is the Qal imperfect third feminine singular of שִׁית with *waw* consecutive and third masculine singular

---

[428] Cf. GKC, § 114 g; Cassel, *Ruth*, 50, n. 1; Sasson, *Ruth*, 167.

suffix ("and she put him on her lap"). חֵיק can refer to the "bosom" of a woman nursing her infant (1 Ki 3:20; cf. 1 Ki 17:19; Prov 5:20; Lam 2:12). But here it refers not primarily to the grandmother's breasts, for Naomi would not nurse the baby (cf. Ruth 1:12), but to her "lap" (*HALOT*, 1; NIV, ESV).

וַתְּהִי־לֹו לְאֹמֶנֶת:—As in 4:13 and 4:15, the combination of הָיָה and the preposition לְ (here on לְאֹמֶנֶת) means "to become." The use of לְ on לֹו is for possession: "she became his guardian." אֹמֶנֶת is the feminine singular Qal participle of אָמַן, which in the Qal occurs only as a participle. Masculine forms can mean "guardian" (2 Ki 10:1, 5; Esth 2:7; *HALOT*, s.v. אמן II, Qal, 1) or "foster-father" (Is 49:23; BDB, s.v. אָמַן I, Qal, 2; cf. Num 11:12). The feminine participle here and in 2 Sam 4:4 means "foster-mother" (BDB, s.v. אָמַן I, Qal, 3) or "guardian" rather than "nurse" (BDB, s.v. אָמַן I, Qal, 3; *HALOT*, s.v. אמן II, Qal, 2).[429]

4:17 וַתִּקְרֶאנָה לֹו הַשְּׁכֵנוֹת שֵׁם—This is, literally, "the neighbors called to him a name." The verb קָרָא (here Qal third feminine plural imperfect with *waw* consecutive) with a person as the indirect object (לֹו, "him") and שֵׁם as the direct object means "to name, give someone a name" (see BDB, s.v. קָרָא I, Qal, 6 f; *HALOT*, Qal, 2 a). The construction with קָרָא and the direct object שֵׁם recurs in the third clause of this verse with the same meaning (see below). The adjective and substantive שָׁכֵן can refer to a fellow "inhabitant" of a town (as in Is 33:24) or a "neighbor" (BDB, 1 and 2, respectively). הַשְּׁכֵנוֹת (feminine plural) refers to the same "women" (הַנָּשִׁים) as in 4:14, hence "the neighboring women."

---

[429] Bush, *Ruth, Esther*, 258–59, notes that here and in 2 Sam 4:4 the word can mean "nurse" in the sense of "one who takes care of or looks after a child" but not in the sense of "wet-nurse."

Ruth 4:13–22

While not necessarily apparent in English, the Hebrew verb (קָרָא) and noun (שֵׁם) here are repeated from 4:11 and 4:14, so the naming of the child is a preliminary fulfillment of the prayers וּקְרָא־שֵׁם, "become famous," in 4:11 (directed at Boaz, who will become famous through his descendants, David and Christ), and וְיִקָּרֵא שְׁמוֹ בְּיִשְׂרָאֵל, "May his name be proclaimed in Israel," in 4:14 (spoken over the child now named).

לֵאמֹר—Despite all the dialogue in Ruth, this is only the third occurrence of the infinitive construct of אָמַר with לְ (the earlier ones were in 2:15 and 4:4). It introduces a quotation of direct discourse and does not itself need to be translated (Waltke-O'Connor, § 36.2.3e).

יֻלַּד־בֵּן לְנָעֳמִי—This short explanation, "a son is born to Naomi," precedes the actual naming (the next clause). Older grammarians generally considered forms such as יֻלַּד to be Pual (BDB, s.v. יָלַד, Pual; GKC, § 52 s). However, as some noted (see GKC, § 52 e), the passive meanings of such forms do not correspond to the active Piel meanings, but to the active Qal meanings. The Piel of יָלַד means "assist a birth as a midwife," and יֻלַּד does not have the corresponding passive meaning; instead it means "to be born," the passive of the Qal meaning. Today grammarians recognize these forms as Qal passive (see Joüon, § 58 a; Waltke-O'Connor, § 22.6). יֻלַּד is third masculine singular perfect. It recurs in other birth announcements: Is 9:5 (ET 9:6); Jer 20:15.[430]

In Jer 20:15 the father is introduced by לְ (יֻלַּד־לְךָ בֵּן, "a son is born to you," that is, "your son is born"), as is Naomi here (לְנָעֳמִי, "to Naomi"). Many other OT verses have forms of יָלַד, "bear, give birth," with לְ prefixed to the name of the father "to" whom the son is born (e.g., Gen 4:18, 26; 10:21, 25; 16:15–16), including Ruth 4:12 (פֶּרֶץ אֲשֶׁר־יָלְדָה תָמָר לִיהוּדָה), "Perez, whom Tamar bore to Judah"; see also 1 Chr 2:4). Thus the construction here may indicate that the neighboring women consider the child to be a son of Naomi (the grandmother) even though Ruth is the actual mother. This verse may be unique in saying that the son is born "to" the mother or grandmother. Alternatively, the לְ could serve as a dative of

---

[430] Campbell, *Ruth*, 167; Hubbard, *Ruth*, 13, n. 32.

advantage ("a son is born *for* Naomi"), as in Is 9:5 (ET 9:6), where the prophet declares, "A Son is born *for us*" (יֻלַּד־לָ֔נוּ יֶ֣לֶד). In Is 9:5 (ET 9:6), the announcement is followed by the naming of the child, as also here in Ruth 4:17.

וַתִּקְרֶ֤אנָה שְׁמוֹ֙ עוֹבֵ֔ד—Literally, this is "And they called his name Obed." This clause has the verb קָרָא and direct object שֵׁם, meaning "to name," as in the first clause of the verse (see the first textual note on 4:17). Here the verb takes a double accusative (two direct objects), as is common with verbs of naming (Waltke-O'Connor, § 10.2.3c, including example 22). The first is שְׁמוֹ ("his name"), and the second is the name itself, עוֹבֵד ("Obed"). This construction (קָרָא followed by שְׁמוֹ and then the name itself) is a formula for naming a newborn son, whether the naming is done by the mother (e.g., Gen 4:25; 19:37; 29:32), the father (e.g., Gen 4:26; 5:28–29), or by others (Gen 25:25; cf. Ex 16:31). The construction recalls two earlier, similar ones with קָרָא and שֵׁם, "become famous" (Ruth 4:11) and "May his name be proclaimed in Israel!" (4:14).

In form, עוֹבֵד ("Obed") is the Qal participle of עָבַד, "to serve," thus meaning "server" or "worshiper," since in the OT עָבַד commonly refers to serving or worshiping the LORD in faith (see BDB, Qal, 4 a). Four other men of the OT bear the name Obed (1 Chr 2:37–38; 11:47; 26:7; 2 Chr 23:1). It could be a shortened form[431] of the theophoric name Obadiah, "worshiper of the LORD" (see *HALOT*, s.v. עוֹבֵד), which is the name of twelve different men in the OT. Compare Micah ("Who is like?"), a short form of Micaiah ("Who is like the LORD?") or Michael ("Who is like God?").

ה֛וּא אֲבִי־יִשַׁ֖י אֲבִ֥י דָוִֽד׃—This is a nominal sentence: "he [was] the father of Jesse, the father of David." אֲבִי is the usual construct form of אָב, "father," with ־ִי being probably an archaic genitival ending (GKC, §§ 90 k; 96 under "Remarks"), though the OT also attests the construct form אַב (Gen 17:4–5). The antecedent of הוּא is the personal name עוֹבֵד, "Obed," at the end of the preceding clause, so "Obed" immediately precedes the formula הוּא אֲבִי־ ("he

---

[431] The first textual note on 4:22 discusses יִשַׁי, "Jesse," another possible shortened name. Cf. Bush, *Ruth, Esther,* 261.

Ruth 4:13–22

was the father of …") that begins this clause. Likewise, a personal name immediately precedes this same formula in Gen 9:18; 19:37–38; 1 Chr 4:11; 7:31. A personal name immediately precedes the fuller formula הוּא הָיָה אֲבִי (which also means "he was the father of …") in Gen 4:20–21. The word order is slightly different in Gen 10:21 (וּלְשֵׁם יֻלַּד גַּם־הוּא אֲבִי כָּל־בְּנֵי־עֵבֶר, "and to Shem were born—also to him, the father of all the sons of Eber"); Gen 36:43 (הוּא עֵשָׂו אֲבִי אֱדוֹם, "he, Esau, was the father of Edom") and 1 Chr 2:42 (מֵישָׁע בְכֹרוֹ הוּא אֲבִי־זִיף, "Mesha, his firstborn, he was the father of Ziph").

The formula הוּא אֲבִי־ ("he was the father of …") is used in narratives to emphasize that a man has significant descendants. This formula is not used in genealogies. Instead of it, Ruth 4:18–22 uses הוֹלִיד (see the second textual note on 4:18).

4:18 וְאֵלֶּה תּוֹלְדוֹת פָּרֶץ—The disjunctive *waw* clause, translated as "*Now* these … ," marks off the genealogy (4:18–22) as a distinct unit (Waltke-O'Connor, § 39.2.3c, including example 12). The genealogy is not a later addition to the book. Rather, it is integrally connected to the preceding narrative (1:1–4:17). The genealogy from Perez to David (4:18–22) is also given in 1 Chr 2:4–15 in a fuller form that includes other sons besides those that were the direct ancestors of David (e.g., it includes six brothers of David).

In the OT the feminine noun תּוֹלְדוֹת (from יָלַד, "give birth) occurs only in the plural construct and usually at the beginning of genealogies. The formula here, אֵלֶּה תּוֹלְדוֹת, occurs elsewhere mostly in Genesis, but also in Num 3:1 and 1 Chr 1:29. The traditional translation of תּוֹלְדוֹת is "generations," beginning an "account of a man and his descendants" (BDB, s.v. תּוֹלְדוֹת, under the root יָלַד). The feminine noun does not refer to the named descendants themselves, who are masculine. Instead, it refers to the "successive generations in the general history of a family … a succession of generations" (*HALOT*, 2 a α).

פֶּרֶץ הוֹלִיד אֶת־חֶצְרוֹן:—"Perez" (פֶּרֶץ) means "bursting forth" from the womb (BDB, s.v. פֶּרֶץ I, 1); see his birth and naming in Gen 38:29. As a common noun, it often refers to a "breach" in a wall (see BDB, s.v. פֶּרֶץ I, 2). הוֹלִיד is the Hiphil third masculine singular perfect of יָלַד, "to give birth." That verb form occurs a total of nine times in 4:18–22. Most of its other occurrences in the OT are in 1 Chronicles.

Feminine forms of the Qal of יָלַד normally refer to women who "give birth" (see the last textual note on 4:13). The Hiphil of יָלַד usually occurs in masculine forms with a causative meaning: the husband "causes a child to be born" by impregnating the mother, hence "to father [a child] from" (מִן, 1 Chr 8:9) the mother. Masculine Hiphil forms of יָלַד are usually translated "to beget" (*HALOT*, Hiphil, 1) or to "father a child" (BDB, Hiphil, 1).[432]

"Hezron" (חֶצְרוֹן), with the diminutive ending וֹ-, might be related to חָצִיר, "grass, herbage," or חָצֵר, "courtyard,"[433] or the homograph חָצֵר, "village." It is spelled "Hezrom" in some LXX manuscripts, the Old Latin, and the Vulgate.[434] The interchange of "n" and "m" occurs with other Hebrew names, for example, Gershon (1 Chr 5:27 [ET 6:1]) and Gershom (1 Chr 6:1 [ET 6:16]).[435]

4:19 וְחֶצְרוֹן הוֹלִיד אֶת־רָם—The generational notices each begin with the conjunction וְ, which need not be translated except for the last one, וְיִשַׁי ("and Jesse ... ," 4:22), which signals the end. On הוֹלִיד, see the second textual note on 4:18. רָם, "Ram," is from רוּם and means "he is exalted" (*HALOT*, s.v. רָם II). It appears as an element in a number of compound Semitic names, for example,

---

[432] Cf. Bush, *Ruth, Esther*, 265–66.
[433] The latter is suggested by Block, *Judges, Ruth*, 734.
[434] Campbell, *Ruth*, 170.
[435] See Campbell, *Ruth*, 170; Sasson, *Ruth*, 187; Hubbard, *Ruth*, 280, n. 1.

Ab*ram*, Am*ram*. His name is spelled identically (רָם) in 1 Chr 2:9, but is given as "Arran" in the LXX Ruth 4:19; "Aram" in the Peshitta and Vulgate of Ruth 4:19 and in Mt 1:3–4; "Aran" in the Old Latin of Ruth 4:19; and possibly "Arni" in Lk 3:33. Some of those spellings may have been influenced by LXX 1 Chr 2:9, which gives Ram, Chaleb, and Aram (Αραμ) as sons of Hezron, whereas MT 1 Chr 2:9 has Jerahmeel, Ram, and Chelubai.[436]

עַמִּינָדָב—"Amminadab" may mean "my people is willing" or "my kinsman/protector is generous."[437] The first element (Am-) may be a homograph of עַם, "people," that means "kinsman" (BDB, s.v. עַם II, under the root עמם I; cf. HALOT, s.v. עַם B) or perhaps "protector" (cf. גֹּאֵל, "kinsman-redeemer"). It occurs frequently in names, for example, *Am*ram and Bala*am*. נָדָב (-nadab) may mean "generous, noble" (BDB), as does the adjective נָדִיב. The cognate noun נְדָבָה can mean "willingness" or refer to voluntary offerings. Nadab was the name of the oldest son of Aaron (e.g., Ex 6:23) and of three other men in the OT (see BDB, s.v. נָדָב).

4:20 נַחְשׁוֹן—"Nahshon," with the diminutive ending וֹ-, may derive from נָחָשׁ, "serpent," and thus mean "little serpent"[438] or "little snake" (HALOT, נַחְשׁוֹן). Or it could be related to נְחֹשֶׁת, "bronze."

---

[436] Cf. Campbell, *Ruth*, 171; Sasson, *Ruth*, 187; Hubbard, *Ruth*, 280, n. 2.
[437] For the later suggestion, see Sasson, *Ruth*, 189; Hubbard, *Ruth*, 282. HALOT, s.v. עַמִּינָדָב, citing Noth, gives "my father's brother has shown himself generous" (Martin Noth, *Die israelitischen Personennamen* [1928; repr. Darmstadt, 1966], 192–93).
[438] Hubbard, *Ruth*, 282.

Ruth 4:13–22

4:20–21 שַׂלְמָה׃ וְשַׂלְמוֹן—Ruth 4:20 ends with "Salmah," but 4:21 begins with his name spelled "Salmon," with a diminutive ending.[439] A few Hebrew manuscripts have שַׂלְמָה in both verses, perhaps because scribes corrected the second occurrence to agree with the first. Most LXX manuscripts have Σαλμών in both verses,[440] as does Mt 1:4–5, but Vaticanus has Σαλμαν in Ruth 4:20–21. The Vulgate has *Salma* in both, in harmony with the Aramaizing שַׂלְמָא in 1 Chr 2:11, 51, 54. In both, the Peshitta has the form that also occurs as Σαλά in Lk 3:32.

Probably שַׂלְמָה ("Salmah") and שַׂלְמוֹן ("Salmon") are variations of the same name, both from the root שׂלם but with different endings. שַׂלְמָה means "garment, clothing," as also does שִׂמְלָה; the two common Hebrew terms are related by metathesis. Alternatively, the meaning could be derived from the Arabic *shillam*, "(little) spark." The father of Boaz is the only one in the OT to bear the name (spelled either way), but similar is שַׂלְמַי in Ezra 2:46 (Qere) and Neh 7:48.

4:21 בֹּעַז—On "Boaz," see the last textual note on 2:1.

עוֹבֵד׃—On "Obed," see the fourth textual note on 4:17.

4:22 יִשַׁי—The etymology of "Jesse" (יִשַׁי; pausal: יִשָׁי) is uncertain.[441] It is spelled אִישַׁי in 1 Chr 2:13. One suggestion is that it derives from יֵשׁ יָהּ, "Yah/the LORD exists" (BDB, s.v. יִשַׁי). More plausible is that it is a shortened form of יִשִּׁיָּה, "Isshiah," the name of a man in Ezra 10:31; 1 Chr 7:3; 23:20; 24:21, 25, which in turn is a

---

[439] See Keil, *Joshua, Judges, Ruth*, 493; Campbell, *Ruth*, 171–72; Hubbard, *Ruth*, 283; Vuilleumier, "Stellung und Bedeutung"; *HALOT*, s.v. *שׂלם.
[440] Cf. Campbell, *Ruth*, 172.
[441] See Sasson, *Ruth*, 190.

Ruth 4:13–22

shortened form of יִשִׁיָהוּ, "Isshiahu" (1 Chr 12:7 [ET 12:6]). Probably יִשַׁי and יִשִׁיָהוּ are derived from the verb נָשָׁה (so BDB, s.v. יִשִׁיָהוּ, under the root נשה II), with the theophoric element יָה or יָהוּ appended, both of which are shortened forms of יהוה, "the LORD." נָשָׁה usually means "to forget," but probably would mean "to forgive" when God is its subject.[442] Thus "Isshiah" may mean "the LORD forgives," and that is as likely a meaning as any also for "Jesse."

---

[442] Cf. *HALOT*, s.v. יִשִׁיָהוּ, which includes "Yahweh caused to forget."

Peer Reviewed

Concordia Publishing House

Similar to the peer review or "refereed" process used to publish professional and academic journals, the Peer Review process is designed to enable authors to publish book manuscripts through Concordia Publishing House. The Peer Review process is well-suited for smaller projects and textbook publication.

We aim to provide quality resources for congregations, church workers, seminaries, universities, and colleges. Our books are faithful to the Holy Scriptures and the Lutheran Confessions, promoting the rich theological heritage of the historic, creedal Church. Concordia Publishing House (CPH) is the publishing arm of The Lutheran Church—Missouri Synod. We develop, produce, and distribute (1) resources that support pastoral and congregational ministry, and (2) scholarly and professional books in exegetical, historical, dogmatic, and practical theology.

For more information, visit:
www.cph.org/PeerReview.

www.ingramcontent.com/pod-product-compliance
Lightning Source LLC
Chambersburg PA
CBHW021758230426
43669CB00006B/113